LEGENDARY LOCALS

OF

EDMOND

OKLAHOMA

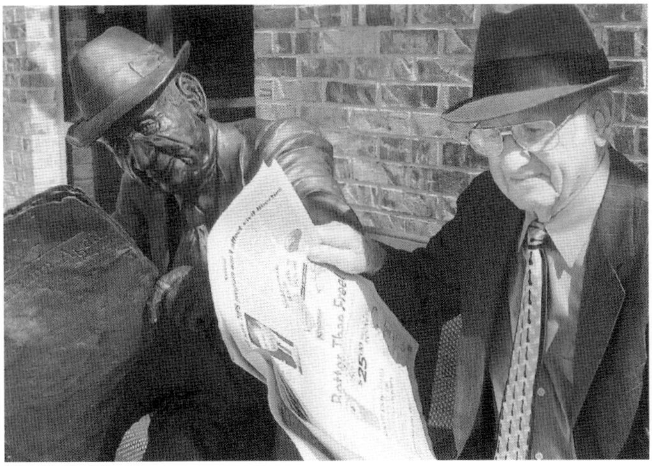

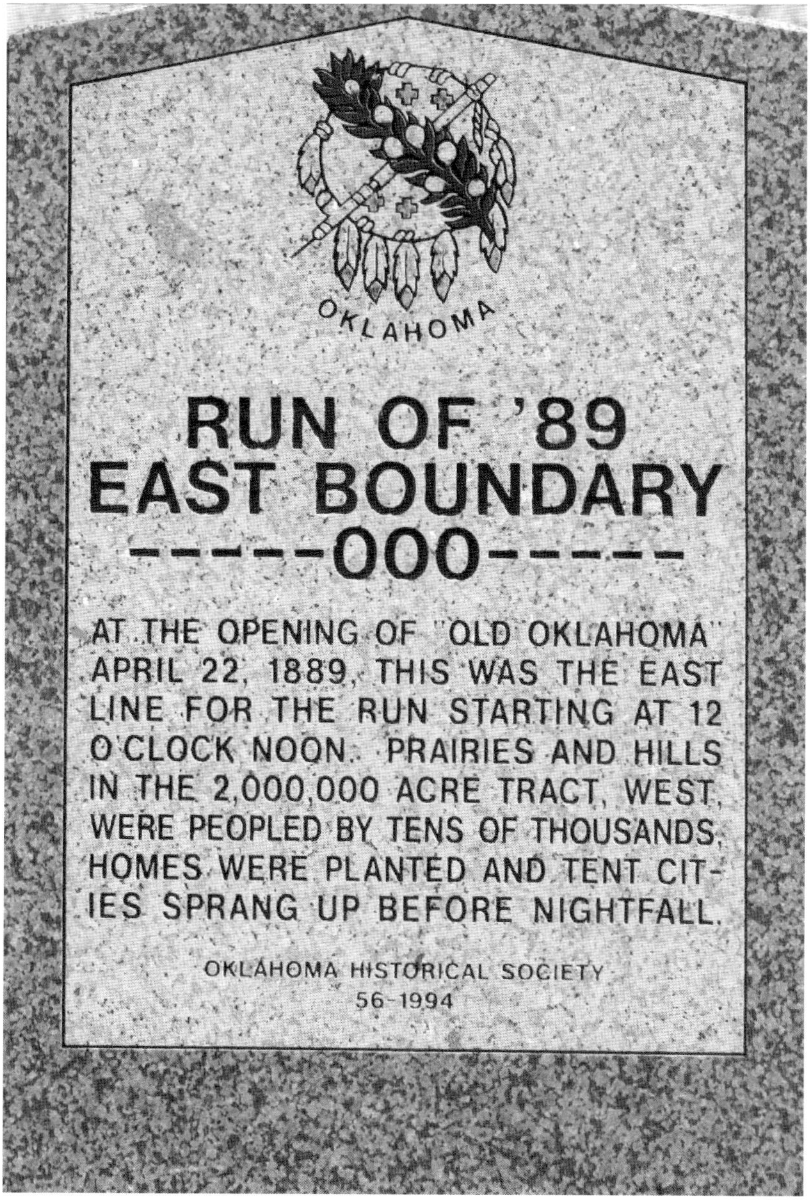

Land Run

It began at high noon on April 22, 1889. Land claims were made, homes staked out, and cities sprang up, Edmond among them. The east boundary was near Arcadia, marked by this Oklahoma Historical Society granite marker on the south side of Route 66, just west of Indian Meridian Road. (Courtesy David Fisk.)

Page One: ***The Reader***

Visitors to Edmond's public library know *The Reader* well. The sculpture was created by Edmond artist Mary Lou Gresham. Edmond boasts more than 130 public works of art, and *The Reader* was one of the first. Pictured is Charles Boldin, who was director of Boys Ranch Town and the model for the piece. See page 112 for more information about him. (Courtesy Ellen Boldin.)

LEGENDARY LOCALS

OF

EDMOND

OKLAHOMA

DAVID RANDALL FISK

LEGENDARY LOCALS

ISBN 978-1-4671-0123-3

Legendary Locals is an imprint of Arcadia Publishing
Charleston, South Carolina

Printed in the United States of America

Library of Congress Control Number: 2013945695

For all general information, please contact Arcadia Publishing:
Telephone 843-853-2070
Fax 843-853-0044
E-mail sales@arcadiapublishing.com
For customer service and orders:
Toll-Free 1-888-313-2665

Visit us on the Internet at www.arcadiapublishing.com

Dedication

For those that have worked tirelessly through the years to preserve the history and memories of the people of Edmond.

On the Front Cover: Clockwise from top left:
Emil Suenram, operator of Farmers Grain (Courtesy Farmer's Grain; see page 79); Lauren Nelson, Miss America 2007 (Courtesy KWTV; see page 57); Shannon Miller, Olympic gymnast (Courtesy Oklahoma Sports Museum; see pages 42-43); Gottlob Fink, banker (Courtesy UCO Library, Archives/Special Collections; see page 17); Charles Boldin, director of Boys Ranch Town (Courtesy Ellen Boldin; see page 112); Ella Turner, child hero (Courtesy Neil Turner; see page 119); Charles Wantland, educator and coach (Courtesy UCO Library, Archives/Special Collections; see page 22); Russell Dougherty, World War II hero (Courtesy Edmond Historical Society Photographic Collections; see page 72); Anita Bryant, singer and beauty queen (Courtesy Anita Bryant; see page 56).

On the Back Cover: From left to right:
Van's bakery drivers pose with owner Everett Van Antwerp, dressed in white with straw hat on head, sometime in the 1940s at the bakery located on Broadway in downtown Edmond. (Courtesy Edmond Historical Society Photographic Collection, see page 81.) Ida Freeman is seen here, in dark dress and hat, at the 1950 ground-breaking ceremony for Ida Freeman Elementary School. (Courtesy Edmond Historical Society Photographic Collection, see page 30.)

CONTENTS

ACKNOWLEDGMENTS

I met a number of interesting people while working on this book and give thanks to all those that helped me gather the information and photographs necessary to complete this project. Numerous histories of Edmond have been published, and I drew upon some of those books and accounts to gain knowledge about the many interesting people of Edmond.

I would like to thank Jena Mottola and the Edmond Historical Society Museum staff, especially Deborah Baker, for their time and efforts in finding old photographs. Thank you to Nicole Willard and staff at the University of Central Oklahoma (UCO) Library, Archives Special Collections, for their professionalism and timeliness, especially Leith Laws. Linda Lynn at the *Oklahoman* did a great job culling images from the vast *Oklahoman* archives. Thanks also go to Richard Hendricks at the Oklahoma Sports Museum; Pam Bell at the Oklahoma City National Memorial Museum; Jennifer Monroe at the Edmond Police Department; the Edmond Fire Department; the City of Edmond; the Edmond Chamber of Commerce; John Greiner at the Oklahoma Military Hall of Fame; and Liz Johnson and Katrina Shaklee at UCO. Also, special thanks to my friend Ray Hibbard, publisher of *Edmond Life and Leisure*, for his continued support and encouragement.

Thanks also to Chris Suenram, Jeff Scoggins, Ellen Boldin, Margaret Self, Pat Hoig, Mary Lou Gresham, Bob Gregg, Kelly Gregg, Beverly Terry, Mike Thompson, Neil Turner, Anita Bryant, Janet Kirk, Martha Hall, Gil and Rhonda Harryman, and many more who provided family and other photographs.

Thanks also go to my editors at Arcadia, Amy Perryman, Jason Humphrey, and Tiffany Frary, who got me started on this whole journey. And thank you to my faithful driver and companion and patient sounding board, Charlene Wolfe. Finally, thank you to all those "characters" that have helped make Edmond a more interesting and better place to live. There are many more people that I wanted to include in this book, but space was limited, so my apologies to those folks.

INTRODUCTION

Edmond sprang to life 125 years ago at 12:05 p.m. on April 22, 1889, when Nanitta Daisey, "Kentucky Daisey," leaped from a train and staked the first claim in what was to become Edmond. The first great Oklahoma land run had begun at noon, and surveyors quickly began laying out the Edmond town site.

Located in the heart of America on historic Route 66, Edmond has grown to be a small city with more than 80,000 residents and lies just north of Oklahoma City, near the interstate crossroads of America of I-35, I-40, and I-44. It is often hard to tell where Oklahoma City ends and Edmond begins.

What was to become Oklahoma was first known as Indian Territory. In 1870, the federal government surveyed part of the territory. Treaties were reached with various Indian nations and reservations were established within Indian Territory. It was later determined that large areas of this region had been left untouched. This land became known as the "Unassigned Lands."

Pres. Benjamin Harrison consulted his cabinet, and they decided that a land rush would be held on April 22, 1889, commencing at high noon. Little did anyone know the magnitude of people that would descend upon the territory borders to take place in the mad dash, or "Harrison's Horse Race," as some called it. Except for earning statehood in 1907, this was, according to most historians, probably the most exciting event in Oklahoma history.

Edmond was home to many firsts in Oklahoma Territory. The first public schoolhouse was completed in 1889. The state's oldest continuous newspaper, the *Edmond Sun*, began publishing on July 18, 1889. St. John the Baptist Catholic Church was dedicated on June 24, 1889, and the Territorial Normal School began in 1891, now the University of Central Oklahoma. The first building the Territorial Normal School used, Old North Tower, still remains a focal point on campus.

Through the first 125 years of its life, a diverse and interesting batch of people has made Edmond home or has had an impact on the community. The first residents were John and Cordelia Steen, who lived with their small son, Charley, in a one-room railroad pump house next to the tracks for more than a year before the 1889 Land Run. At that time, only one freight train passed through Edmond, which served as a coaling and watering stop for the passing trains.

From early founders and builders such as Milton "Kicking Bird" Reynolds, founding editor of the *Edmond Sun*, to present-day leaders like bank executive and former college president Roger Webb, current mayor Charles Lamb, and many more, a very interesting batch of "legendary locals" have made Edmond what it is today. A thriving community and great place to live, Edmond has been listed in many places as being a top 10 place to live.

Edmond's crime rate is always one of the lowest among Oklahoma's cities, according to FBI Uniform Crime Reports. Former mayor Saundra Naifeh, who was the first woman mayor of the city, said in a 2002 news story in the *Oklahoman*, "Edmond has always been held to a high standard by the people and businesses who call it home. This ranking exhibits the exceptional job our citizens have done in building this city."

The official "Edmond Visitor's Guide," produced by the Edmond Convention and Visitors Bureau, states, "Prominently located on Rt. 66, (which runs right through town on Second Street) the glory days of the 'Mother Road' brought fame to many Edmond restaurants. The Wide-A-Wake Café, the 66 Highway Café, the Lone Elm, and Royce's are just a few. Those are gone now, but other wonderful restaurants now call Edmond home. . . . Today, more than 200 restaurants serve travelers ranging from fast food to elegantly gourmet."

Edmond is known nationwide for its challenging golf courses. The private Oak Tree National has hosted several PGA championship events, including the 1988 US Open. The USGA Senior Open is scheduled in 2014 at Oak Tree. Golfers Dr. Gil Morgan, Bob Tway, Scott Verplank, Doug Tewell, Mark Hayes, Willie Woods, and Dave and Danny Edwards call Edmond home.

Professional bowlers are not unfamiliar to Edmond. The 1989 US Open was held at Boulevard Bowl, as were several Hammer Opens and Choice Hotel Classic tournaments. Hall of Fame bowler Gary Dickinson lives in Edmond and is still active on the Senior Tour.

Edmond has several major events every year, including LibertyFest, Edmond's Fourth of July festival, which spans 10 days with events ranging from a car show and a kite fest to a road rally, all capped by a spectacular fireworks finale. The Edmond Arts Festival, held downtown each May, attracts hundreds of artists and exhibitors from around the country and grows bigger each year. The University of Central Oklahoma hosts the Endeavor Games, a national competition for athletes with physical disabilities.

Edmond is becoming known as a city of statues and art. Almost 150 world-class sculptures are scattered like jewels throughout the city. Dozens of them line the streets and rest tucked away at parks, schools, and businesses across the Edmond landscape. Perhaps the most famous is the spectacular 18-foot, 7-inch-tall bronze Shannon Miller statue created by Edmond sculptor Shan Gray that is located in Shannon Miller Park, adjacent to the Edmond Public Library.

On a sadder note, Edmond was also the site of the post office massacre on August 20, 1986, in which 14 people were killed and 6 wounded by Patrick Sherrill, a disgruntled postman, who then killed himself. A memorial to the victims stands next to the downtown post office where it happened.

The city was the subject of a US Supreme Court case during the 1990s in which a Christian cross was depicted on the city seal, raising issues concerning the First Amendment of the US Constitution. In May 1996, the Supreme Court let stand a Federal Appeals Court ruling that ordered the city to remove the cross from the seal.

On the following pages, business people, doctors, preachers, everyday folks, educators, lawmen, heroes, athletes, civic leaders, politicians, future leaders, celebrities, musicians, Miss Americas, moms, and many more people that have had an impact on or call Edmond home can be found.

Some of these include Shannon Miller, America's most decorated Olympic gold-medalist gymnast (now a proud mom); NBA basketball star Blake Griffin; retired NFL standout Kelly Gregg; NFL quarterback Brandon Weeden; Roger Webb, University of Central Oklahoma's 19th president; police chief Bob Ricks (a former FBI agent known from the Waco standoff); retired fire chief Gil Harryman and his wife, Rhonda, a former teacher of the year; former Miss America Allison Brown; Karen Silkwood, the Kerr-McGee whistleblower; and many more.

Edmond has blossomed into a small city rather than a town as far as population goes, but residents continue to be proud of its heritage and small-town character and values.

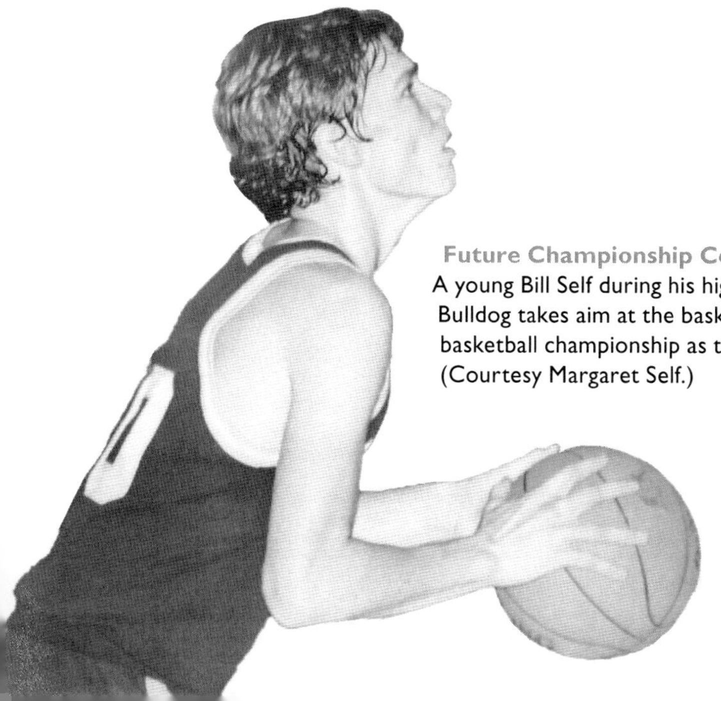

Future Championship Coach
A young Bill Self during his high school days as an Edmond Memorial Bulldog takes aim at the basket. Self went on to win the NCAA basketball championship as the coach of the University of Kansas. (Courtesy Margaret Self.)

CHAPTER ONE

Founders and Builders

The land rush on April 22, 1889, brought a number of hearty and ambitious souls to Edmond. It took men and women with will power and courage to create a town and build a community where barren land once sat. Oklahoma City and Guthrie had 10,000 people by the end of the first day of the run; Edmond had about 150.

First residents John and Cordelia Steen led the way and were joined by early business leaders and town builders, including Milton Reynolds, founder of the *Edmond Sun*; developer Anton Classen; Robert Galbreath, first lawman; and the Kunc family, who farmed land east of town.

Jennie Forster began the town's first library above a grocery store. John Mitch and Richard Thatcher were vital to the establishment of a college in Edmond. Developer Harry Clegern, newspaperman A.D. Dailey, and banker Gottlob Fink were major influences.

For the first few decades, Edmond went through many growing pains, eventually became a thriving and growing place thanks to the early founders and community builders.

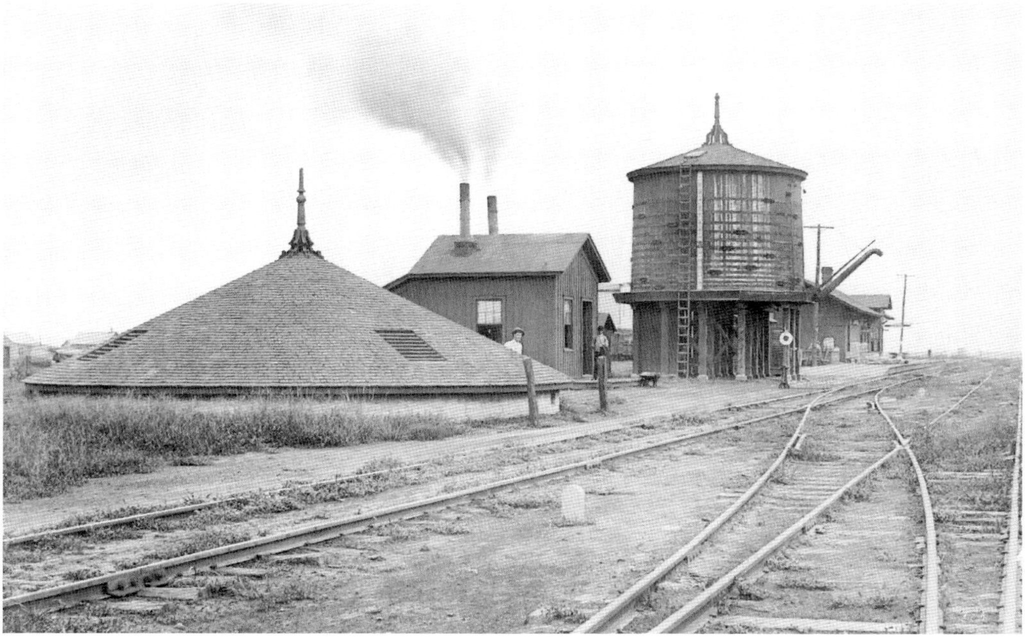

Edmond S. Burdick

Burdick was a freight agent for the Atchison, Topeka & Santa Fe Railroad. Burdick began his railroad career in 1881 and worked for several railroad companies. He was an assistant right-of-way agent at that time, when station points along the Arkansas City extension were being named by the Santa Fe Railroad. After bearing the designation of Mile Marker 103, its depot shown above, the area was renamed Edmond in 1887 by Santa Fe officials. A few years after the Land Run of 1889, the *Edmond Sun* reported that Burdick "was very pleased to see the town that was named after him doing so well." Pictured below are some earlier settlers of Edmond. (Both, courtesy UCO Library, Archives/Special Collections.)

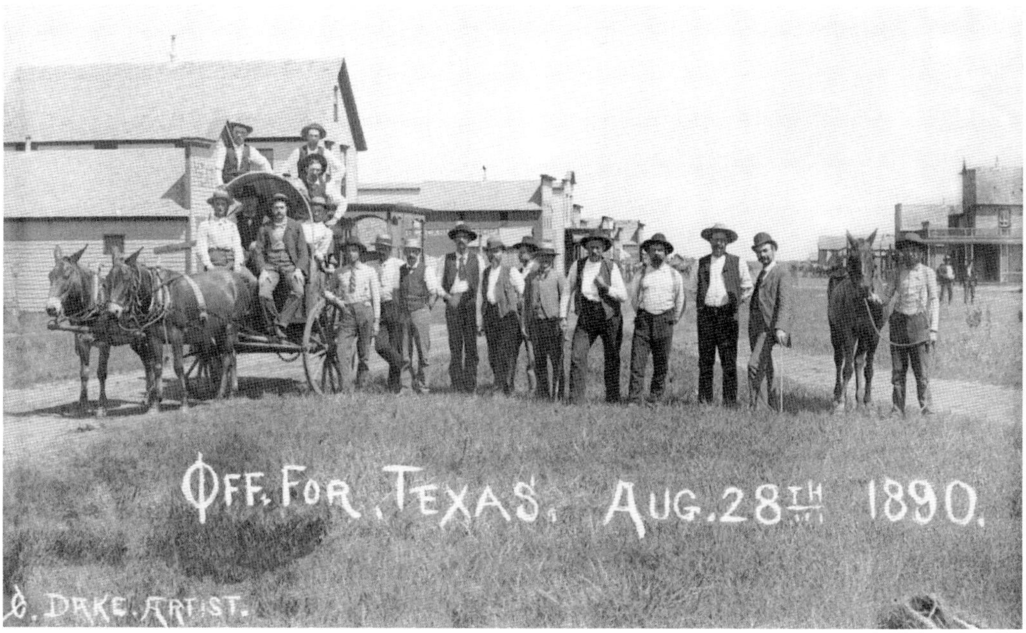

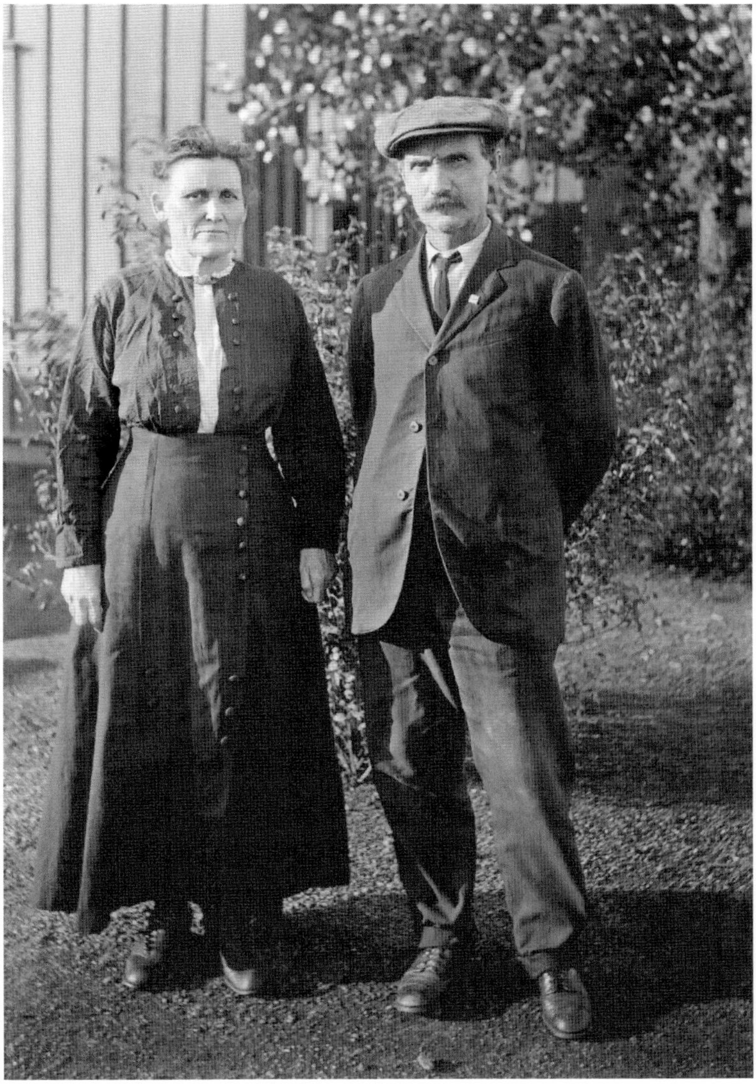

John and Cordelia Steen

Steen worked for the Santa Fe Railroad and was brought in from New Mexico in 1887 to complete a well at what was to become Edmond a few years later. The project was under way when the laying of the track was completed, connecting Arkansas City, Kansas, and Gainesville, Texas, on April 26, 1887. The well was 128 feet deep, 30 feet across, and lined with 110 carloads of rock. When the well was finished, a pump house was built, and Steen's family joined him. Steen, with his wife, Cordelia, and their toddler son, Charley, lived in the one-room pump house until after the Land Run of 1889. According to James Crowder's book *Historic Edmond*, "They were the only permanent residents of Edmond. They watched for one passenger train and one freight train that arrived from each direction every day." The entire north-south route through Oklahoma began full service on June 12, 1887. Ranches in the Kickapoo and Iowa lands used Edmond for shipping cattle and receiving supplies. Turner's general store, 29 miles to the east in Wellston, also used Edmond as a receiving point. George Haas, a Santa Fe engineer when the line opened, later recalled that the only place the crew could get anything to eat was at Edmond. Once they knew when they would arrive, they would telegraph the Steens "to have some grub ready for us." (Courtesy UCO Library, Archives/Special Collections.)

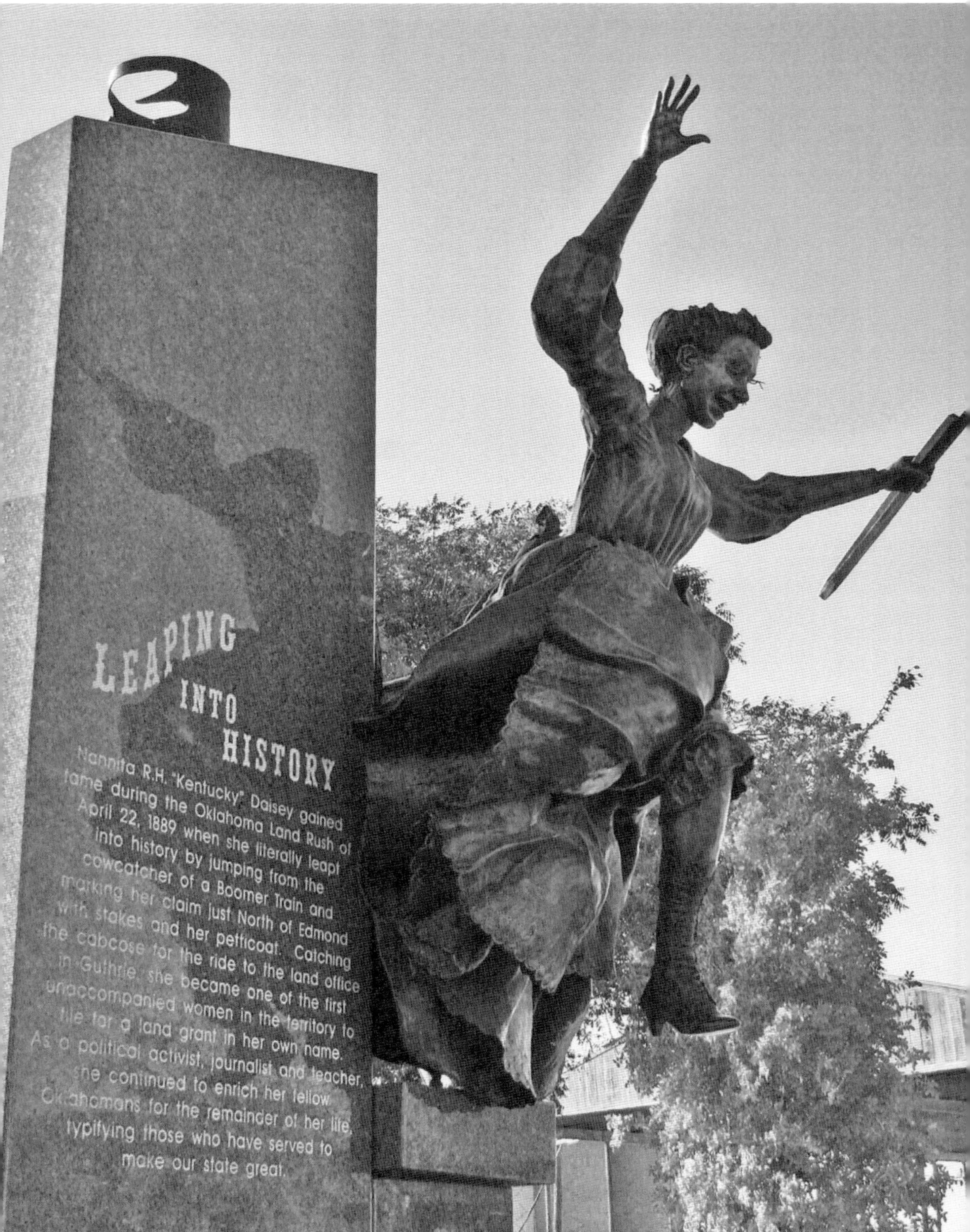
LEAPING
INTO
HISTORY
Nannita R.H. "Kentucky" Daisey gained
fame during the Oklahoma Land Rush of
April 22, 1889 when she literally leapt
into history by jumping from the
cowcatcher of a Boomer Train and
marking her claim just North of Edmond
with stakes and her petticoat. Catching
the caboose for the ride to the land office
in Guthrie, she became one of the first
unaccompanied women in the territory to
file for a land grant in her own name.
As a political activist, journalist and teacher,
she continued to enrich her fellow
Oklahomans for the remainder of her life,
typifying those who have served to
make our state great.

Nanitta R.H. Daisey (OPPOSITE PAGE)
Best known as "Kentucky Daisey," Nanitta R.H. Daisey was one of the most colorful participants in the Land Run of 1889. Visitors at the Festival Market Place are greeted by a statue that depicts the dashing pioneer jumping from a train to stake her claim in Edmond. On the morning of April 22, 1889, Daisey, who was a correspondent for the *Dallas Morning News*, rode in the first train on the Santa Fe tracks coming north from Purcell. Legend has it that as the train raced into the Unassigned Lands at 20 miles per hour, Daisey made her way into the confidences of the engineer, who allowed her to climb outside the train. There are varied accounts of Daisey's actions. According to historian Stan Hoig, "she leaped from her perch on a locomotive's cowcatcher and ran to make a homestead claim north of Edmond Station." When the train reached a point near the present location of Boulevard and Covell Road, it slowed to take a curve, and Kentucky Daisey jumped off, raced over a ditch, and stuck her claim stakes into the ground. Then, she reportedly got back aboard the train before it passed her by. According to information from the Edmond Historical Society Museum, that feat gained her local, regional, and even national notoriety when it was reported in newspapers around the country. The legend grew from its tamer, original accounting in the *Dallas Morning News* by a reporter who witnessed the event into a tall tale embellished by Kentucky Daisey herself and other publications from 1889 to well after her death in 1903. (Courtesy David Fisk.)

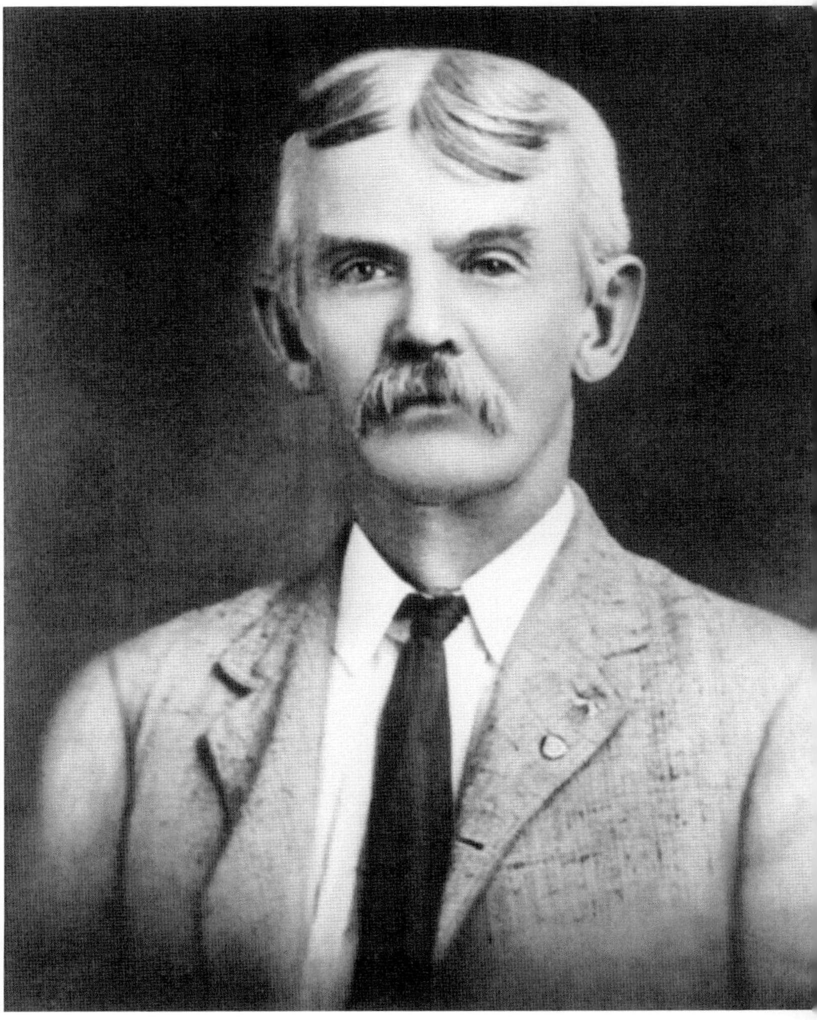

Richard Thatcher
Thatcher survived Andersonville prison as a teen during the Civil War before moving to Edmond in 1890, where he bought the Central Hotel. Thatcher was appointed in 1891 to be the first head of the Territorial Normal School, now University of Central Oklahoma. A 33rd Degree Mason, he was the second master of Edmond Masonic Lodge and principal of the Edmond schools in 1894–1895. He died in Edmond in 1909 of tuberculosis. (Courtesy UCO Library, Archives/ Special Collections.)

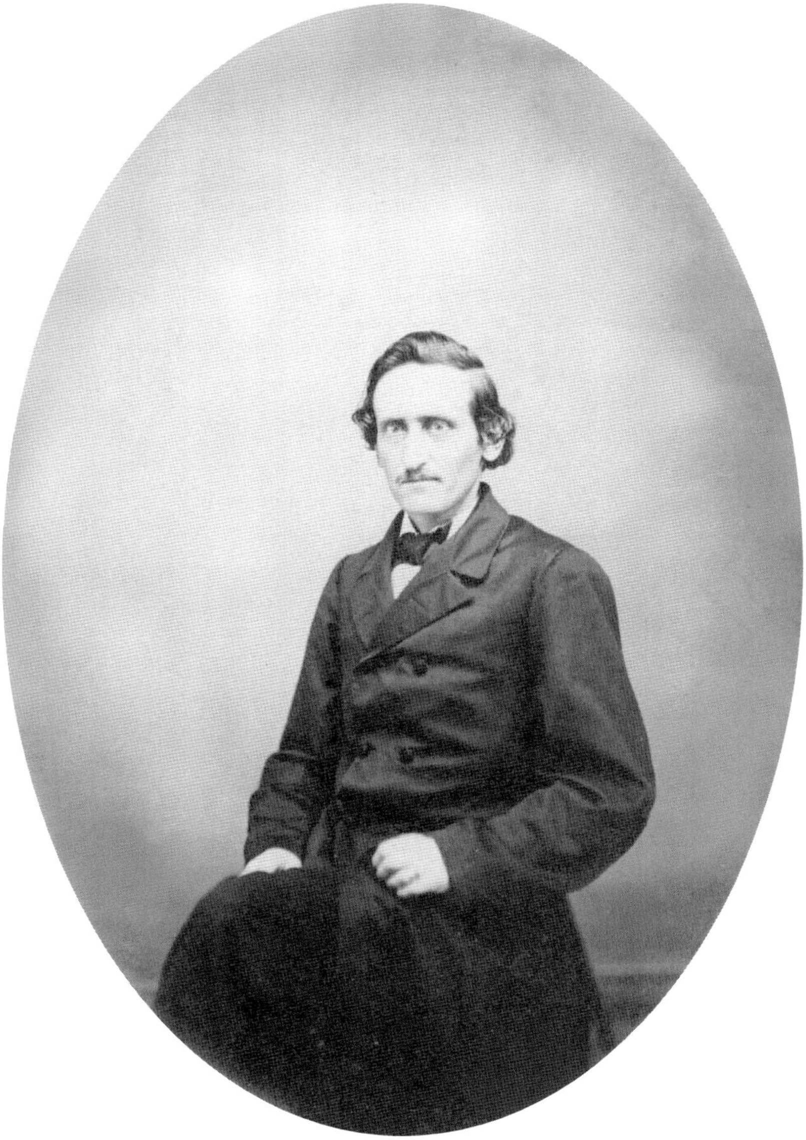

Milton W. Reynolds
Reynolds, known as "Kicking Bird" Reynolds, founded the *Edmond Sun* in 1889 after ditching an effort to start a newspaper in Guthrie. Established in a one-room building on the east side of Broadway just south of Second Street, the first issue of the paper was published on July 18, 1889, making the *Edmond Sun* is the oldest and longest-running newspaper in Oklahoma. In his book *Edmond: The First Century*, historian Stan Hoig called Reynolds "probably the most famous man to make the Run of 1889." A Michigan native, Reynolds was a news correspondent in Michigan, Nebraska, and Kansas and went to Washington, DC, to promote legislation for the opening of the Oklahoma lands. Edmond's public golf course bears the name Kickingbird. Reynolds reportedly took the name from a Kiowa chief he had met during an 1867 treaty in Kansas. He fell ill in 1890 while traveling in a political campaign to win a seat in the First Territorial Legislature. He returned home and, exhausted, died in August 1890. Hoig said Reynolds's description of Oklahoma as the "Land of the Fair God" has been often quoted by historians. (Courtesy UCO Library, Archives/Special Collections.)

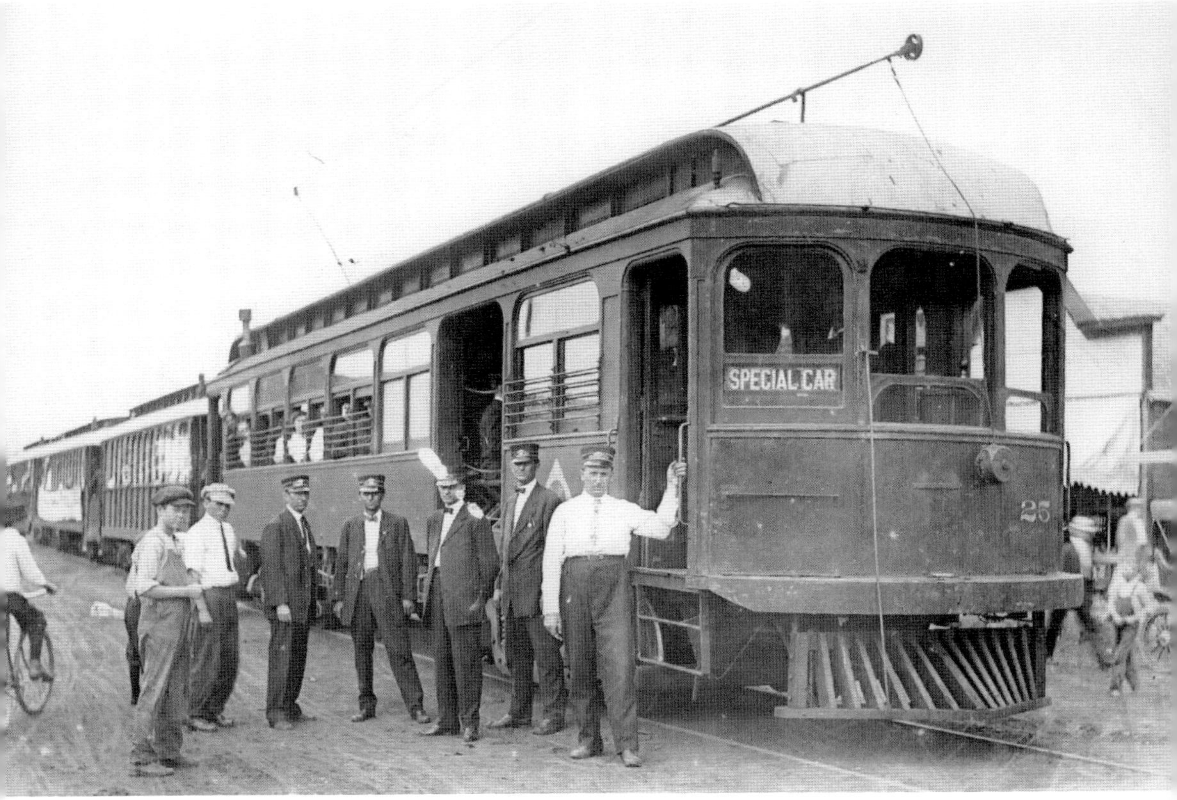

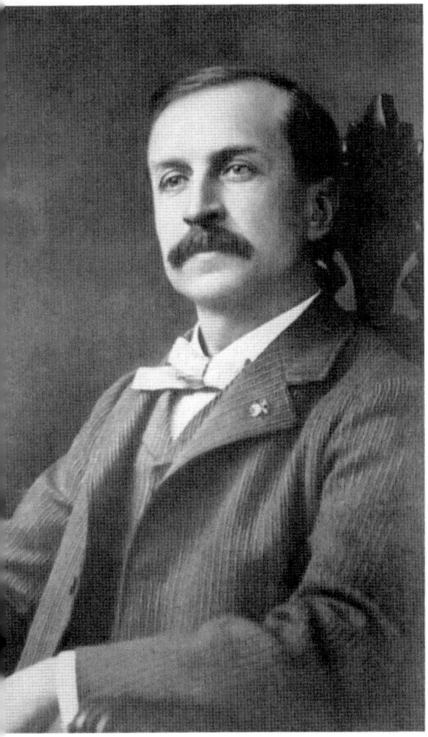

Anton Classen

Classen was an important man in Edmond long before he made his mark as an Oklahoma City civic leader, where one of the main boulevards bears his name. Two years after graduating from the University of Michigan's law school, Classen made the Land Run of 1889, living briefly in Guthrie. The town had too many lawyers for his practice to be viable, so he moved to Edmond. Classen, a man who wore many hats, is considered one of the most important men in Edmond's early years, historian Lucille Warwick said when the Classen's Grove plaque was dedicated at the Edmond Public Library. He was a benefactor, businessman, publisher of the *Edmond Sun*, postmaster from 1890 to 1893, and city attorney, and he helped establish the legal township of Edmond. Classen donated the original 40 acres for the Territorial Normal School, which is now University of Central Oklahoma. Historian Bob Blackburn said Classen was the secretary of the county's first public library and was behind the planting of trees and shrubbery in the first of Edmond's parks and along Boulevard Avenue. Classen later brought the interurban railway to Edmond as president of the Metropolitan Street Railway Company. (Both, courtesy UCO Library, Archives/Special Collections.)

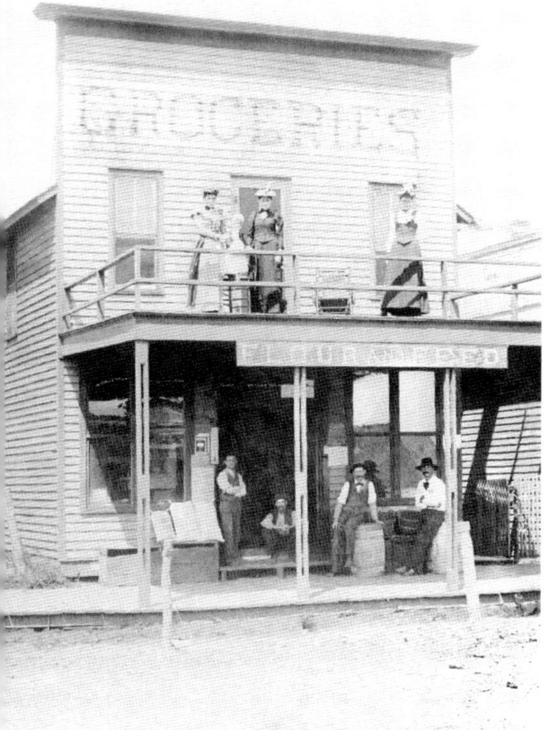

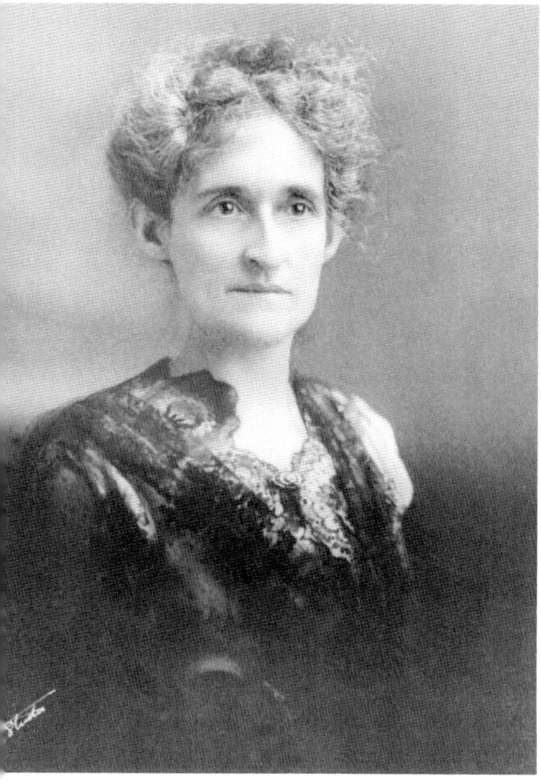

Jennie Forster

Forster and her husband, George, arrived in Edmond on the day of the land run in 1889. Together with George Angerman, they operated Forster and Thompson Dry Goods & Groceries at the corner of Broadway and Second Street. Operating out of a tent, it was the first grocery in Edmond. The first tree in Edmond was reportedly planted in front of their store. The grocery store was also the first library in Edmond, opened by Jennie Forster with books she had brought with her on their journey to Edmond. She was the first president of the Ladies Aid Society and School Aid Society. The Ladies Aid Society helped secure funds to build the first public schoolhouse in Oklahoma Territory. (Above, courtesy Edmond Historical Society Photographic Collection; below, courtesy UCO Library, Archives/Special Collections.)

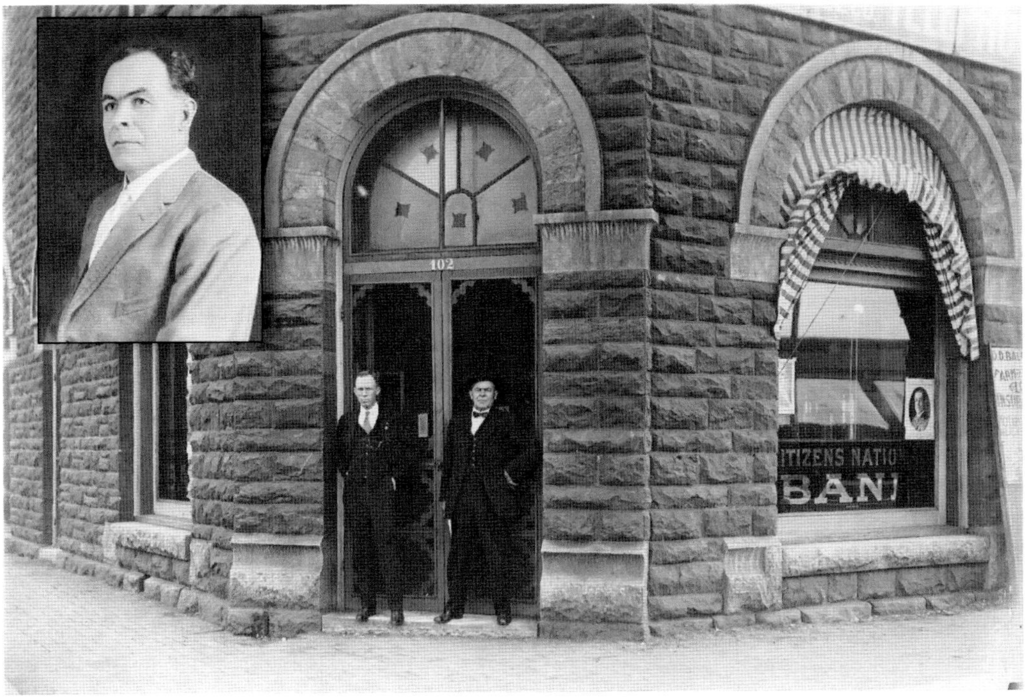

Gottlob Heinrich Fink

A prominent businessman in real estate and banking, Fink was elected mayor in 1929 and served until he died from a brain hemorrhage in 1930. In 1890, when he was 23, he came to Indian Territory and claimed land 10 miles west of Edmond near Western and Memorial Roads. He was an organizing officer of Citizens' State Bank in 1901 and served as cashier until becoming bank president in the 1920s. He helped organize Farmers State Bank in 1907; the two banks were consolidated in 1912. He helped acquire land for Old North and Evans Hall at Central State College. All four of his daughters graduated from the Territorial Normal School in Edmond. Fink Park on Second Street is named for him. The *Edmond Sun* said his goal as mayor was "to give Edmond the best administration in its history." (Above, courtesy Edmond Historical Society Photographic Collection; inset, courtesy UCO Library, Archives/Special Collections.)

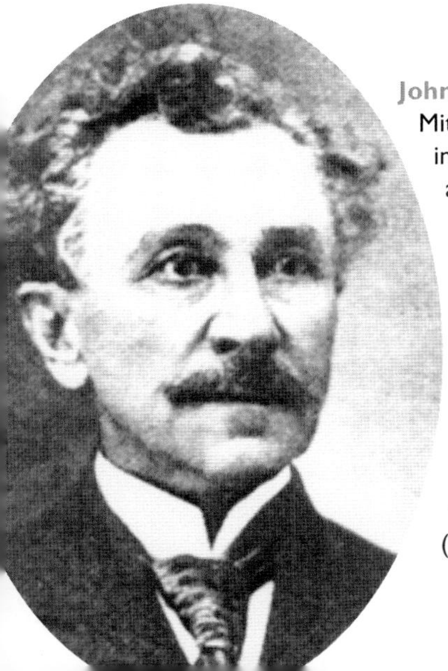

John Louis Mitch

Mitch Park's namesake, Civil War veteran John Mitch, arrived in Edmond in 1889 to stake his claim. He was a cashier at the Bank of Edmond and helped set up Edmond's second bank, the People's Bank. He was mayor in 1890–1891 and was a supporter of parks and beautification. He spearheaded the location of the Territorial Normal School, earning the nickname "Father of the Normal School." He was on the committee to establish the first public education school in the territory for grades one through eight. He plowed land at Broadway and Campbell Street and planted 1,000 trees to beautify the town and create Edmond's first park. The current downtown post office building sits on that land. Today, Mitch Park is comprised of 300 acres of land on Covell Road. When the park opened in 1994, a headline in the *Edmond Sun* stated "Mitch Would Have Been Pleased with Park." (Courtesy UCO Library, Archives/Special Collections.)

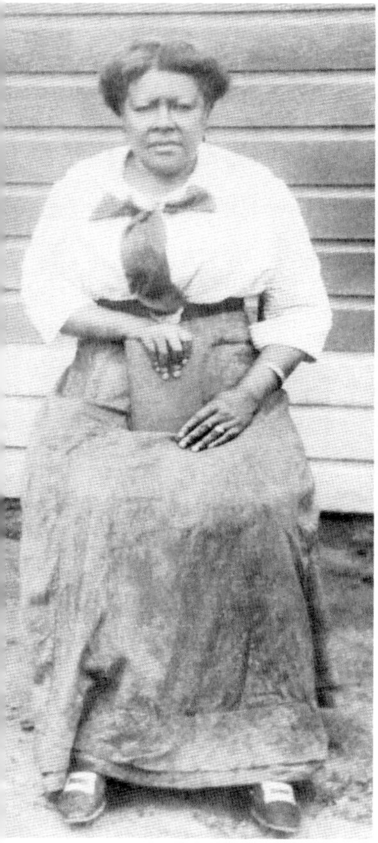

John and Ophelia Gower

Gower and his family made the Land Run of 1889 and on September 19, 1889, applied for a homestead certificate for 160 acres on land east of Edmond. The black family lived in an earthen dugout initially. Information from the Edmond History Museum indicates that the area where the Gowers settled was known as Nonsey. Gower was a stonecutter, and his wife, Ophelia, was a mid-wife. In November 1889, they gave up a small part of their homestead to establish the Gower Cemetery. Located on Covell Road between Post Road and Douglas Boulevard, this one-acre site holds more than 500 gravesites and is still active. The Gowers dedicated the land because, prior to this, there was not a cemetery for African Americans in the area. The cemetery holds significance because of its association with black settlers who lived near the area on their original homesteads. The first burial was in 1896, and the cemetery allowed "burial of all people." A back portion of the cemetery holds paupers and homeless of all races. Few of the original markers remain or are legible. Succeeding generations of Gowers maintained and cared for the cemetery, which was placed in the National Register of Historic Places in 1991. Their granddaughter, Myrtle Gower Thomas, sought help from the City of Edmond to maintain the site during the late 1980s. The city declined and suggested the Edmond Historic Preservation Trust be approached about the matter. This helped lead to the eventual designation of historic stature, even though the Preservation Trust also declined to take over maintenance. Thomas told the *Edmond Sun*, "I just knew that I wanted the cemetery to be a tradition on my family to help those who could not help themselves." Rev. John Petusky of St. John the Baptist Catholic Church in Edmond blessed the monument for the site in 1994. Family members still maintain the site as of this writing. (Left, courtesy UCO Library, Archives/Special Collections; below, courtesy David Fisk.)

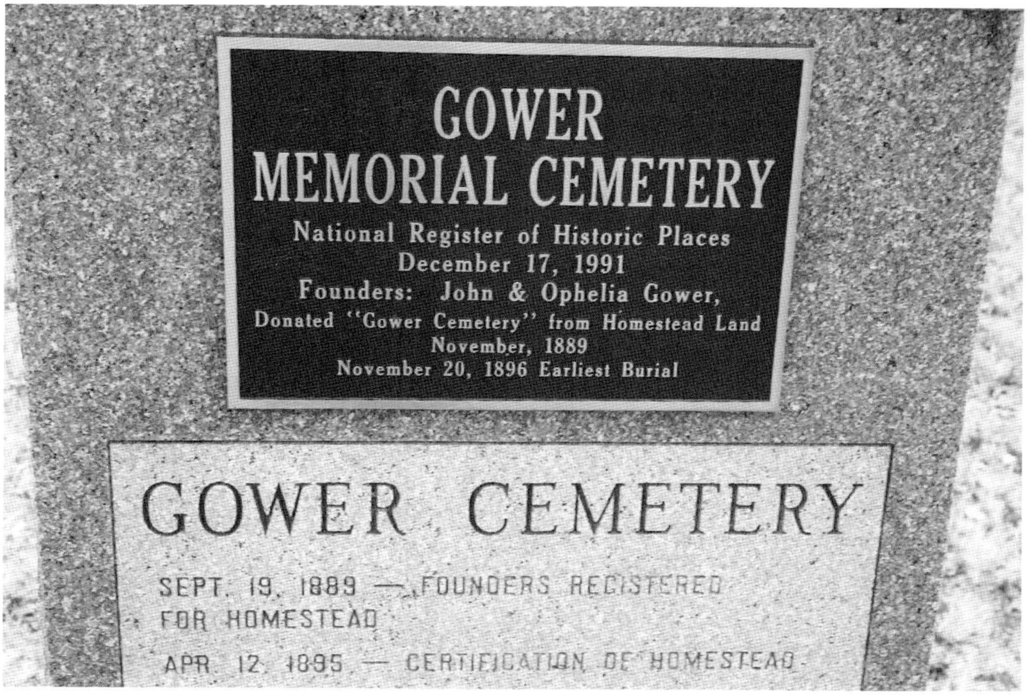

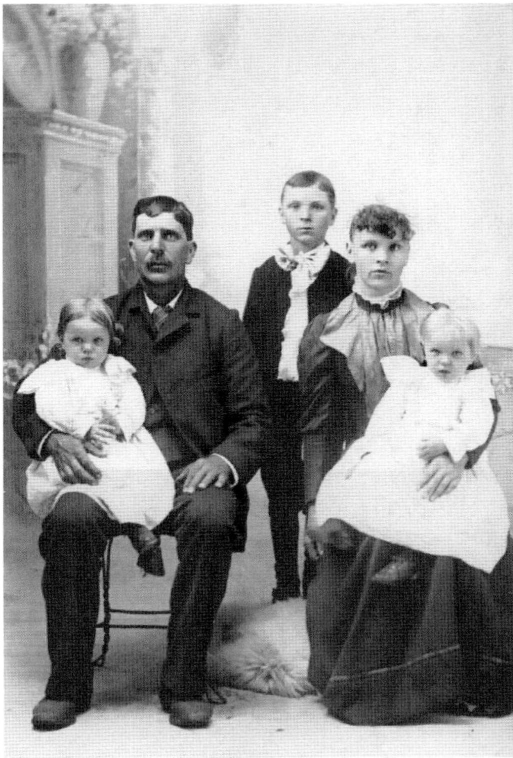

Kunc Family

For almost 100 years, the pioneer Kunc family continuously occupied the farmland they settled in 1889 at the southwest corner of Second Street and Sooner Road. James and Katherine Kunc, along with their one-year-old son, William, made the run and homesteaded land there, living in a dugout until they could build a house, below. James Kunc helped build the first Catholic church, providing tools and equipment. He also helped construct the Fairview country school at Danforth and Sooner Roads, where Fairview Baptist Church is today. In 1923, they sold an acre of land on the northeast corner of the property to Everett Bradbury. Bradbury established a campground and filling station on what became known as Bradbury Corner. The intersection was the junction of US Highway 66 (Route 66) and US Highway 77. In 1925, Bradbury moved across the highway and added a general store to the famous location. The Kunc homestead remained in their family until 1982, when William's son Stanley sold the property. Fox Lake addition sits on land where the Kuncs once raised corn. Members of the Kunc family remained active in the community during their years in Edmond. (Both, courtesy Edmond Historical Society Photographic Collection.)

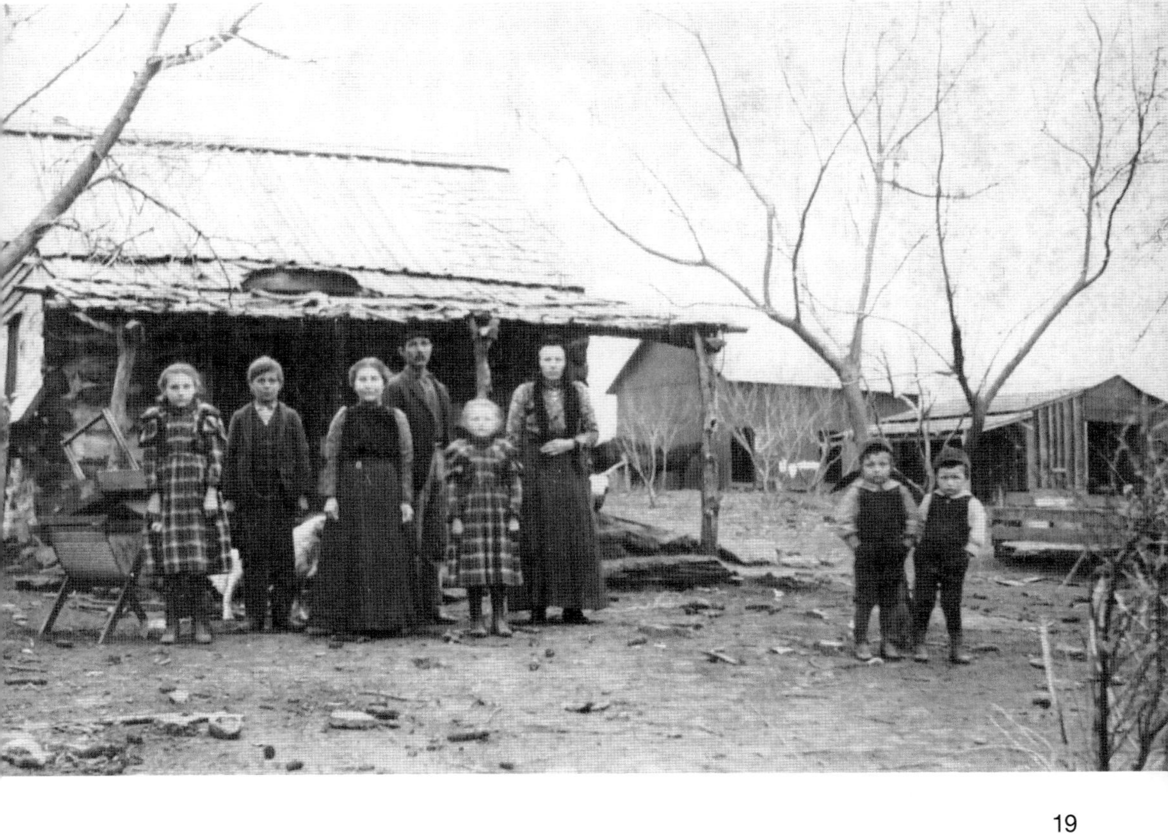

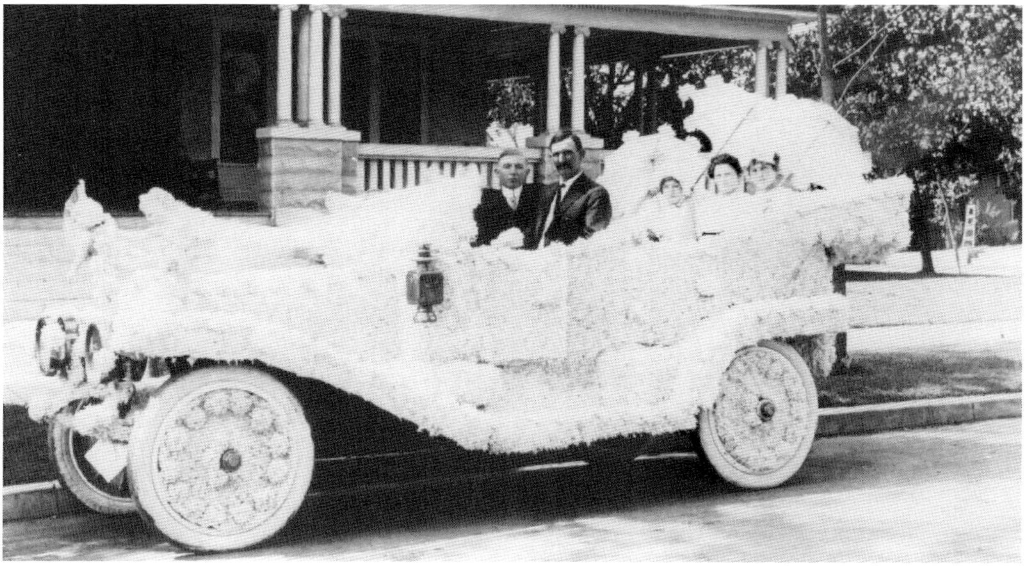

Robert Galbreath

A pioneer, adventurer, and wildcatter, Galbreath, riding in car above, was the first provisional town marshal of Edmond, as well as a Deputy US Marshal. This was before he became rich and famous in 1905, when he drilled a gusher of an oil well on Ida Glenn's farm in Tulsa County, which became known as the "Glenn Pool" oil field. It proved to be the richest the world had yet known. In his book *Glenn Pool*, his son, Frank Galbreath, called his father the "Papa" of early-day Oklahoma Oil. (Courtesy Edmond Historical Society Photographic Collection.)

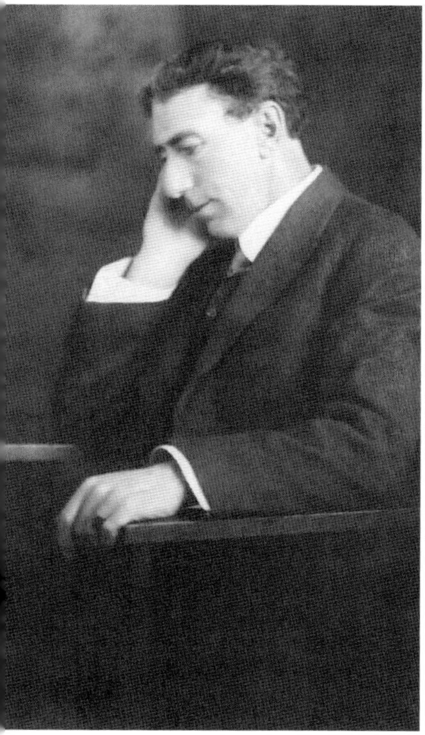

A.D. Dailey

Dailey became publisher and editor of the *Edmond Sun* in 1905 and ran the paper for 32 years. He wrote strong editorials supporting a bond drive to build a new high school, as well as urging change in the way the city was governed. After his death in 1937, his widow, Winifred, took the reins as editor. The statue at right stands in front of the present *Edmond Sun* office. (Right, courtesy David Fisk; left, courtesy UCO Library, Archives/ Special Collections.)

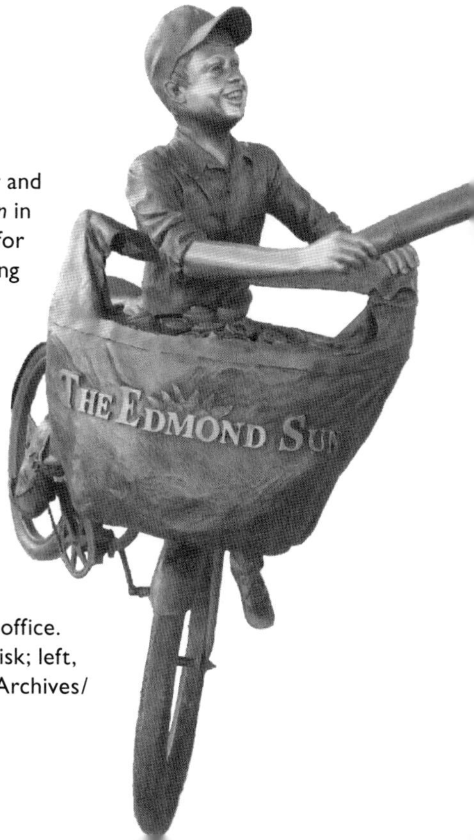

CHAPTER TWO

Teachers, Preachers, and Healers

Being home to the third largest university in Oklahoma, Edmond has many top educators, noted historians, gifted doctors, and dedicated ministers. College presidents have helped create a continuing learning atmosphere in Edmond, and countless citizens attend an array of churches. Once a town with one hospital, three first-class medical centers now serve Edmond and area residents.

Legendary college coaches Charles Wantland and Dale Hamilton led the way for men's athletics at Central State (now UCO). Emma Plunkett was a leading health and physical education proponent at the school, and Virginia Peters followed in her footsteps while coaching and mentoring many young women. Well-known teacher Ida Freeman paved the way in Edmond public schools for people like Supt. George Rowley; Principal Oretha Moulder; basketball coach Mike de la Garza; special education teacher Rhonda Harryman; and many other dedicated educators. The early founders and presidents at Central State passed the torch down through the years to modern-day university presidents Bill Lillard, Roger Webb, and George Nigh, all who brought much growth and change to UCO.

Historians Lucy Jeston Hampton, Reba Collins, and Stan Hoig made sure future generations maintained a sense of history with their research, writing, historical fact finding, and preservation. Turn-of-the-century doctors John W. Howard and Arthur M. Ruhl cared for their patients equally, regardless of social standing. Later, Dr. W.H. Roberts founded Parkside Osteopathic Hospital, which closed after Edmond Memorial Hospital was opened in 1967.

Rev. Jimmy Hylton helped bring the familiar huge cross that overlooks Edmond just east of I-35. In 2013, Rev. Mateen Elass led his First Presbyterian congregation in a break from the Presbyterian Church (USA). Dennis Newkirk has guided growth at Henderson Hills Baptist Church and helped swing a deal to sell church land for a new hospital. Until his death, First Baptist's senior pastor Alan Day led his flock in an always-growing path, including relocation. Former NFL and Memorial High School football star Paul Blair now leads the congregation at Fairview Baptist Church. Countless religious leaders help thousands of church-going Edmond citizens live their lives in a meaningful way.

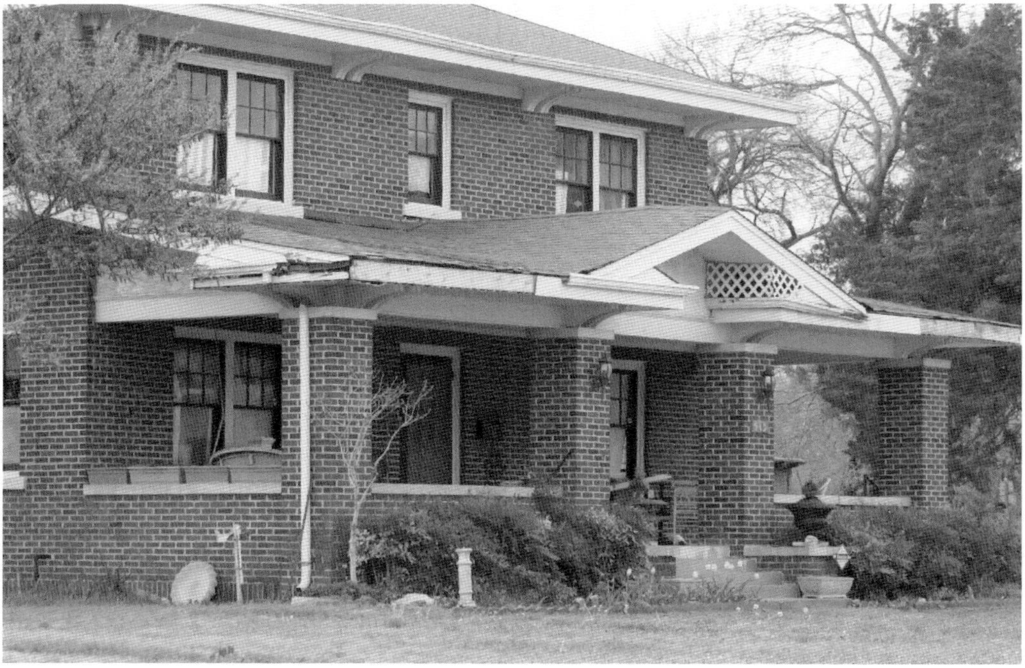

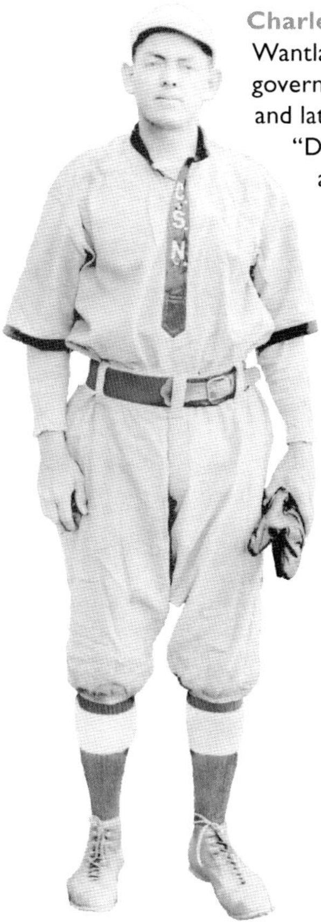

Charles W. Wantland

Wantland was a great athlete and perhaps the only coach ever fired by a governor. He was the first four-sport letterman at the University of Oklahoma and later a football coach at Central State College. Wantland's son David said, "Dad was that natural athlete, not unlike Jim Thorpe." He also served as the dean of men at Central State. The university football stadium bears his name. His wife came up with the name "Bronchos" for the college's mascot. He founded the Letterman's Club in 1922 and built the Bronchos into a football powerhouse. Shown above is the house the Wantlands lived in as it appears today. Wantland was also a businessman, opening a garage at Second Street and Broadway in 1919 in the building that houses the *Edmond Sun* today. In 1930, he voiced support for an Oklahoma City oilman, Frank Buttram, who was opposing "Alfalfa Bill" Murray for governor. Several days after being elected, Murray showed up in Edmond and "fired Charley Wantland," according to son David. The college president, Dr. John Mitchell, was also fired. Wantland, who never coached again, went into the oil business. (Above, courtesy David Fisk; left, courtesy UCO Library, Archives/Special Collections.)

Dale Hamilton

Frank Boggs, a legendary sports writer, said in the *Oklahoma City Times*, "Dale Hamilton is really as much a part of the Central State campus as Old North Tower." Hamilton served the college for 44 years. When he died in 2002, then UCO president Roger Webb said, "Dale Hamilton was one of the legends of the university. It's hard to imagine UCO without remembering Coach Hamilton." He was known only as "Coach" to many; the Bronchos never had a losing season in his 12 years as football coach. He earned 12 letters in three sports at then Central State College in the 1930s. He became the athletic director in 1941. He received numerous honors, including induction into the NAIA and UCO Halls of Fame. In 1993, Broncho Field House was renamed Hamilton Field House. (Right, courtesy UCO Library, Archives/Special Collections; below, courtesy David Fisk.)

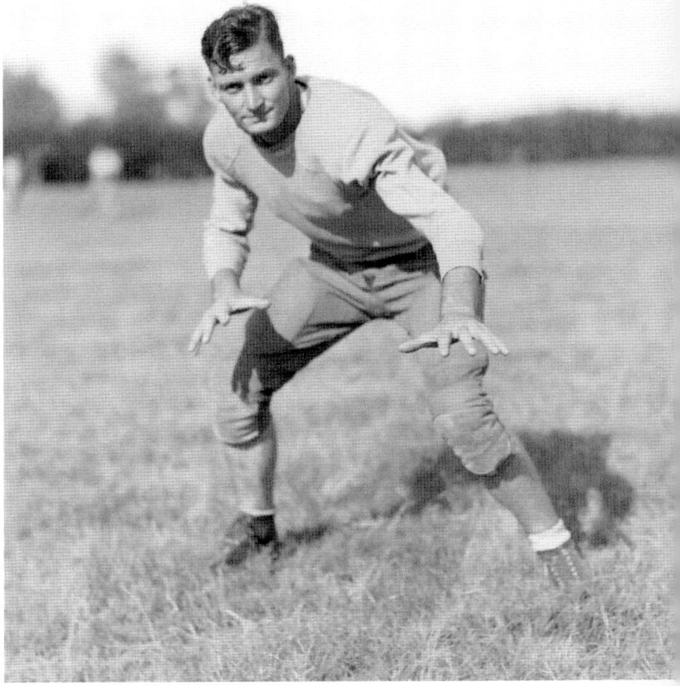

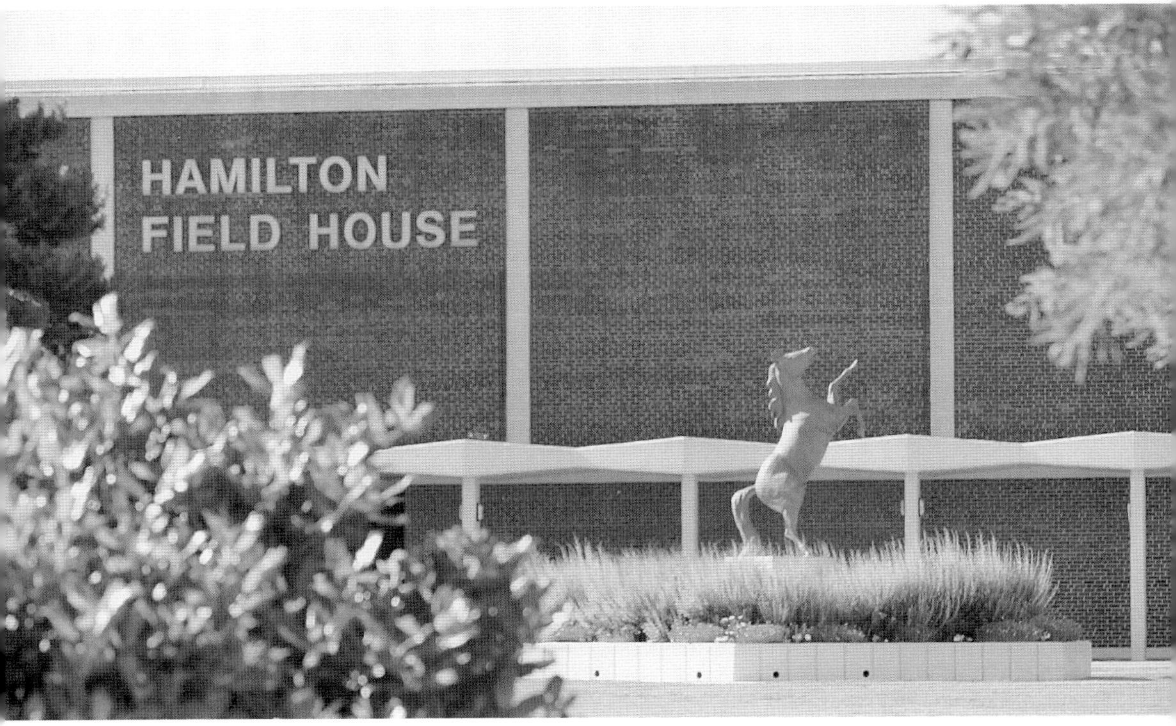

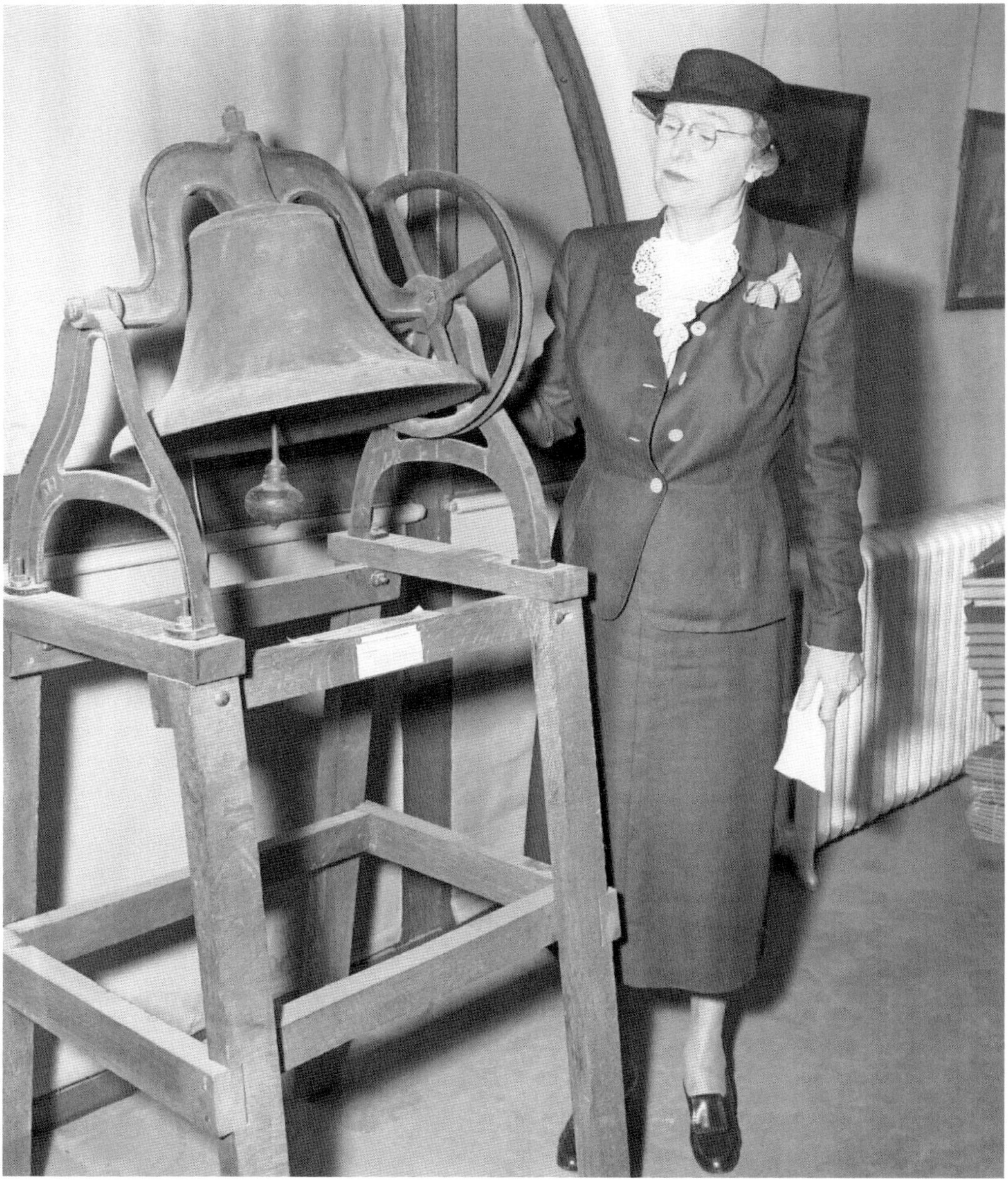

Lucy Jeston Hampton

Founder of the first historical society in Edmond, Hampton taught history for 48 years at Central State College (CSC). In 1915, she founded the Laboratory of Original Evidence, a historical museum at Central State (now UCO). She remained the curator until her retirement. She came to CSC in 1910 as a history professor, retiring in 1958. She was a charter member of the Woodrow Wilson Society in 1929 and instrumental in getting a granite marker placed at 19 North Broadway, where Central State's first classes were held in 1891. She was in demand as a public speaker and in 1936 was named one of the most outstanding women in Oklahoma by the *Daily Oklahoman.* A Central State article after her death said she saw history as "ideas of the past, grappled and projected into the future. An individualist herself, Miss Hampton also stressed 'Integrity, respect for honest labor and generous use of organized knowledge with awareness and sympathy for others.' " (Courtesy UCO Library, Archives/Special Collections.)

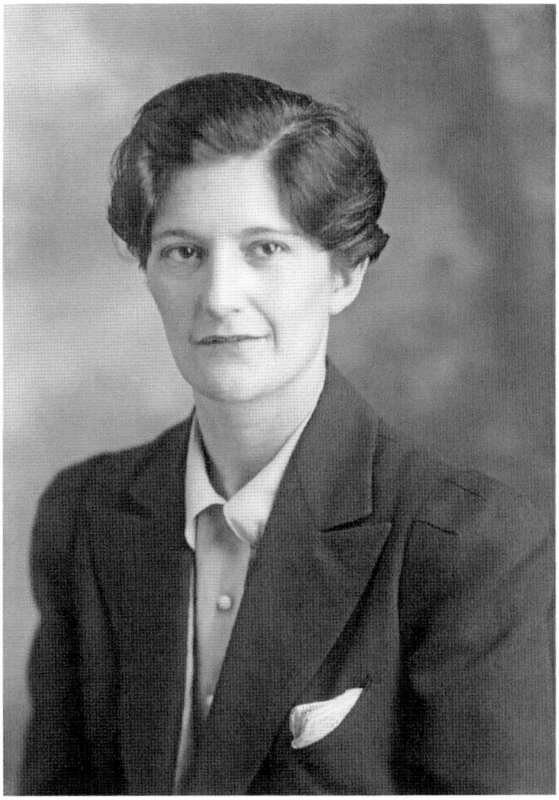

Emma Plunkett
During her 38-year career at Central State Teachers College, she established a nationally recognized health and physical education program at the school, now known as UCO. She was chair of the Department of Health and Women's Physical Education, where her philosophy was, "I will not be associated with mediocrity." She was involved in many college and community organizations and was also a public speaker and patron of the arts. Plunkett came to Edmond in 1928 and taught there until retiring in 1968, when she moved to Ponca City to live with her sister, also a teacher. Local educators told reporter Jim Killackey of the *Oklahoman*, "She was a woman well ahead of her time." When she died in 1997 at age 95, she became one of the largest donors to UCO, leaving $1 million to the school to be used for scholarships for female students. (Courtesy UCO Library, Archives/Special Collections.)

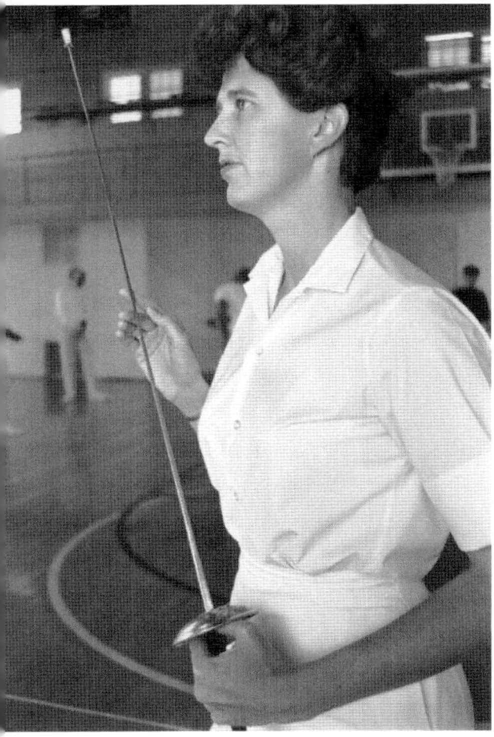

Virginia Peters
Peters came to the University of Central Oklahoma to play basketball in 1953 on a $40 scholarship. After graduation, she taught a year in Oklahoma City and then returned to the college in 1958, where she stayed 34 years as a coach, mentor, and administrator in the health and physical education department, retiring in 1992. An interesting part of Peters's legacy included teaching fencing at the request of legendary department head Emma Plunkett. When the college merged the men's and women's physical education and athletic departments in the 1970s, Peters was named the first chairperson. Probably the only time a professor was ever confronted by a gunman on the Edmond campus was when an enraged student burst into her office, apparently seeking another teacher. The man held a gun to her face and she heard it click. It failed to fire, and she was able to summon help, leading to the man being caught. (Courtesy UCO Library, Archives/Special Collections.)

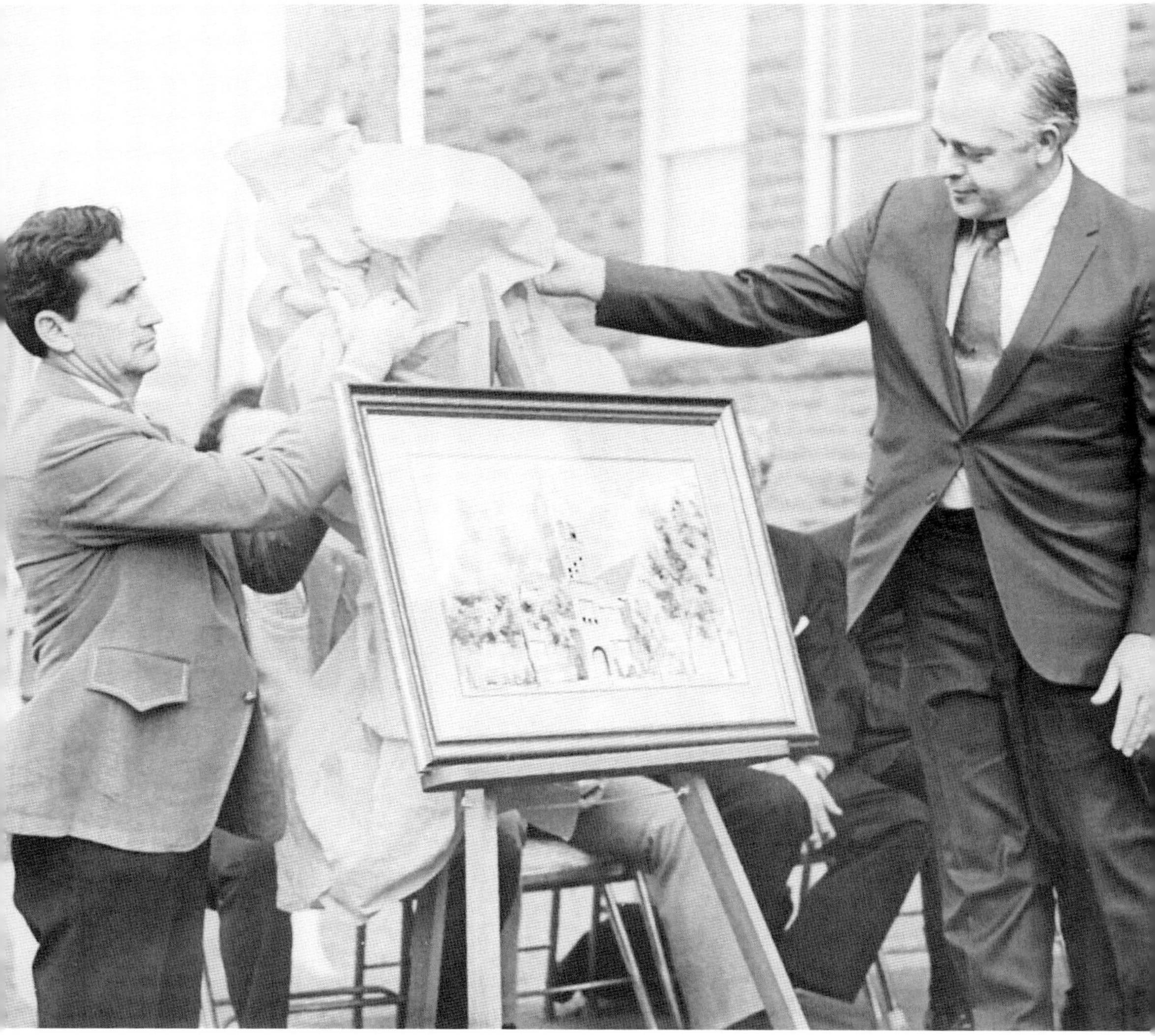

Stan Hoig

Hoig moved to Edmond in the 1960s from Houston, where he had been a publications editor for a private business, to teach at Central State College after getting his MA degree at Oklahoma University. A member of the Edmond Hall of Fame, he taught journalism at Central State until he retired in 1986. An "Old West" expert and historian, Hoig wrote more than 25 books, including local histories *Edmond: The First Century*, *The Early Years of Edmond*, and *In the Shadow of Old North Tower.* He became interested in the Cheyenne Indians and wrote several books dealing with them, including *The Cheyenne Indians* and *Peace Chiefs of the Cheyennes*. He penned *The Sand Creek Massacre*, *The Battle of the Washita* and *Sequoyah: The Cherokee Genius*. His list of literary and educational honors is long. He was inducted into the Oklahoma Hall of Fame in 1989 and Oklahoma Journalism Hall of Fame in 1994. His wife, the former Patricia Corbell, is retired from a teaching career in Edmond schools. Hoig died in 2009 at the age of 85. He is pictured at left as he helps to unveil the *Old North* painting with artist Gene Hartsell. (Courtesy Pat Hoig.)

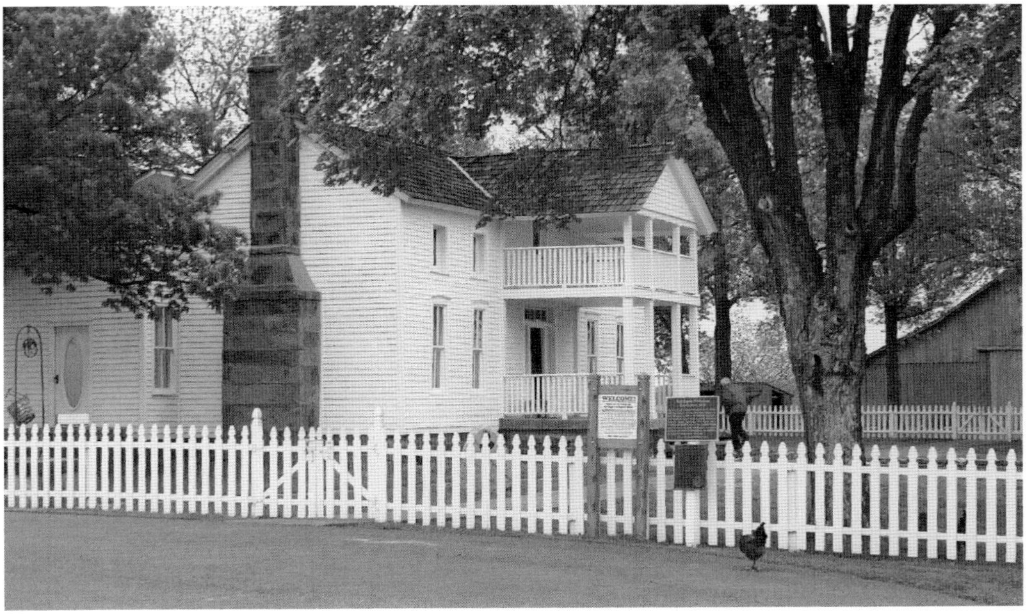

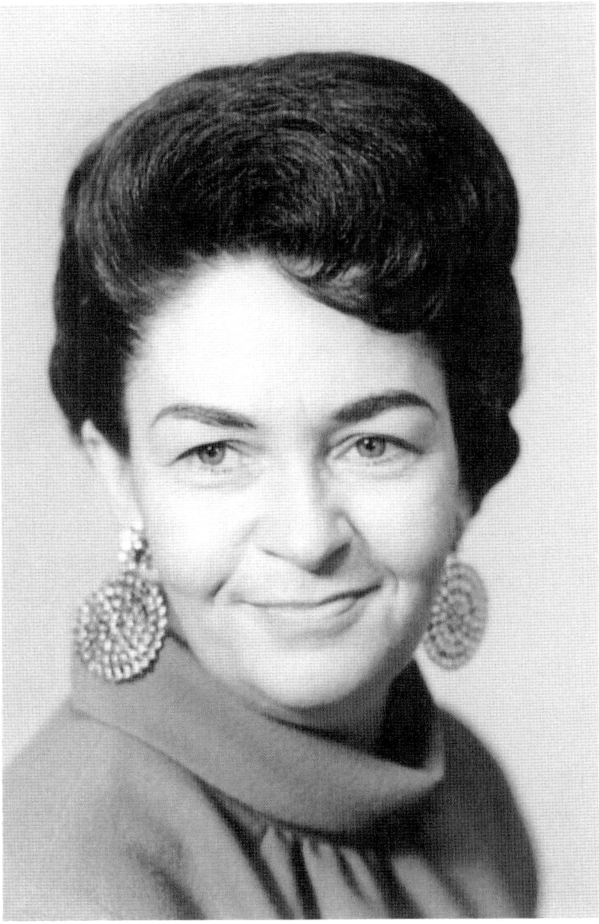

Reba Collins
Collins was director of the Will Rogers Memorial Museum in Claremore, Oklahoma, from 1975 to 1991. One of the world's foremost scholars on Will Rogers, Collins wrote seven books and hundreds of articles about him. She was raised on a farm north of Edmond, where she attended Rock Mound School. She was a journalism professor for many years at Central State University and also the director of university relations. She wrote articles and book reviews for many newspapers, including the *Edmond Sun* and *Daily Oklahoman*. She is a member of the Oklahoma Historians Hall of Fame and Oklahoma Journalism Hall of Fame. She came up with the idea of turning Will Rogers's birthplace in Oologah, Oklahoma, into a working ranch, recreating the period after his birth in 1879. (Below right, courtesy UCO Library, Archives/ Special Collections; above, courtesy David Fisk.)

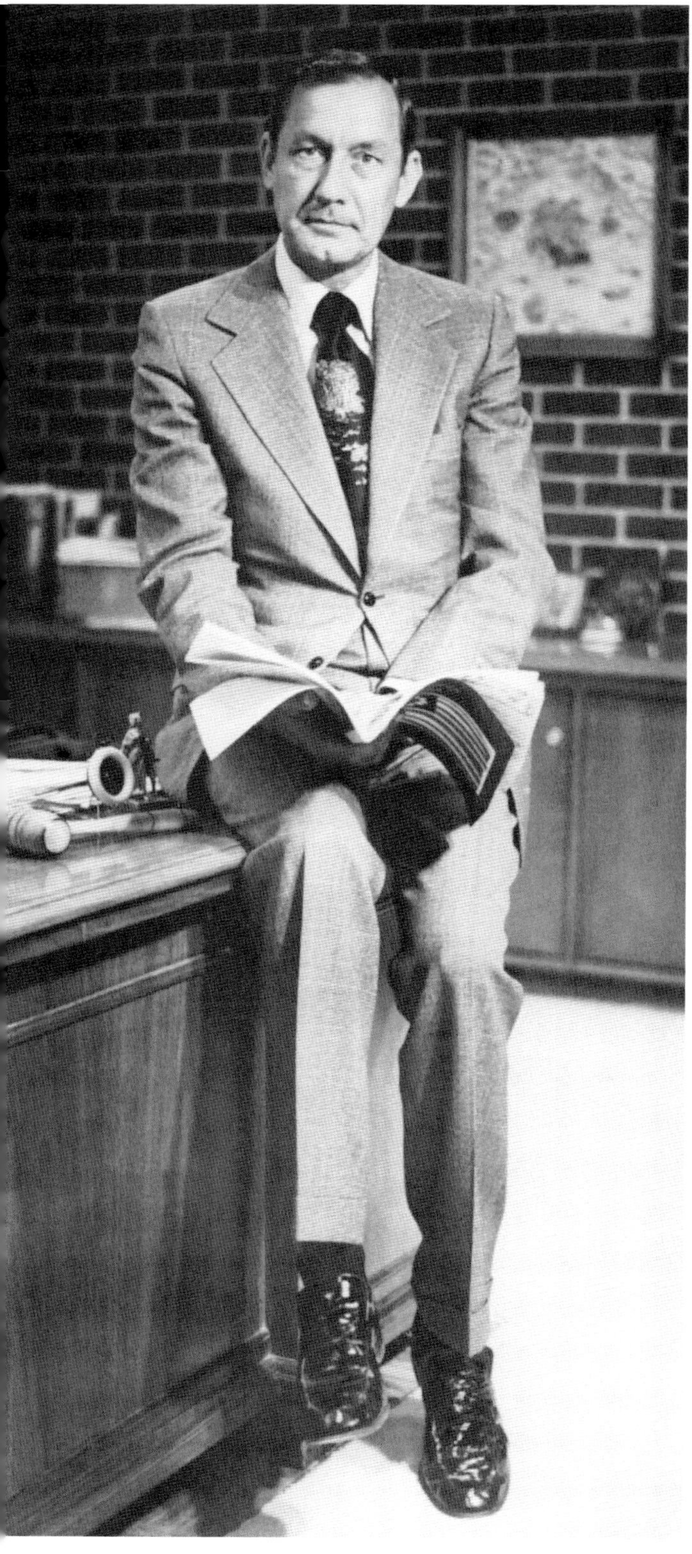

Bill Lillard

Lillard made quite an impact on Central State University during his 17-year tenure as college president from 1975 to 1992. Lillard was the man who gave the university its modern name and oversaw the construction of several new campus buildings. Lillard helped to change CSU's name to the University of Central Oklahoma and worked to expand the campus with the addition of several buildings and degree programs. Lillard also received several accolades during his presidency, particularly for his work in increasing the university's financial resources, his efforts in promoting the participation of women in higher education, and his pushing university enrollment above 13,000 for the first time. Lillard's tenure was not without challenges. Halfway through his tenure, Lillard survived an attempt by then-regent Ed Livermore and members of the CSU faculty to block renewal of his contract. The board of regents ultimately voted to renew Lillard's contract. He retired in 1992 and was succeeded by Pres. George Nigh. Nigh named the Lillard Administration Building after his predecessor and predecessor's wife. Lillard was 87 when he died in 2012. UCO president Don Betz said, "President Lillard and his late wife, Mary Helen, served Central with grace and distinction for 17 years, leaving behind a legacy that will long be remembered in the community and beyond." Betz called him "one of this university's great leaders." Before coming to UCO, he was superintendent of the Oklahoma City School District. Lillard and his wife shared a love for athletics. Mary Helen was a long time physical education instructor for Oklahoma City Public Schools, and Lillard was an avowed ice hockey fanatic. "I am a hockey hound myself, but Mary Helen doesn't care much for hockey," Lillard said in a 1974 article published in the *Vista*. (Courtesy UCO Library, Archives/Special Collections.)

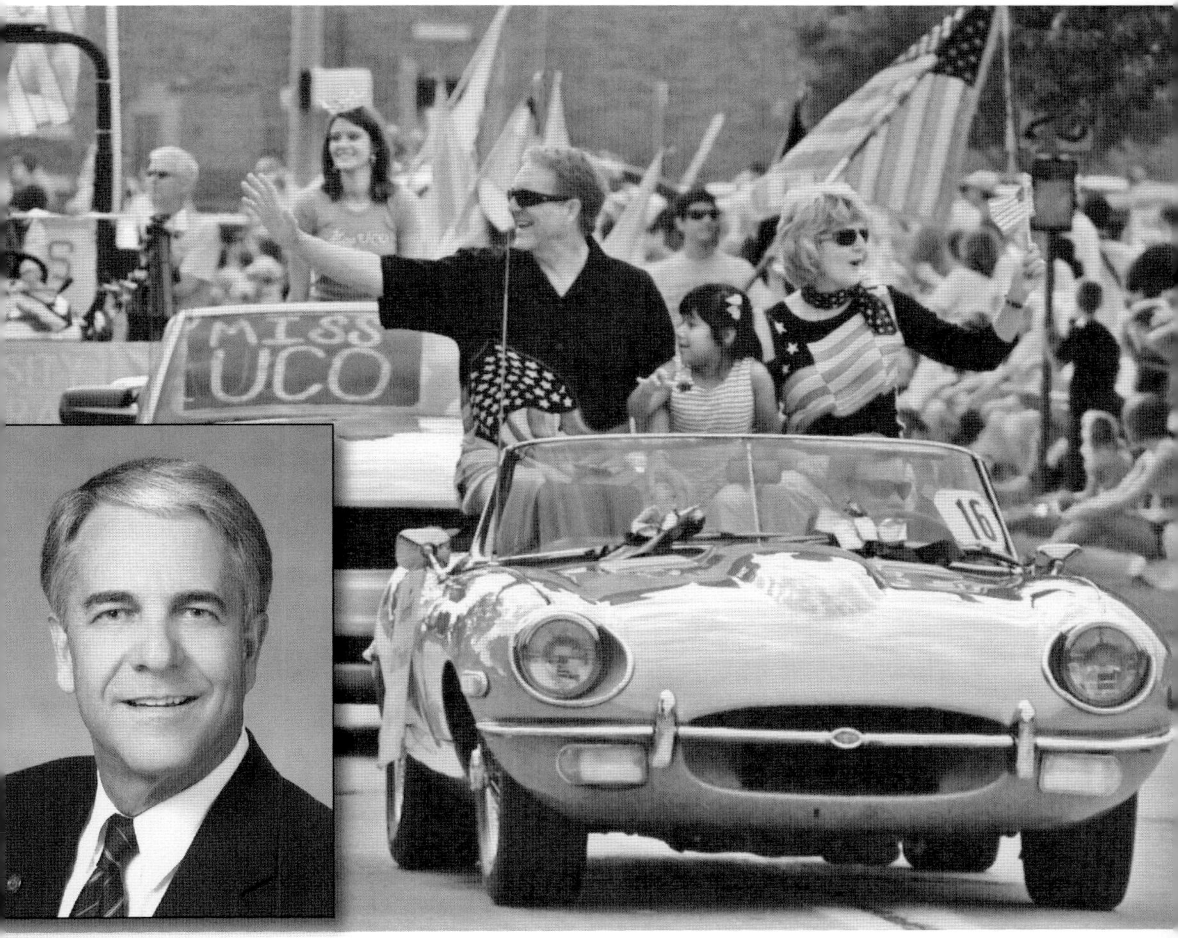

Roger Webb

If there was ever a candidate for a Citizen of the Decade award, Webb, retired president of Oklahoma's third largest university, would be at the top of list. Webb was at the helm of the University of Central Oklahoma from 1997 until 2011. He was named Edmond's Citizen of the Year in 2009. Since stepping down from the top spot at UCO, Webb has been serving on the board of Citizen's Bank. As the 19th president of the school, Webb left a deep imprint, leading UCO through some of its greatest years of growth and development. His impact on Edmond and UCO is immense. He was instrumental in bringing the Oklahoma State Bureau of Investigation (OSBI) Crime Lab to Edmond and creating the UCO Forensic Science Institute across the street from the OSBI lab. He made UCO one of the premier forensics and criminal research facilities in the world. He convinced UCO grad Dwight Adams to lead the program. Adams came back to Edmond from the FBI and brought on board many former crime lab directors and other personnel, including bomb experts, with him. The future of music took a new direction with another Webb project. His vision brought about the creation of the new Academy of Contemporary Music (ACM) at UCO, located in Oklahoma City's historic Bricktown. The academy is the only American affiliate of the original academy in England. ACM continues to grow at a fast pace, with students beating on the doors to enroll. Webb helped coordinate the establishment of the teaching/entertainment venue known as the UCO Jazz Lab. His efforts brought together the City of Edmond, businessman Mark Neighbors, and UCO. Neighbors donated land near the university campus for the building. Webb helped set up Tres Amigos Productions to bring in artists such as Judy Collins, Boz Scaggs, Jerry Jeff Walker, Steve Tyrell, and other contemporary musicians. (Courtesy David Fisk; inset, courtesy *Edmond Life and Leisure*.)

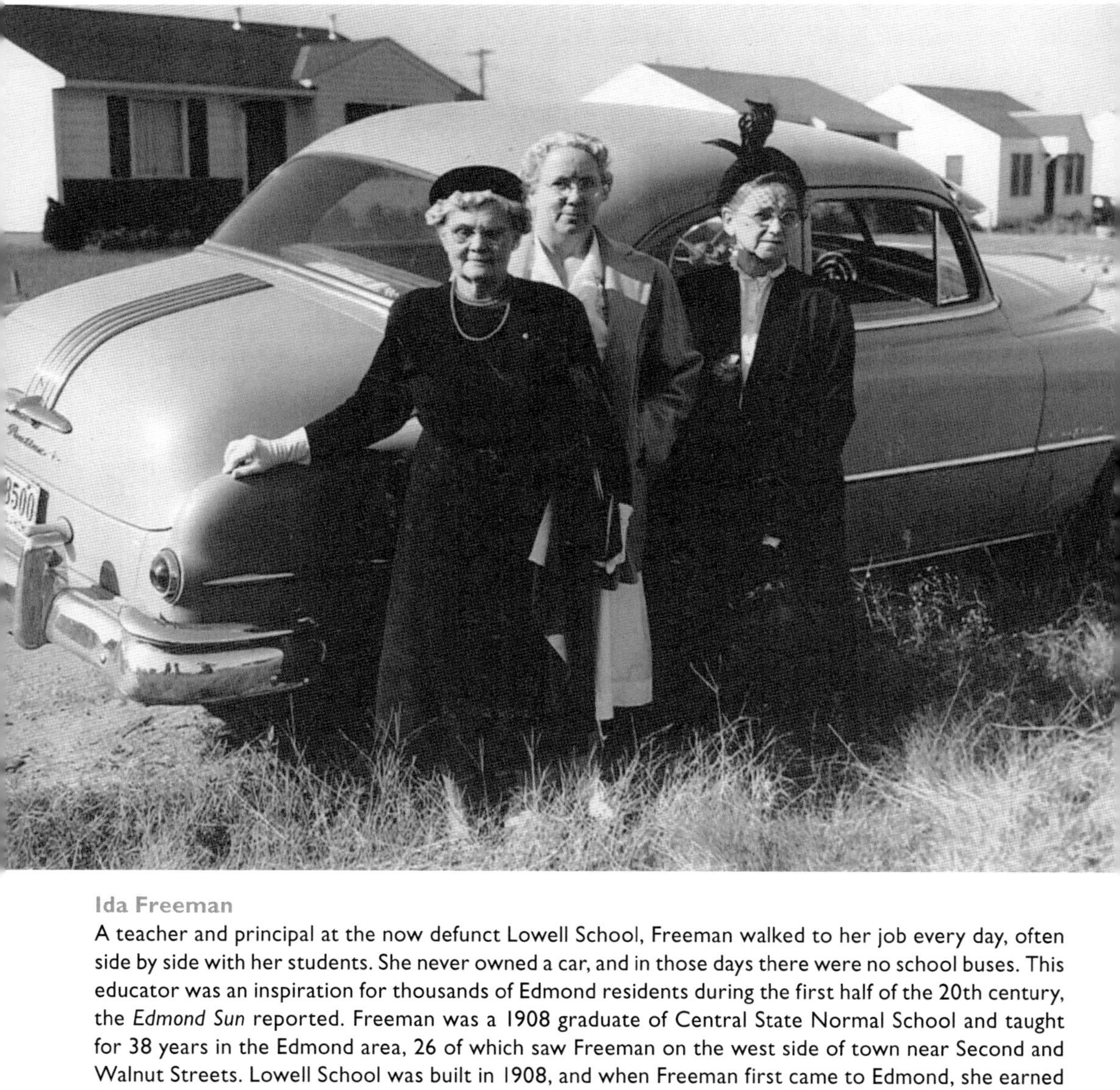

Ida Freeman
A teacher and principal at the now defunct Lowell School, Freeman walked to her job every day, often side by side with her students. She never owned a car, and in those days there were no school buses. This educator was an inspiration for thousands of Edmond residents during the first half of the 20th century, the *Edmond Sun* reported. Freeman was a 1908 graduate of Central State Normal School and taught for 38 years in the Edmond area, 26 of which saw Freeman on the west side of town near Second and Walnut Streets. Lowell School was built in 1908, and when Freeman first came to Edmond, she earned $55 a month. In 1950, a new school, Ida Freeman Elementary, was named for her. Freeman, left, is shown above at the ground-breaking ceremony with her sister Estella Boone (center) and Carrie Freeman (right), her brother's wife. "Miss Ida" was proud of a huge pecan tree that shaded her yard at her home on First Street near University Drive. In 1915, she gave her students hundreds of pecans to plant, some of which still stand. (Courtesy Edmond Historical Society Photographic Collection.)

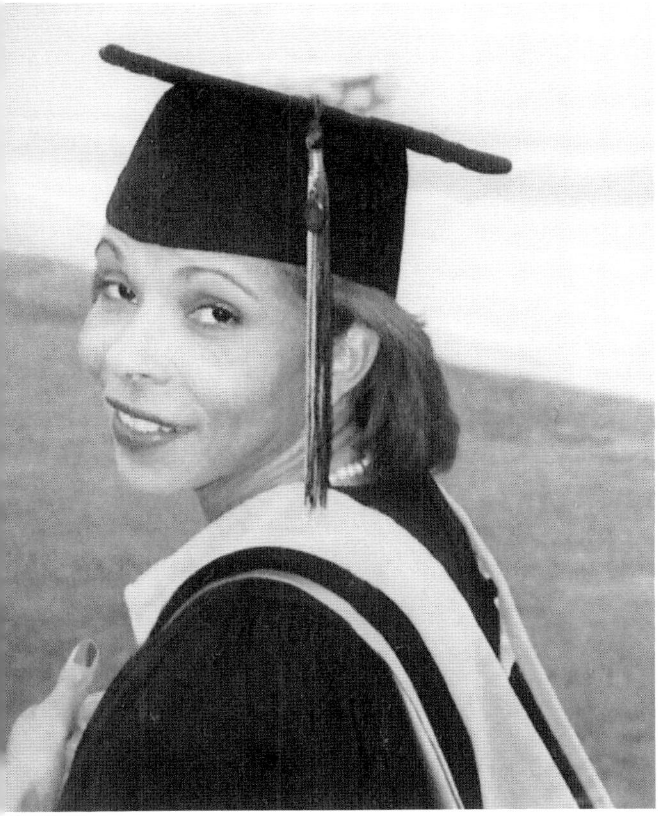

Oretha Moulder

Edmond Public Schools' first black administrator, Oretha Moulder, began in 1976 as a fifth-grade teacher at Russell Dougherty Elementary. She taught at Cimarron, Northern Hills, and Clegern, where she was principal. Diagnosed with cancer in 2000, she retired as principal of Charles Haskell in the fall semester and died a month later. Former superintendent George Rowley told the *Edmond Sun* that he "hired Moulder because she was the 'best-qualified candidate' to teach at Russell Dougherty." A Langston University graduate, Moulder earned her master's degree in education at Central State University. School superintendent Charles Goin called her a " 'great lady' who never allowed cancer to best her spirit or faith." (Courtesy the Moulder family.)

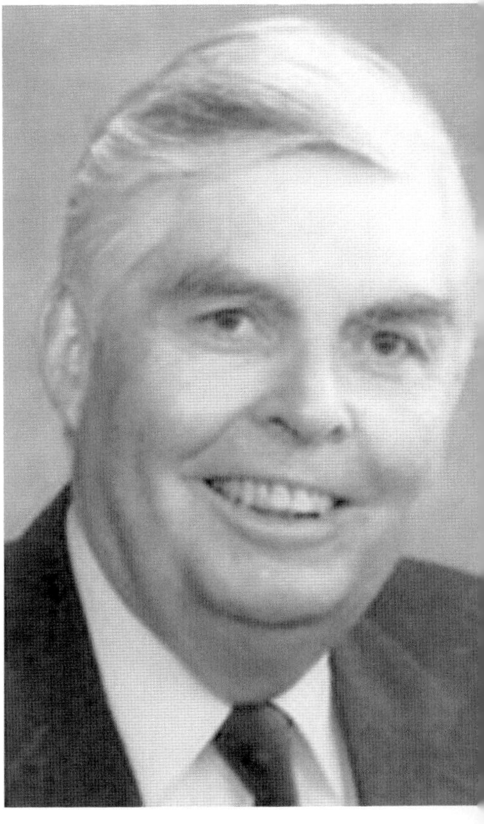

George Rowley

Rowley came to Edmond from Blackwell, Oklahoma, to be superintendent of the school district, a post he held almost 15 years. During his tenure, he was responsible for construction of new schools including Chisholm, John Ross, Haskell, North Mid-High, Sequoyah, Cimarron, and more. Edmond's Citizen of the Year in 1987, Rowley steered growth of the district from 4,800 to 11,600 students. An honorary member of the Edmond Educational Endowment, he initiated many new programs, including an arts-in-education program and advance placement classes. He was an educator in Oklahoma for 39 years before retiring in 1988. (Courtesy Edmond Public School District.)

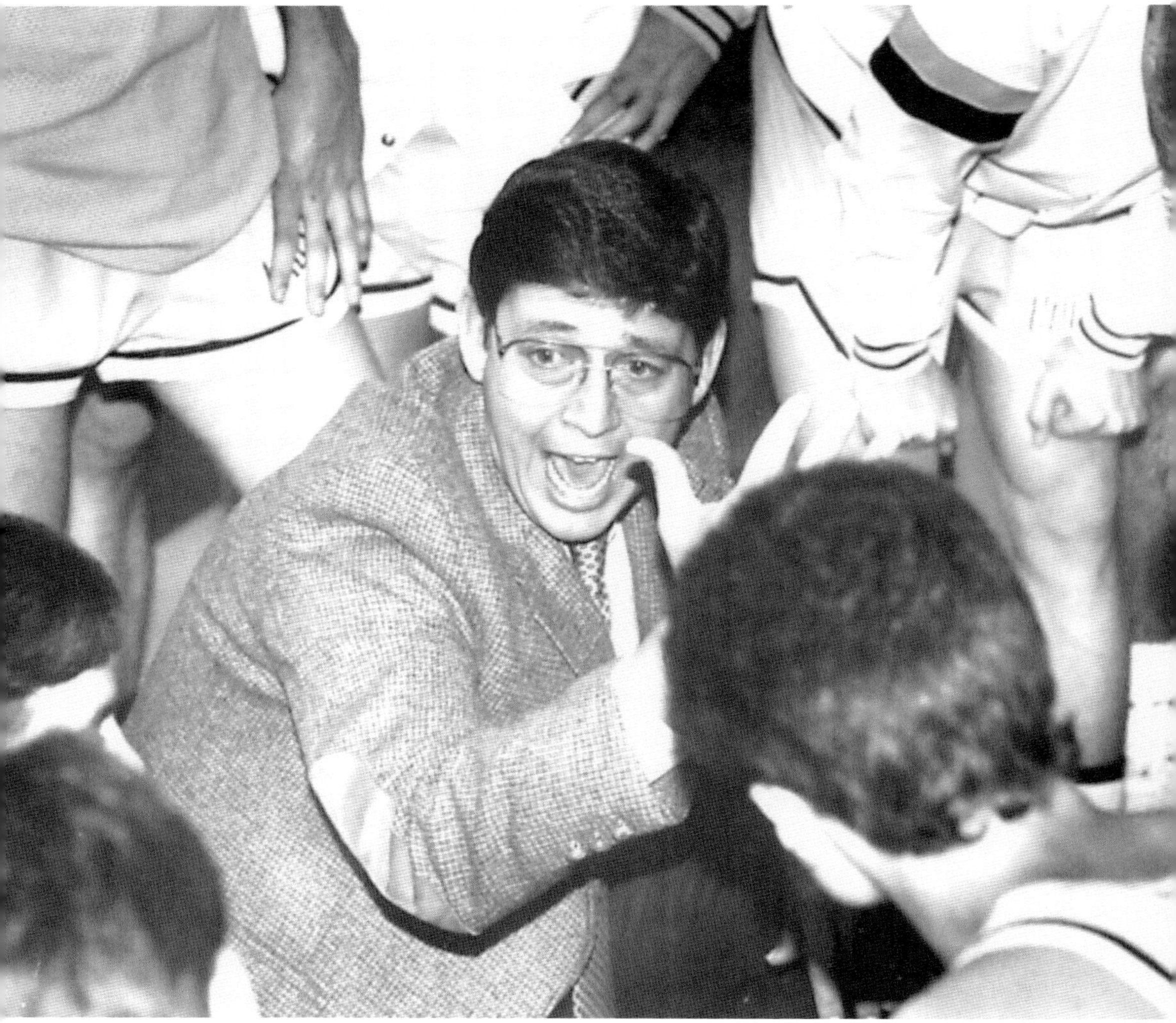

Mike de la Garza

"Just try to win the next game" is the advice former Edmond Memorial High School basketball coach and athletic director de la Garza has for other coaches. He used that approach during his more-than-40-year career, including 22 years coaching the Memorial Bulldogs. The peak of his success came with the state championship in 1993 as coach and then again in 2011 as athletic director. The 1993 team went 27-2, and the championship was the 303rd win for de la Garza in Edmond. His Bulldogs made the state tournament 11 times from 1979 to 1994. In 2011, he was inducted into the Oklahoma Coaches Association Hall of Fame. He also taught business at Memorial, and his former students and players are not shy about piling on their praise for him. One former player summed it up with, "I had no other teacher who cared more about his players and his job than Coach." Before coming to Edmond, he coached several years at Mount St. Mary in Oklahoma City. (Courtesy the *Oklahoman* archives.)

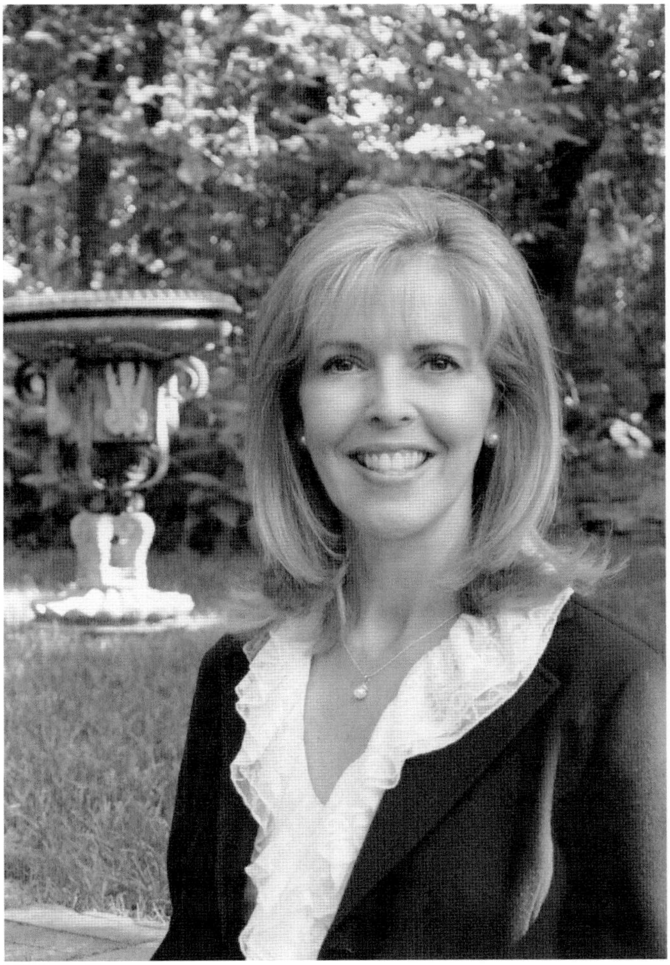

Rhonda Harryman
"Special" describes Harryman, the first Edmond educator to hold the honor of being Oklahoma State Teacher of the Year, representing 48,000 teachers. Harryman taught special education in Edmond schools and the University of Central Oklahoma for almost 30 years and was Edmond's Teacher of the Year in 1991–1992, earning the Oklahoma title that year. Harryman told judges, "Because I believe every child can learn, regardless of background or handicapping condition, teaching special needs children is the most rewarding career I can imagine." Harryman often dressed as characters from books to help tell stories to her students at Cross Timbers and Russell Dougherty. Harryman and her husband, Gil, Edmond's fire chief for 11 years, coached Edmond Special Olympic teams for 16 years. For 35 years, the Harrymans have worked with boys at the Edmond Boys Ranch, serving as positive role models, tutoring, taking them on trips, and just having fun. They are involved with many activities at Henderson Hills Baptist Church, including the Ministries of Jesus and Special Ministries, where they help children with developmental disabilities. For Valentine's Day in 1999, the *Edmond Sun* ran a contest called "How I Met My Valentine." The Harrymans won hands-down with their heart-warming entry. The entry described "a tale of two people, burned by previous relationships, who united to lift up not only themselves but the community around them." The couple met through friends on a blind date; they were engaged after the third date. Gil had told Rhonda she could go with him for his "night out with the boys." She did, and it was to Boys Town Ranch, where he helped mentor young boys. Harryman told her friends, "Just because I met this guy doesn't mean I have to marry him." The rest of the story is history. (Courtesy Rhonda Harryman.)

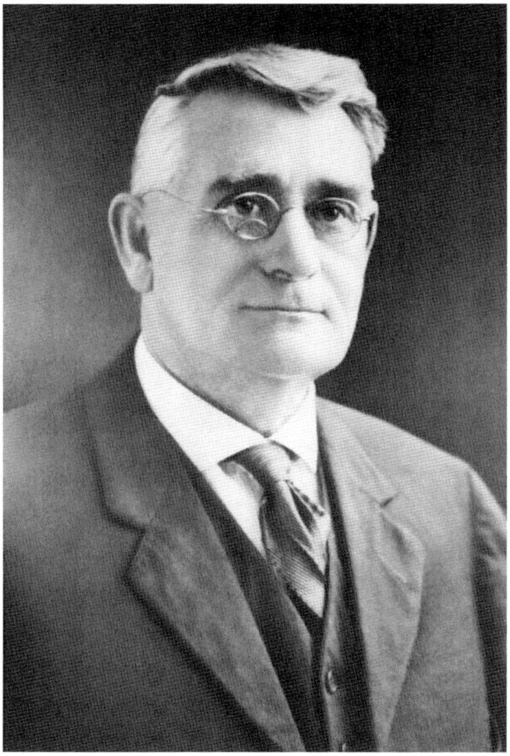

Dr. John Woodville Howard

Dr. Howard arrived in Edmond just a few months after the 1889 land run with his son, seeking a drier climate than Kentucky. His wife and daughters soon joined him at the farmland he acquired at what is now Broadway and Coffee Creek Road. He established an excellent reputation as a pioneer doctor and opened Howard Drug Store in downtown Edmond, which he operated until retiring in 1920. According to information from his relatives in material in the UCO Library Archives, Howard travelled by horseback or used a two-wheel cart to tend to the sick in the 1890s. Howard was elected to represent the Edmond area in the Territorial Legislature and introduced the bill that led to having Central Normal School (now the University of Central Oklahoma) located in Edmond. (Courtesy UCO Library, Archives/Special Collections.)

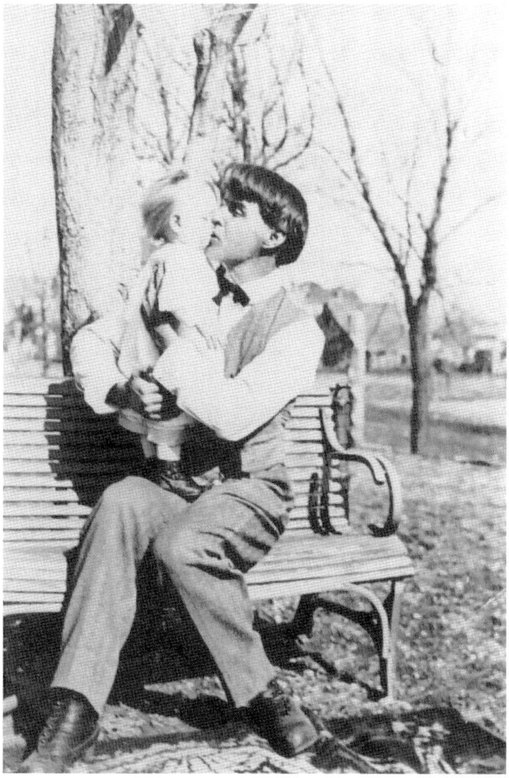

Dr. Arthur Masters Ruhl

Ruhl was a country doctor for more than a third of a century. He came to Edmond around 1900, where he practiced medicine until his death in 1936. Today, Edmond residents often drive by the house he built back in 1908 at the corner of First Street and University Drive, home to Arcadian Inn Bed and Breakfast. A newspaper obituary said, "No matter whence the call came, the lowly cabin or the mansion, Dr. Ruhl always responded. He gave his services as cheerfully in the humble home without compensation as in the homes of the more pretentious." Martha Hall, owner of the Arcadian Inn, said he was well known for having saved a boy's arm in a tractor accident. (Courtesy Edmond Historical Society Photographic Collection.)

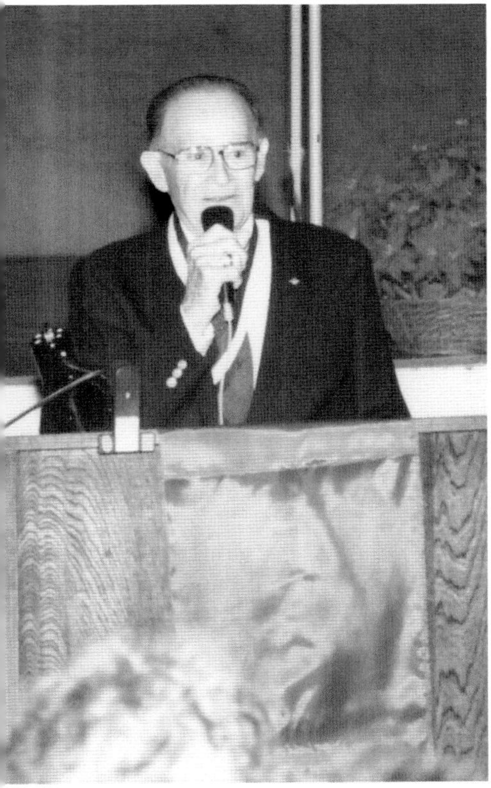

Dr. W.H. Roberts

In 1937, Dr. Roberts packed his new Chevy and left Missouri, looking for a college town in Oklahoma to establish a practice. He found Edmond and spent the rest of his life here. The first thing he did was offer free physical exams to the Central State football team. He became a lifelong Broncho fan, missing only four games in 54 years. His first office was above the Broncho Theatre at 20 North Broadway. At times, he was the only doctor in town. He operated two maternity homes that were the first licensed medical facilities in Edmond. In the 45 years he practiced medicine in Edmond, he said he delivered more babies than the total population of the town the year he arrived.

In 1950, he opened the Parkside Osteopathic Hospital at 101 East Fourth Street, and he operated it until closing it in 1967, when Edmond Memorial Hospital was opened. He was chief of staff there and a team physician for Edmond High School's Bulldogs for more than 40 years. He was inducted into the Edmond Hall of Fame in 1986 and named the Oklahoma Osteopathic Association Doctor of the Year in 1986. A longtime Edmond Chamber of Commerce member, he was a charter member of Edmond Rotary Club. (Left, courtesy UCO Library, Archives/Special Collections; below, courtesy David Fisk.)

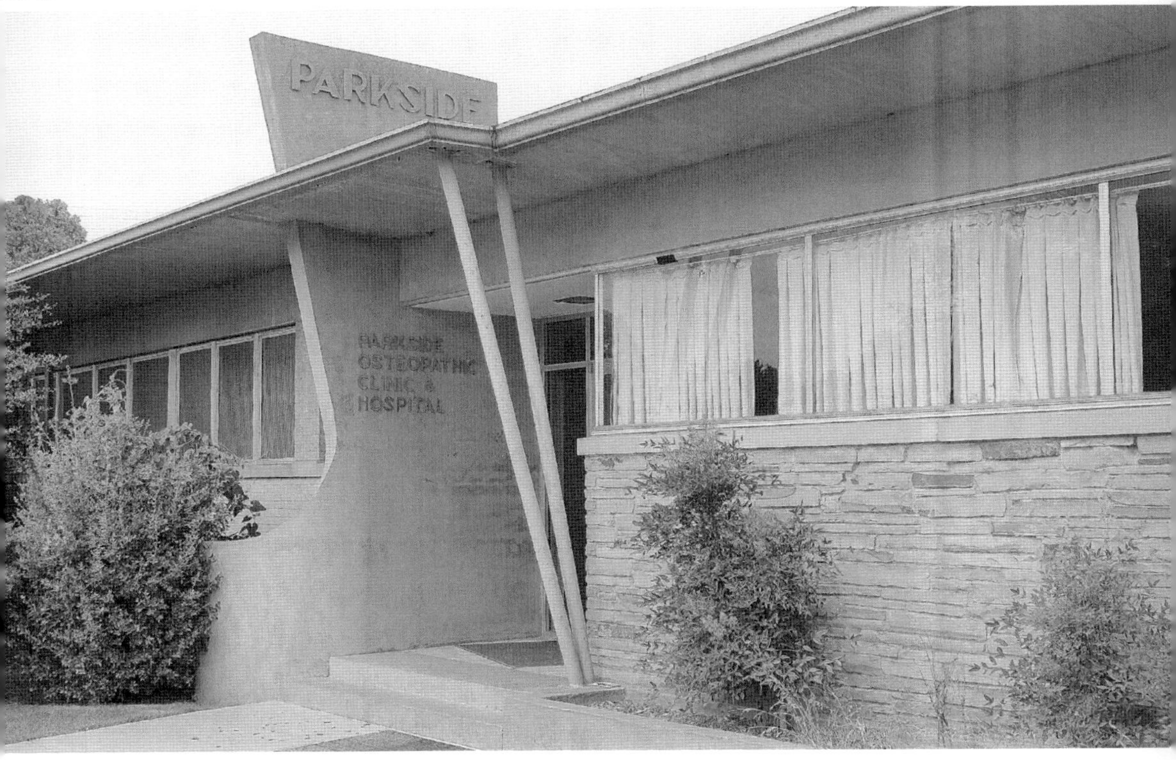

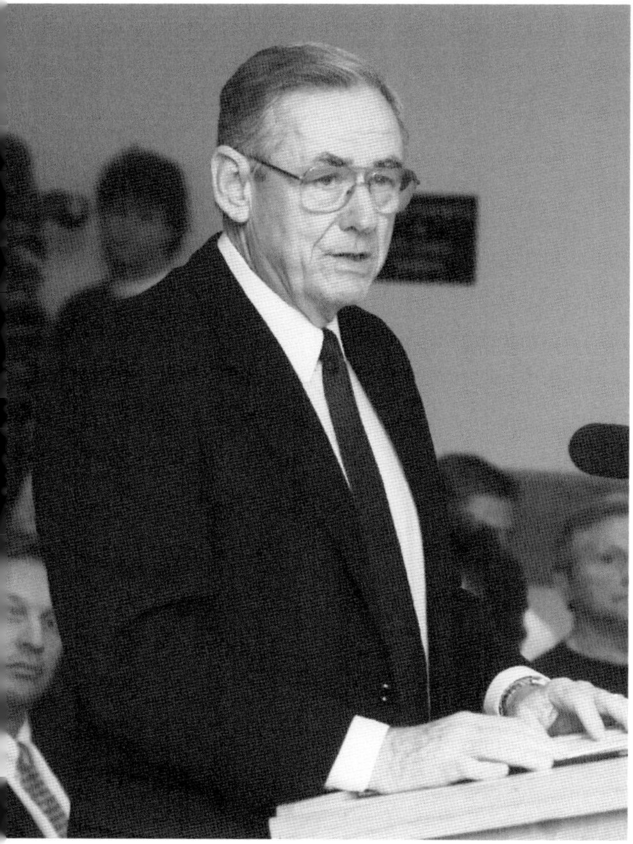

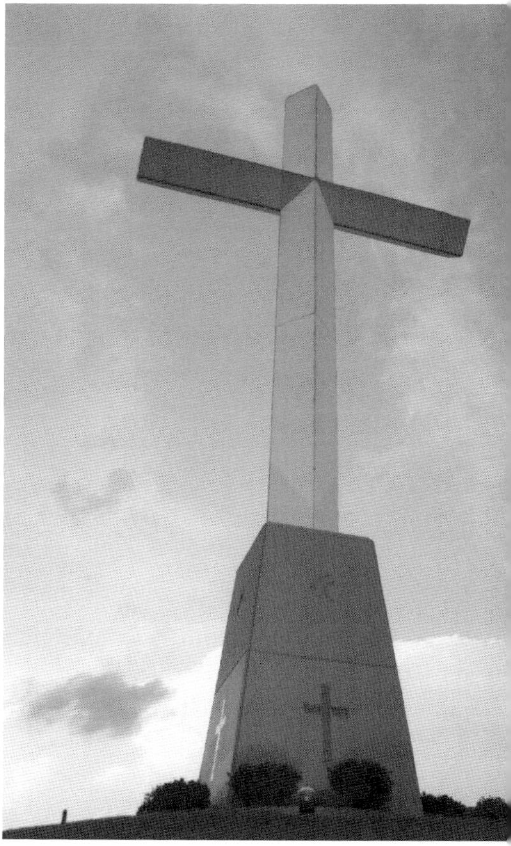

Rev. Jimmy Hylton

In 1995, Hylton became senior pastor of MetroChurch. Three years later, he saw the fulfillment of the church's dream as a huge white concrete cross was built at the church high above Interstate 35 and Second Street. The 100-foot-tall cross sits atop a 37-foot-tall base and can be seen from miles away. Edmond's city council originally denied the church a permit for the cross but after much debate approved a permit in 1997. A lawsuit challenging the action brought an injunction, barring the church from building the cross. In October 1997, District Judge Niles Jackson dismissed the suit, and a permit was issued a few days later. Private donations of $1.5 million helped fund the project. (Left, courtesy the *Oklahoman* archives; right, courtesy David Fisk.)

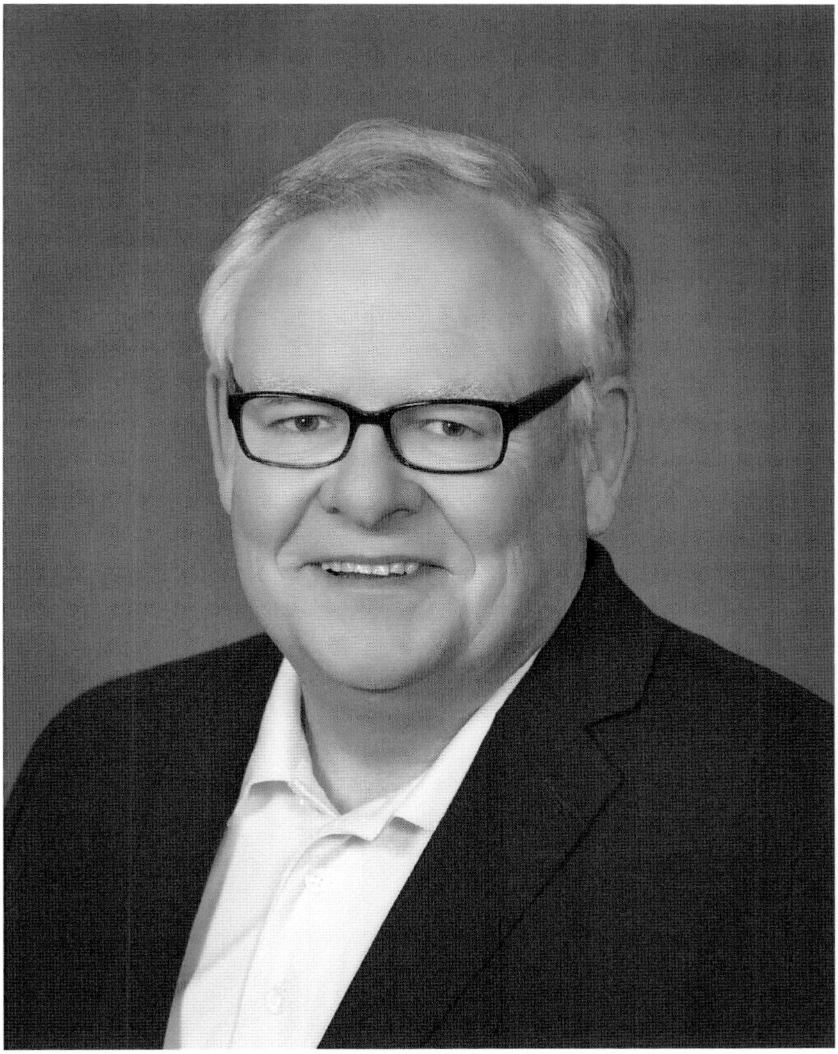

Rev. Dennis Newkirk

Henderson Hills Baptist Church turned 50 in 2014, and Senior Pastor Newkirk has been with the church almost half that time, joining HHBC in 1992. Since then, church membership has grown to 5,500, making it one of the largest congregations in Oklahoma. Under his leadership, the church began following a document it produced called the "Ten Principles of Ministry." The church formed a leadership council in 1996 called the Elder Council. In 1999, a proposal to merge with MetroChurch was nixed, and attendance declined slightly. Healing took place over a period of years, and the church grew steadily. In 2001, when the church was running out of room at its original location at 2300 South Boulevard Street, he led a "Time for Sacrifice" fund-raising program for a new 2,500-seat worship center. He guided the church in its move in 2004 to its new I-35 and Fifteenth Street location and was later instrumental in the $5.3-million sale of church-owned land for the new Integris Hospital, which opened north of the church. Newkirk's idea for a free medical clinic took shape, and in 2002, Ministries of Jesus opened its doors. Newkirk has two books to his credit: *No gods but God*, a book about confronting modern-day idolatry, and *Glimpses of God's Glory*, which combines his passion for God, travel, and photography as he shares his favorite photographs and devotional writings. Newkirk grew up in Phoenix, Arizona, and worked in insurance before becoming a minister. (Courtesy Henderson Hills Baptist Church.)

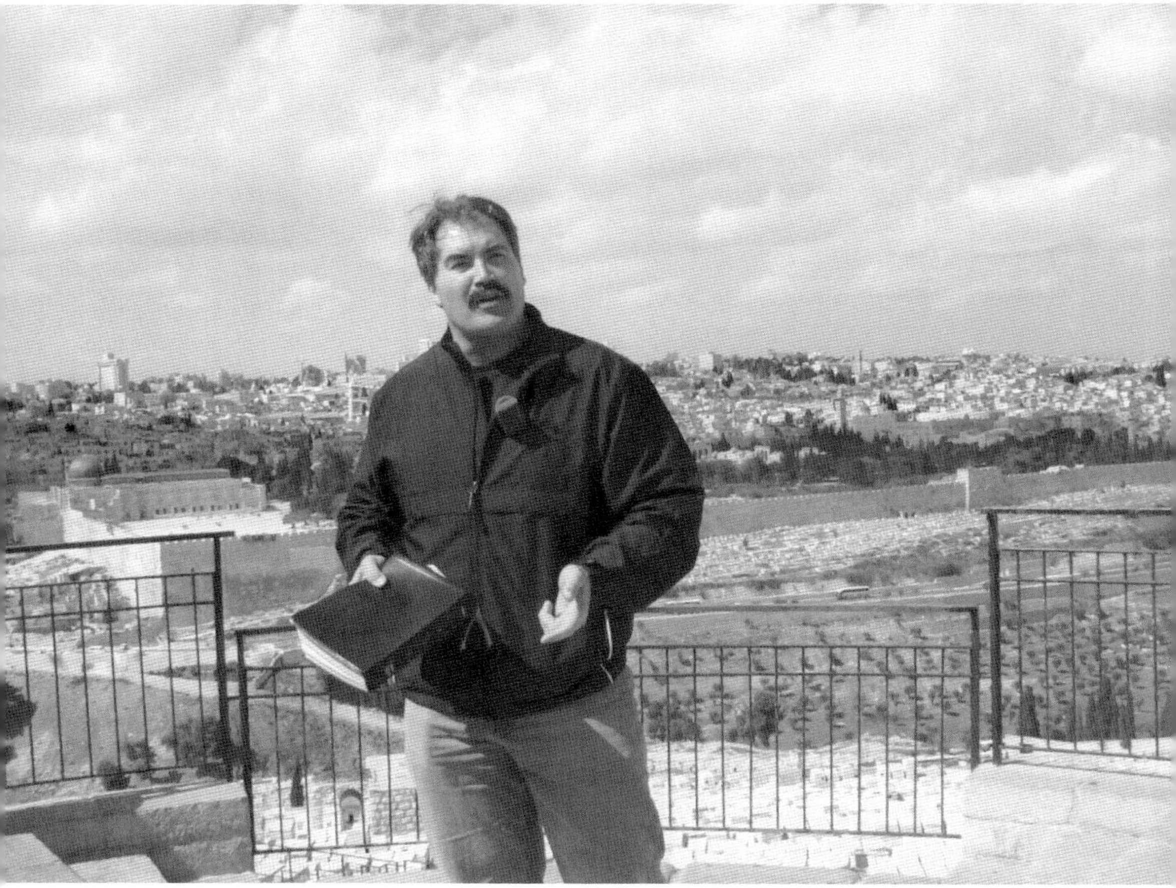

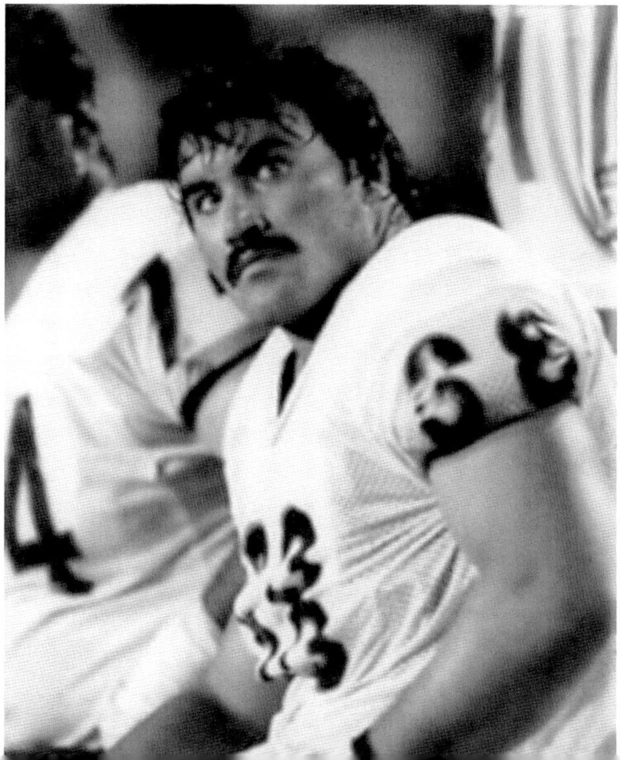

Rev. Paul Blair

From the gridiron to preaching the word of God, Blair has travelled a long road. The former NFL and Memorial High School football star ran a close and controversial Republican primary campaign for the state senate in 2012, losing by about 1,000 votes to incumbent Clark Jolley. The owner of Blair Vending and Coffee, he is also pastor of Fairview Baptist Church. He was a driving force in organizing Reclaiming America for Christ and Reclaiming Oklahoma for Christ. He played with the Chicago Bears, Denver Broncos, and Minnesota Vikings before retiring in 1990 because of knee injuries. (Both, courtesy Paul Blair.)

Rev. Mateen Elass

First Presbyterian Church of Edmond senior pastor Elass led his congregation as it voted to split ties with the Presbyterian Church (USA) and join the Evangelical Covenant Order of Presbyterians. In a historic 815-95 vote, the church cut ties with the denomination over theological differences. The action was called the most significant in the history of the church, which was established following the Land Run of 1889. Elass told the *Edmond Sun*, "I think this vote, a huge landslide vote, is a vindication of the direction that the leadership felt God was calling this congregation to move forward." Elass was born to a Muslim father and American mother, was raised in Saudi Arabia for more than a decade, and was schooled in western philosophy and psychology. Elass became a Christian when he was 20 and paid a high cost for his new faith: isolation from his father for many years. He became a minister and came to Edmond's First Presbyterian in 2007. He had been senior pastor at a church in Illinois before that. (Right, courtesy Mateen Elass; below, courtesy David Fisk.)

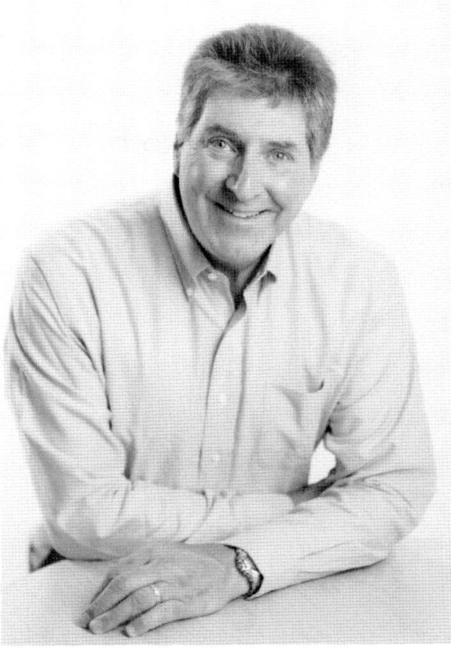

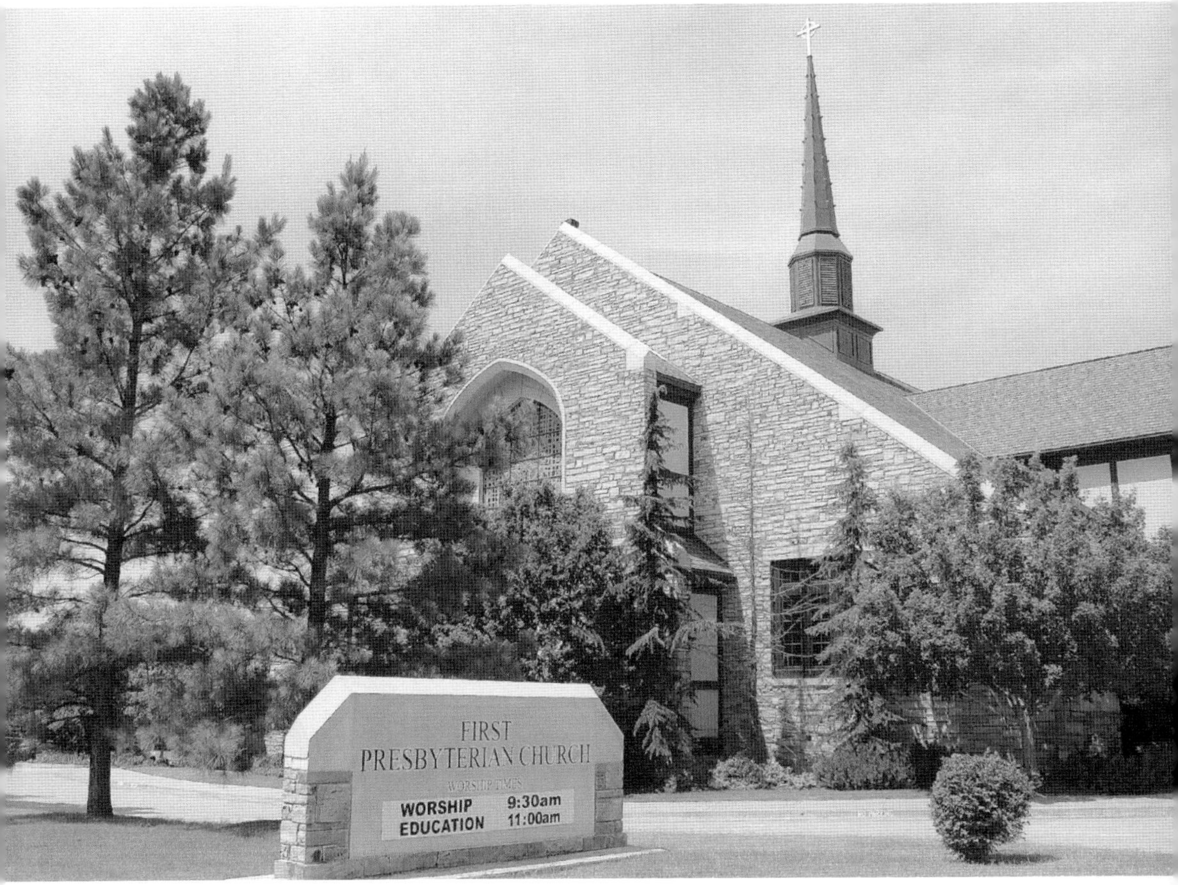

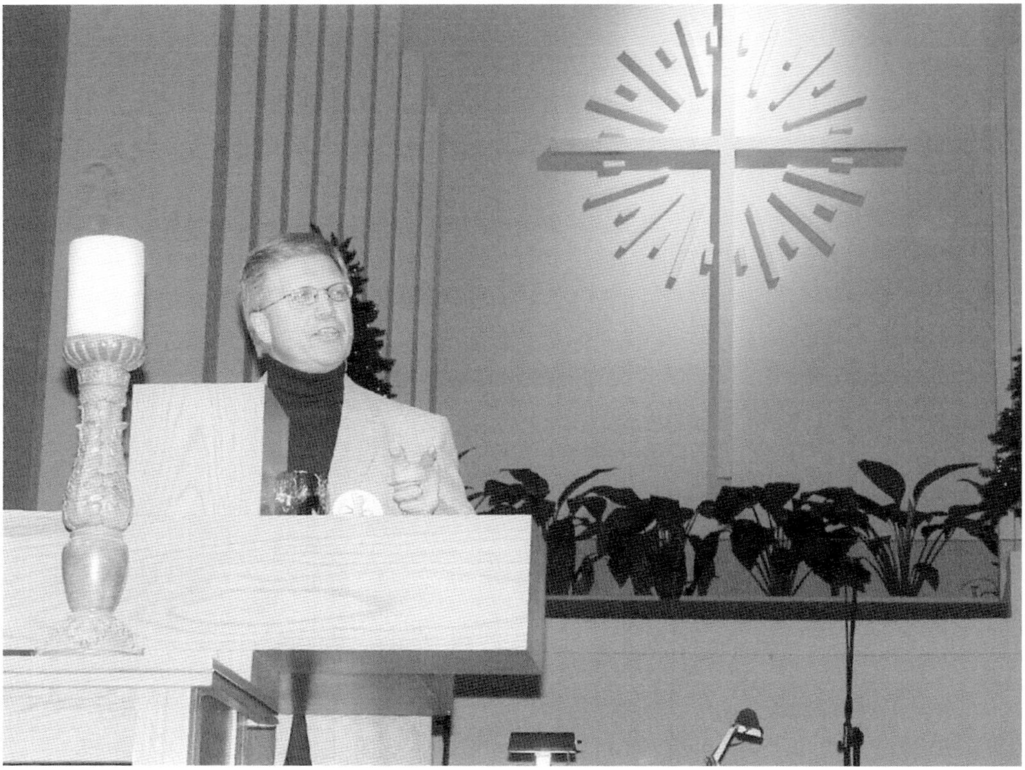

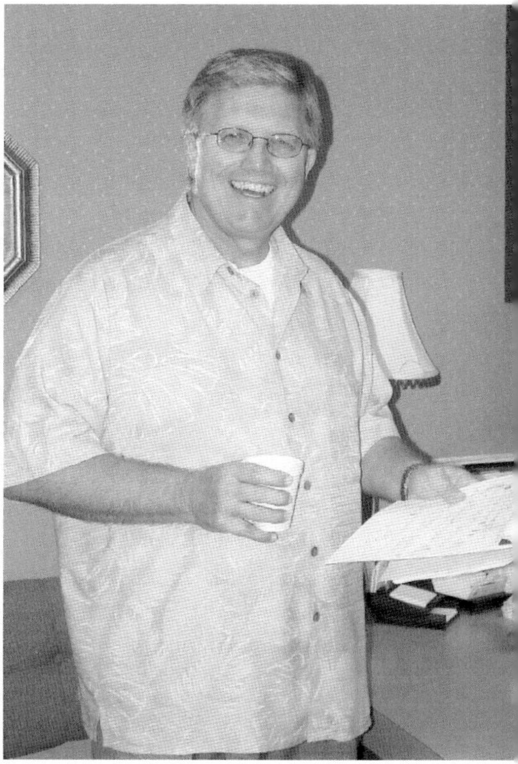

Rev. Alan Day

Day had just celebrated 25 years ministering to his congregation at Edmond's First Baptist Church when he was killed in a motorcycle accident in 2011. Day was senior pastor at the church and had been a pastor since 1968, serving at churches in Louisiana, Texas, Mississippi, and Oklahoma. The associate pastor of First Baptist, Keith Haygood, told the *Oklahoman*, "Day would want his death to lead people to Christ. . . . Alan Day was a godly man, he was a man of great faith, and he spent his life encouraging people to make themselves ready." Day came to First Baptist in 1985 when longtime pastor Eugene Stockwell stepped down. He emphasized and encouraged the church to do special mission projects. In 1986, church members voted to relocate the church to Thirty-Third Street and Bryant Avenue. They kicked off a long campaign to raise money to build the $6.7-million complex, and Day helped steer that journey. A new church was dedicated on May 5, 1993. Day was a former board member of the Southern Baptist International Mission Board and a vice chair of the Oklahoma Baptist University trustee board. (Both, courtesy First Baptist Church.)

CHAPTER THREE

Jocks and Stars

Edmond has had more than its share of famous athletes and celebrities, Olympian Shannon Miller perhaps being the most famous. Beauty queen Anita Bryant is another whose name is familiar to many from her long singing career. Professional golfers, baseball players, football stars, basketball players, rodeo champions, bowlers, actors, beauty queens, sculptors, musicians: you name it, Edmond has them.

The University of Central Oklahoma can boast former Miss America Lauren Nelson. Television viewers can see Jim Beaver in shows like *Justified* and *Deadwood*. Sculptor Shan Gray captured the grace and beauty of Miller with his statue in Shannon Miller Park. Horseshoe Road has taken its music worldwide, while Garrett "Big G" Jacobson plays the blues for many area fans.

Local high schools have produced a number of athletes and coaches that have made their mark professionally. Bill Self, University of Kansas national championship basketball coach, first starred at Memorial High School under legendary coach Mike de la Garza. NBA superstar Blake Griffin led Oklahoma Christian to basketball glory while being coached by his dad before starring at the University of Oklahoma.

Kelly Gregg made his mark in the NFL after starring at not one but two Edmond high schools. Brandon Weeden, Reggie Smith, Paul Blair, and numerous others have gone from Edmond schools to college and professional stardom. Cal McLish and Jim Gentile had notable major-league careers, with others like Ty Hensley perhaps heading in that direction.

And then there is UCO wrestler Ray Clemons, who led the US wrestling team to Berlin for the controversial 1936 Olympics. Clemons is still the only UCO athlete to have been in the Olympics.

Edmond is known nationwide for its challenging golf courses. The private Oak Tree National has hosted several PGA championship events, including the 1988 US Open. The USGA Senior Open is scheduled in 2014 at Oak Tree. Golfers Dr. Gil Morgan, Bob Tway, Scott Verplank, Doug Tewell, Mark Hayes, Willie Woods, and Dave and Danny Edwards call Edmond home.

There are many others and not enough room to write about them all, but Edmond is bursting at the seams with notable stars and athletes.

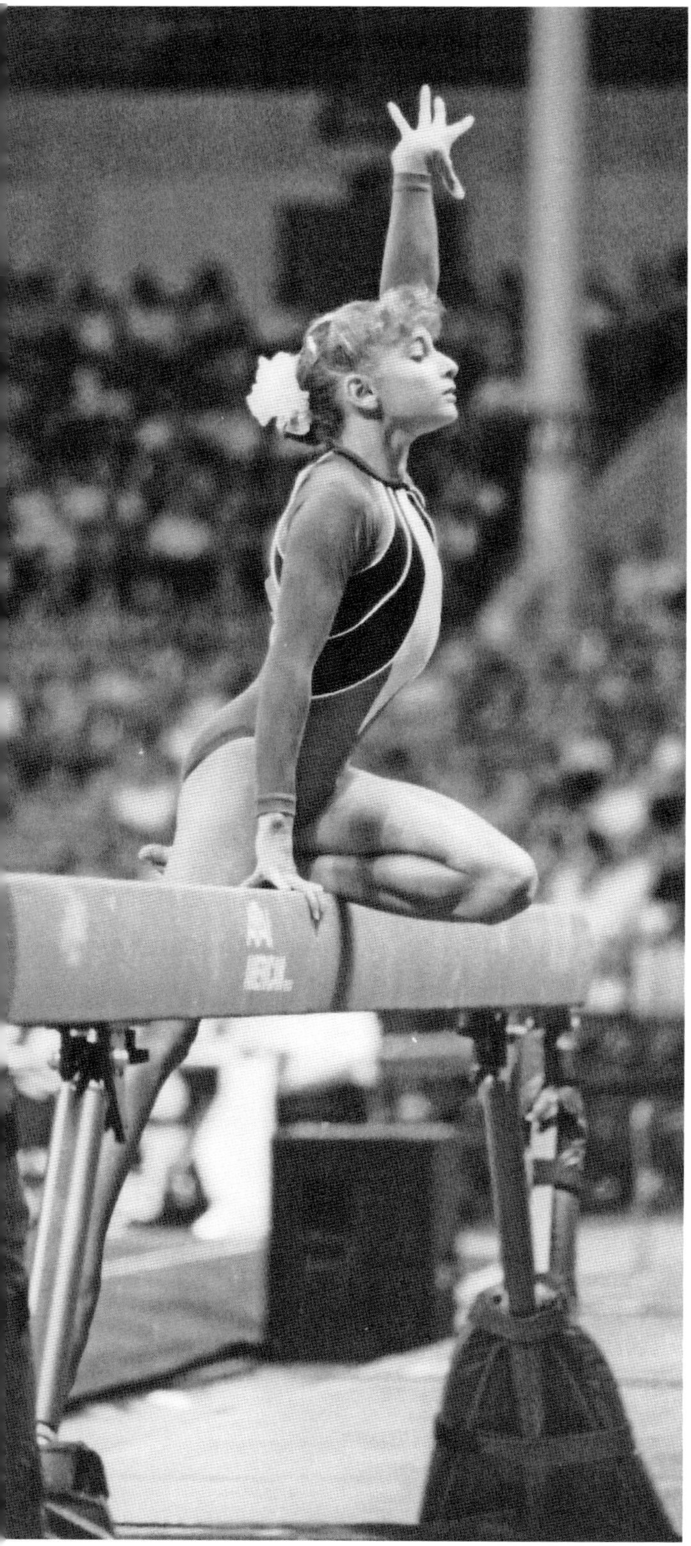

Shannon Lee Miller
(LEFT AND OPPOSITE PAGE)
America's most-decorated gymnast, Miller won seven Olympic medals and nine world championship medals as a teen. She is also a two-time world all-around champion. As an infant, the Missouri native moved to Edmond with her parents, Claudia and Ron Miller. She studied gymnastics for four years when, at the age of nine, she and her mother traveled to Russia to participate in a gymnastics camp. As a 12-year-old, she finished third at the 1989 Olympic Festival. She trained with coach Steve Nunno, who later became the Oklahoma University women's gymnastics coach. As a 15-year-old in the 1992 Summer Olympics, she barely missed capturing the gold medal in the all-around competition. She won two silver and three bronze medals. And that was after she broke her elbow just months before the Olympics. Her chase for a gold medal ended in the 1996 Olympics, when she anchored the "Magnificent Seven," which captured team gold. She also took the individual gold medal on the balance beam. Edmond held huge parades to welcome the star home after both Olympics. Miller is the only woman, in any sport, to be inducted into the US Olympic Hall of Fame twice, as an individual and for her team. In 2007, she became the seventh American to be inducted into the International Gymnastics Hall of Fame at a ceremony in Oklahoma City. "When you start out, it's not really something you think about," Miller said. She told an *Oklahoman* reporter, "I wasn't the most talented or the strongest, but I always tried to work the hardest." The Edmond North High School graduate spends her time as a mother and motivational speaker, discussing leadership and aspects of success. She is president of Shannon Miller Foundation, a group dedicated to fighting childhood obesity. (Both, courtesy Oklahoma Sports Museum.)

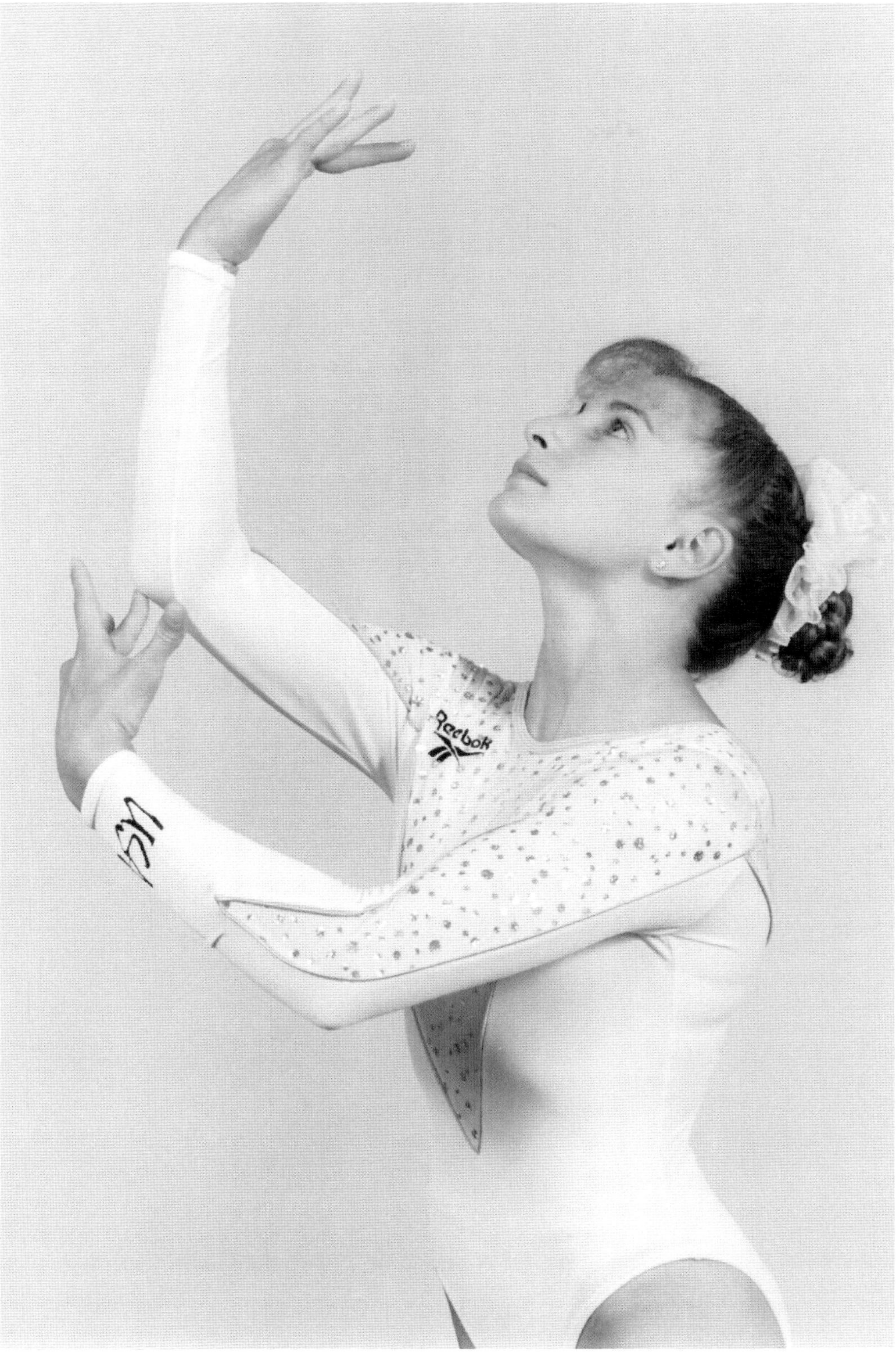
Reebok
USA

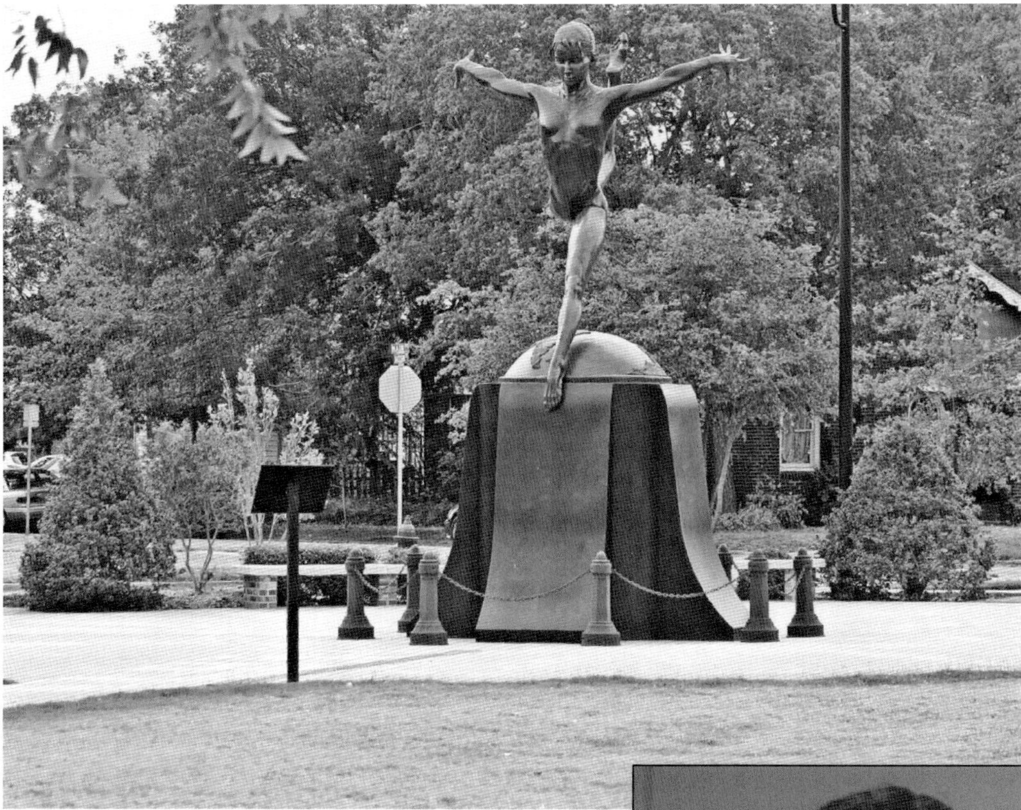

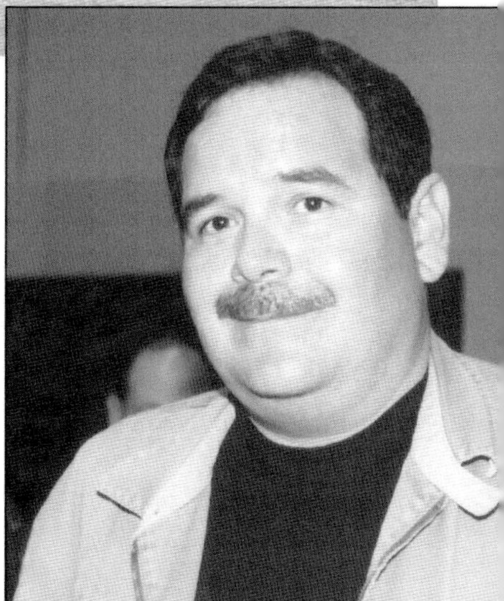

Shan Gray

Gymnast Shannon Miller earned her fame in the Olympics. Edmond artist Gray captured the Edmond athlete's grace and form in an 18-foot bronze statue that shows Miller poised on a balance beam in Shannon Miller Park, near the Edmond Library. Gray sculpted the statue in the Oklahoma Sports Museum in Guthrie. Gray uses his timeless vision to, as he puts it, "Express the human endeavor." Gray was also one of several artists that competed to create the American Indian statue for the Oklahoma Capitol. Gray, who studied at Oklahoma State University and then the University of Central Oklahoma, didn't get that job, but he is working on a monument called *The American*, which would be a more-than-20-story structure near Tulsa. It depicts a bald eagle landing on the upraised arm of a Native American warrior. Gray, who is part Osage, has been working on the project since 2004, and plans for the final location were taking shape in 2013. Gray has created many statues familiar to Oklahomans, including the James Garner statue in Norman, the Warren Spahn statue at the Sports Museum in Guthrie, and a bust of heart transplant doctor Nazih Zuhdi at Integris Health Baptist Medical Center in Oklahoma City. (Above, courtesy David Fisk; right, courtesy Oklahoma Sports Museum.)

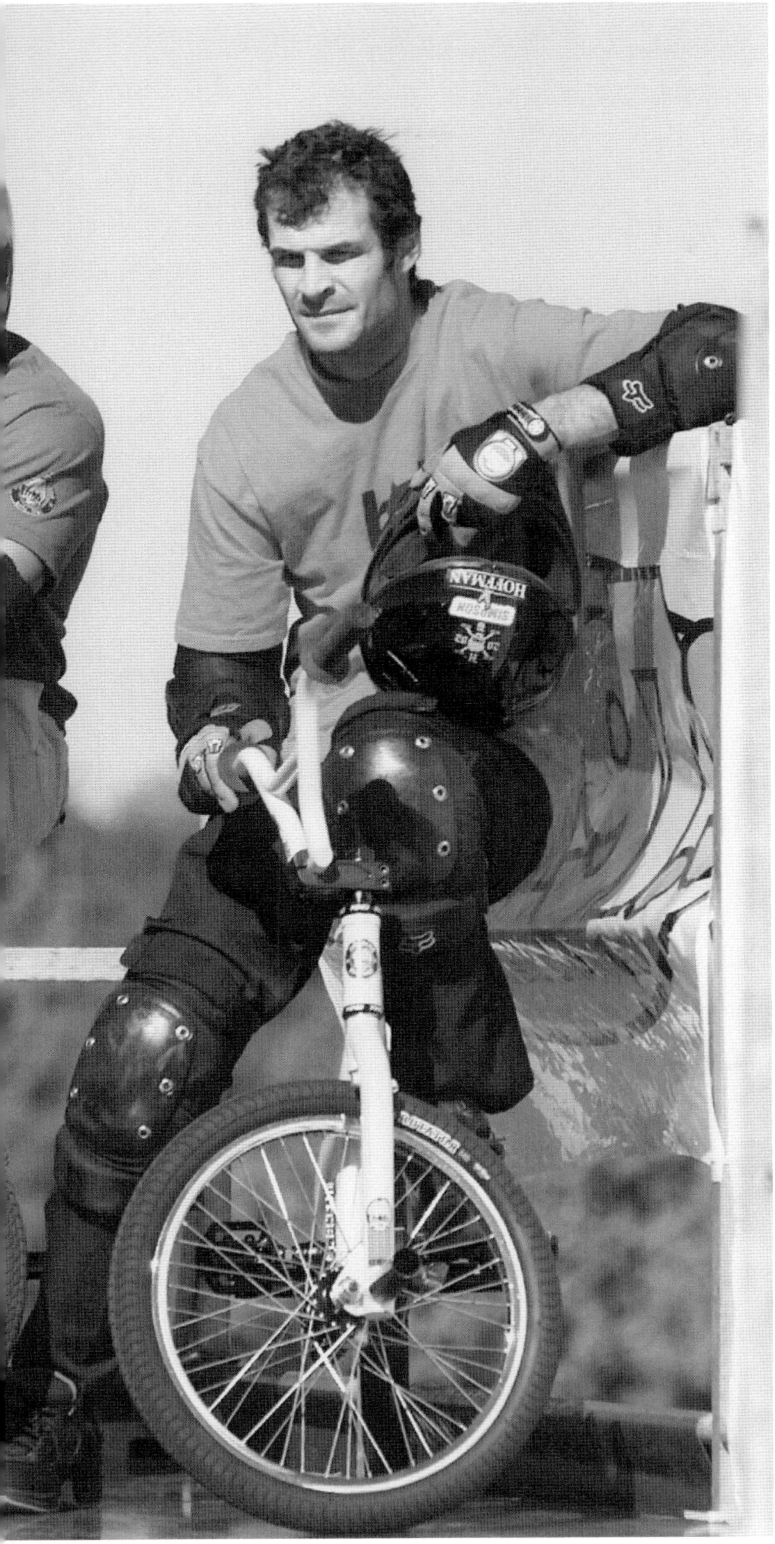

Mat Hoffman
Riding a bike was not enough for 10-year-old Edmond schoolboy Mat Hoffman. He began creating spectacular tricks and stunts on his bicycle and turned professional at age 16. A key player in the development of freestyle bicycle motocross (BMX) as a sport, Hoffman, now in his 40s, is known as the "godfather" of BMX. He turned his hobby into a multimillion-dollar business venture. He is president and CEO of Edmond-based Hoffman Enterprises, which has several companies, including Hoffman Bikes and Hoffman promotions. He is nicknamed "the Condor," and his autobiography is called *The Ride of My Life*. (Courtesy the *Oklahoman* archives.)

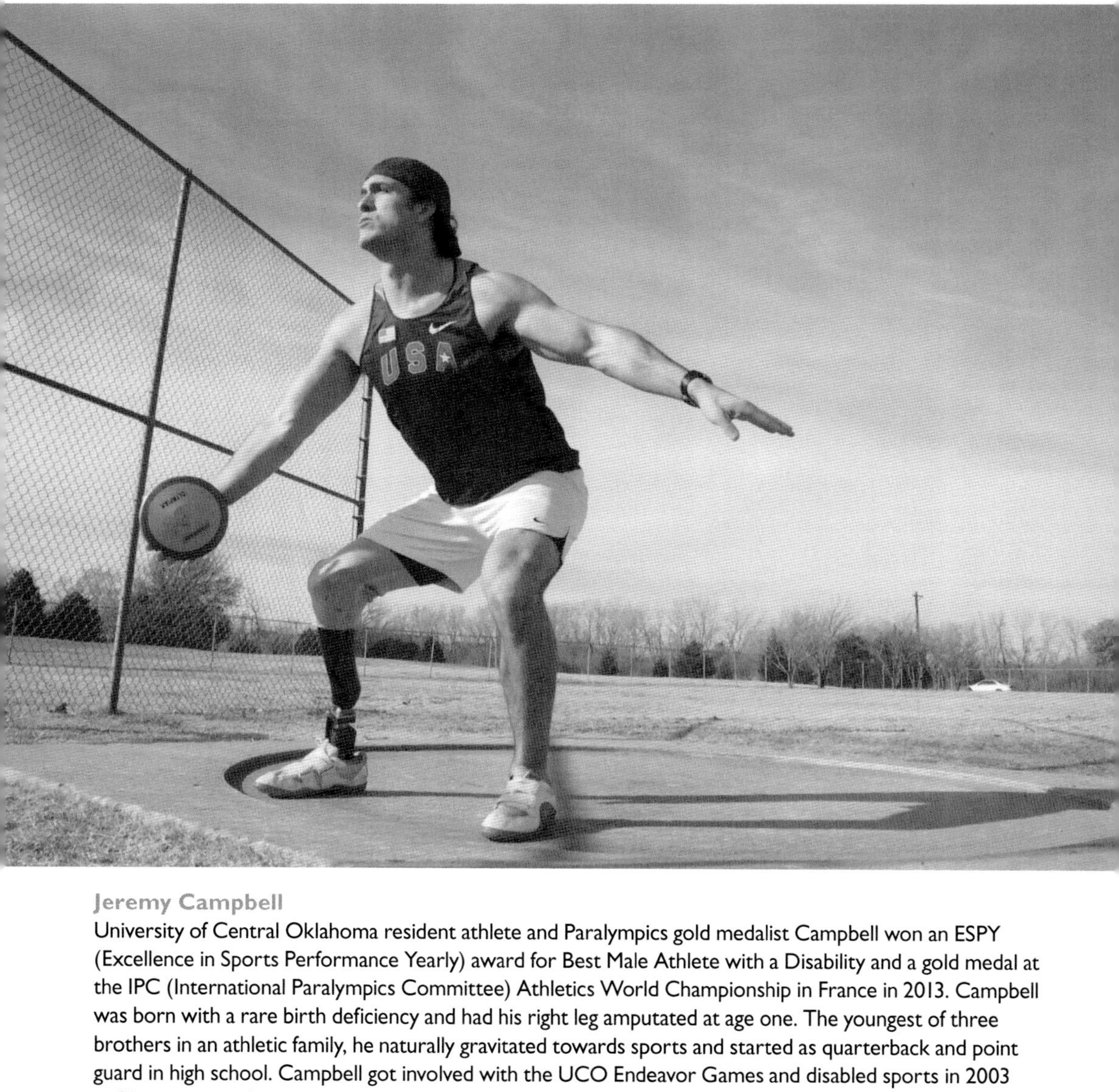

Jeremy Campbell
University of Central Oklahoma resident athlete and Paralympics gold medalist Campbell won an ESPY (Excellence in Sports Performance Yearly) award for Best Male Athlete with a Disability and a gold medal at the IPC (International Paralympics Committee) Athletics World Championship in France in 2013. Campbell was born with a rare birth deficiency and had his right leg amputated at age one. The youngest of three brothers in an athletic family, he naturally gravitated towards sports and started as quarterback and point guard in high school. Campbell got involved with the UCO Endeavor Games and disabled sports in 2003 and has competed ever since. He is a three-time Paralympic gold medalist, winning his first two in the 2008 Beijing Games, where he shattered the world record in the pentathlon and set an American record in the discus. After 2008, he focused on the discus. At the Endeavor Games in 2012, he became the only Paralympic athlete to break the 60-meter/200-foot barrier, shattering the world record with a throw of 63.46 meters. He ended the year by taking gold in the 2012 London Paralympic Games. Cable television network ESPN presents the ESPY Awards annually, recognizing individual and team athletic achievement and other sports-related performance. Campbell was recognized alongside athletes like the Miami Heat's Lebron James, tennis star Serena Williams, and Olympic swimming icon Michael Phelps. "I am so excited and honored to have won the ESPY. I was not expecting it, so it caught me off guard, which made it that much more exciting," Campbell said. UCO became an official US Olympic Training Site in 2009 and has been an official US Paralympics Training Site since 2005. At UCO, athletes can train for Olympic volleyball and archery and any Paralympic sport. Campbell was the first athlete to be inducted in to the UCO Endeavor Games Hall of Fame. (Courtesy UCO Wellness Center.)

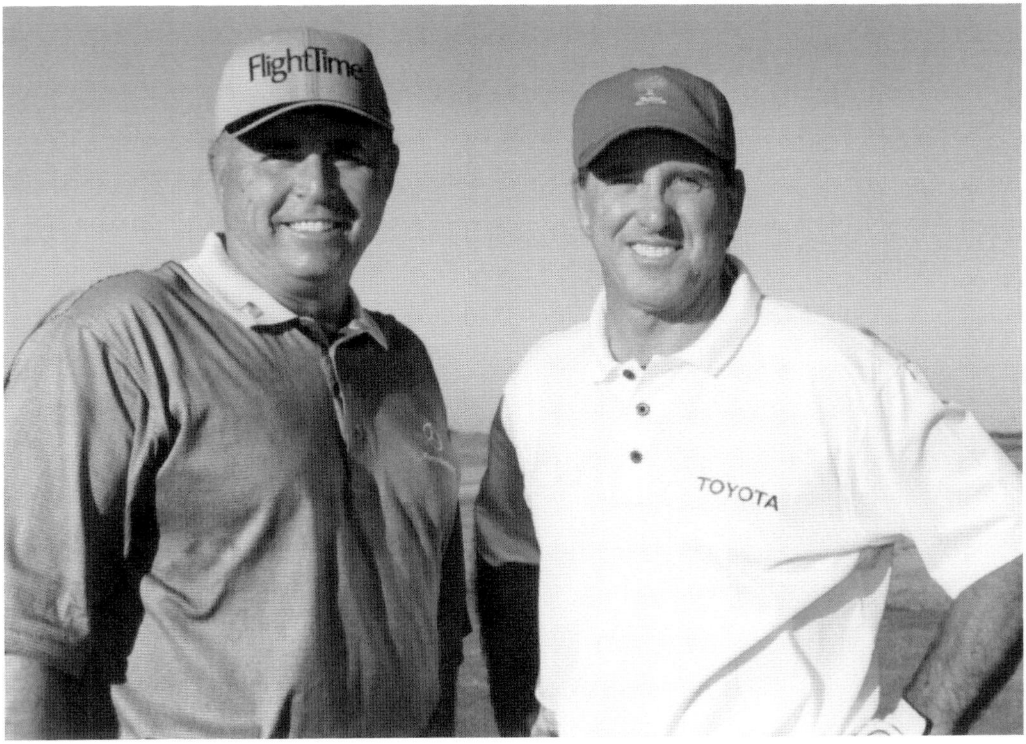

"The Oak Tree Gang"

Known for its many beautiful golf courses, Edmond is home to a number of professional golfers. "The Oak Tree Gang" includes Doug Tewell, left, and Gil Morgan, right, as well as Willie Wood, Bob Tway, and now Scott Verplank. Homegrown pros Dave and Danny Edwards, Mark Hayes, and up-and-coming pro Kevin Tway, son of Bob Tway, are also based out of Oak Tree. In 2010, Tewell became the first athlete to join the Edmond Hall of Fame. Tewell rose from his job as assistant golf pro at Kickingbird to be winner of 12 PGA tour tournaments. He helped bring professional tournaments to Edmond. In four decades, Morgan has won more than 40 professional championships. The US Senior Open is to be held at Oak Tree in 2014. (Courtesy Oklahoma Sports Museum.)

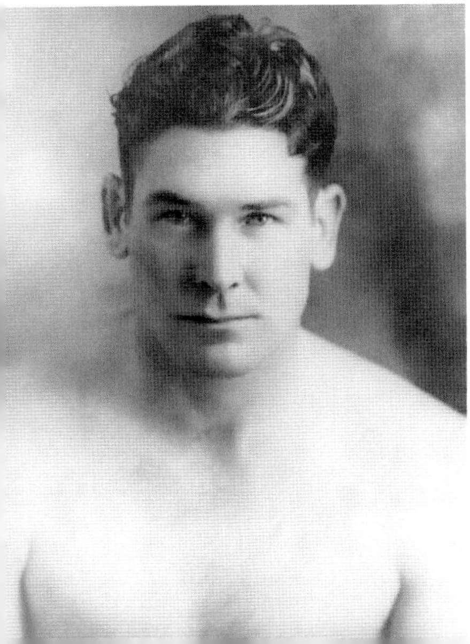

Ray "Duke" Clemons

"On to Berlin" was the chant three-time All-American Clemons led his 13 American wrestling teammates in as they urged the United States to participate in the 1936 Olympics in Hitler's Berlin. Thankfully, the USA did take part in the games, and Clemons, at 191 pounds, finished fifth without a medal. To this day, he remains the only athlete from the University of Central Oklahoma to compete in the Olympics. In 1990, he became one of the first members of the UCO Athletic Hall of Fame. (Courtesy UCO Library, Archives/Special Collections.)

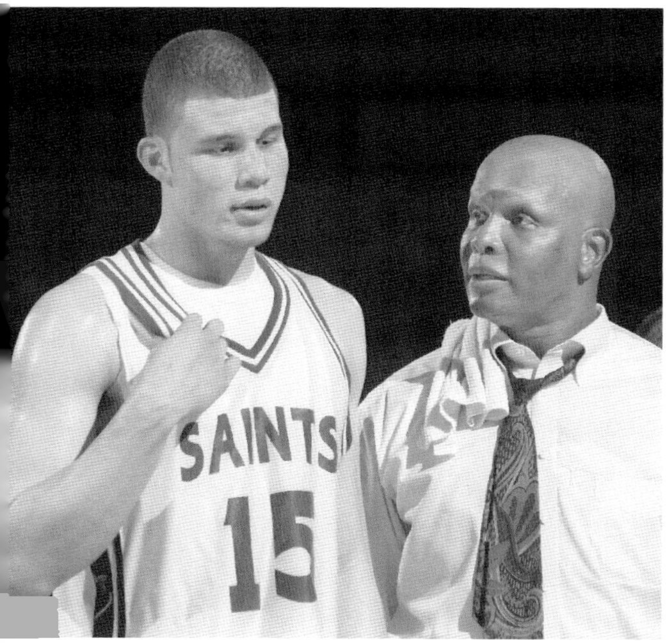

Blake Griffin
Before his current role as NBA superstar for the Los Angeles Clippers, Griffin, left, led Edmond's Oklahoma Christian School to four straight state basketball championships. He and older brother Taylor were coached by their father, Tommy Griffin, right. His freshman year, the Saints were a perfect 29-0. The following year, big brother Taylor was Oklahoma's Player of the Year as the team again won state. Blake went on to earn those honors his junior and senior year, when the team rolled over Pawnee 81-50 for the state title. He starred at the University of Oklahoma for two years, where he was AP Player of the Year his sophomore year. Griffin went on to the NBA where, after missing a season due to injury, he was Rookie of the Year in 2010–2011. (Courtesy the *Oklahoman* archives.)

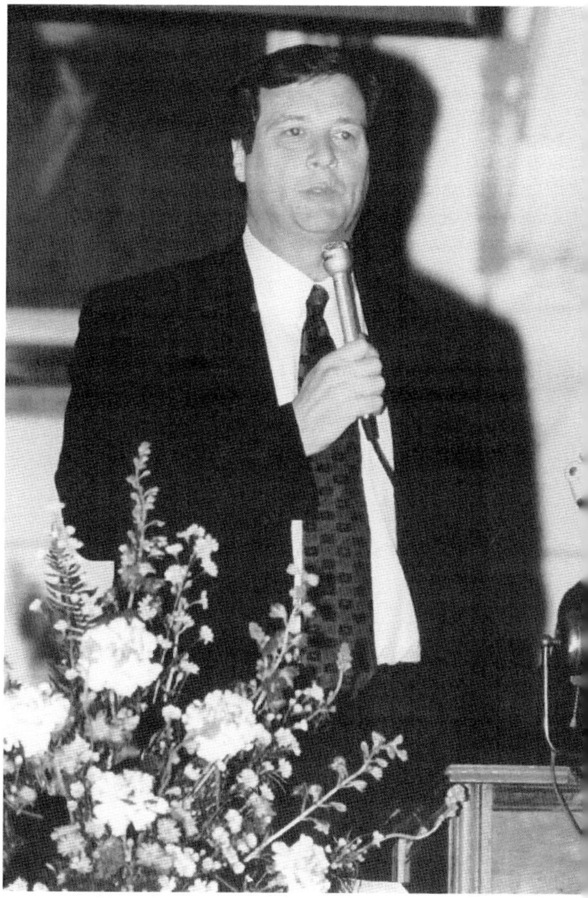

William B. "Bill Teegins" Tietgens
On a bitter cold night in 2001, a small plane carrying members of the Oklahoma State men's basketball team crashed near I-70 in Colorado. Teegins of Edmond was sports director for KWTV News 9 in Oklahoma City and a passenger on the plane when it went down during a snowstorm. All 11 people on board, including some Oklahoma State University players and coaches, were killed. He was the voice of the OSU Cowboys football and basketball teams for years, as well as Sportscaster of the Year in Oklahoma a record eight times. His widow, Janis, told Ed Murray of KWTV, "Even when he wasn't on the air, his joking nature was infectious. You know when your first date is to a baseball game, you know that he is a sports nut." (Courtesy Oklahoma Sports Museum.)

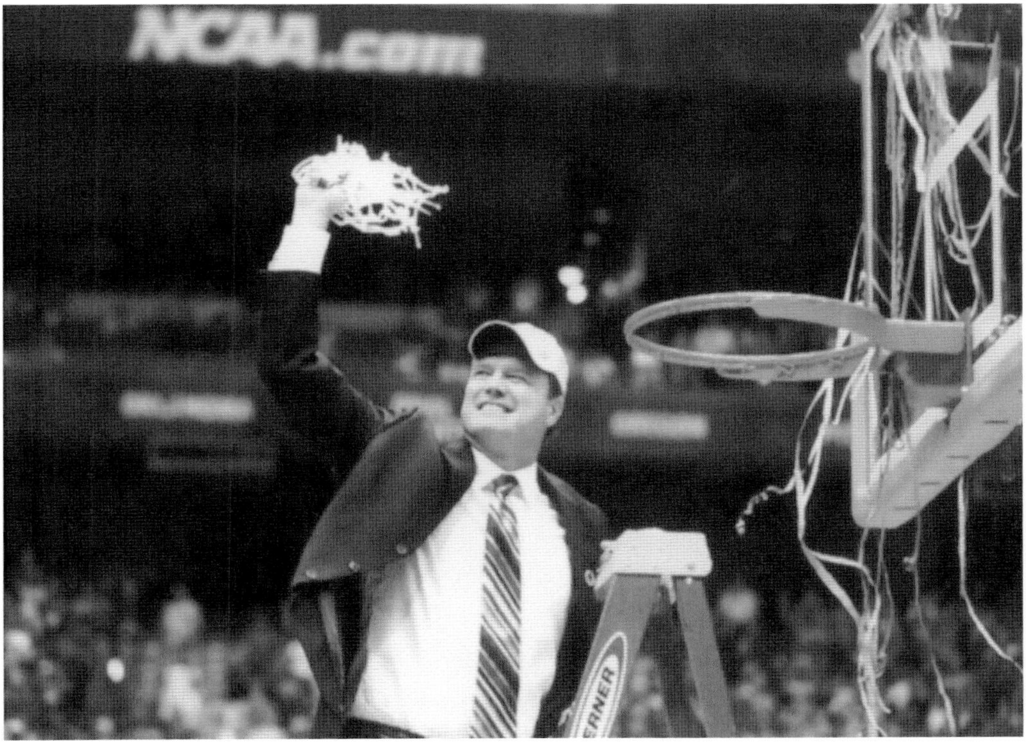

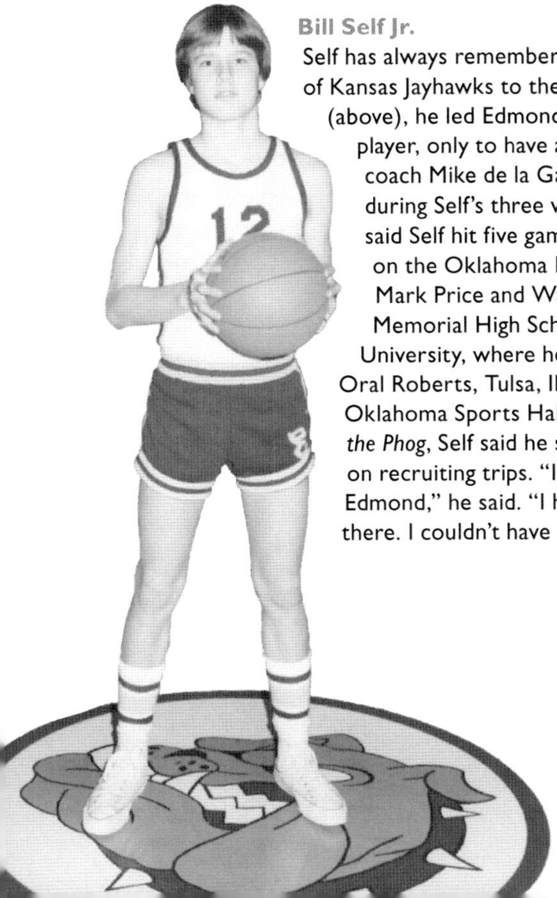

Bill Self Jr.

Self has always remembered his roots. Years before coaching his University of Kansas Jayhawks to the 2008 NCAA national basketball championship (above), he led Edmond Memorial High School to the state playoffs as a player, only to have a state crown elude them. Playing for legendary coach Mike de la Garza, the "Cardiac Bulldogs" went a combined 65-18 during Self's three varsity seasons. During his senior year, de la Garza said Self hit five game-winning shots. During the summer, Self played on the Oklahoma Rams AAU team that included future NBA stars Mark Price and Wayman Tisdale. He was also selected as Mr. Edmond Memorial High School. Self played college ball at Oklahoma State University, where he coached from 1986 to 1993, before coaching at Oral Roberts, Tulsa, Illinois, and then Kansas. Self was inducted into the Oklahoma Sports Hall of Fame in 2013. In John Rohde's book *At Home in the Phog*, Self said he still gets back to Edmond from time to time, mostly on recruiting trips. "It's not home for me anymore, but I loved living in Edmond," he said. "I had a great childhood and I loved going to school there. I couldn't have had more fun." (Both, courtesy Margaret Self.)

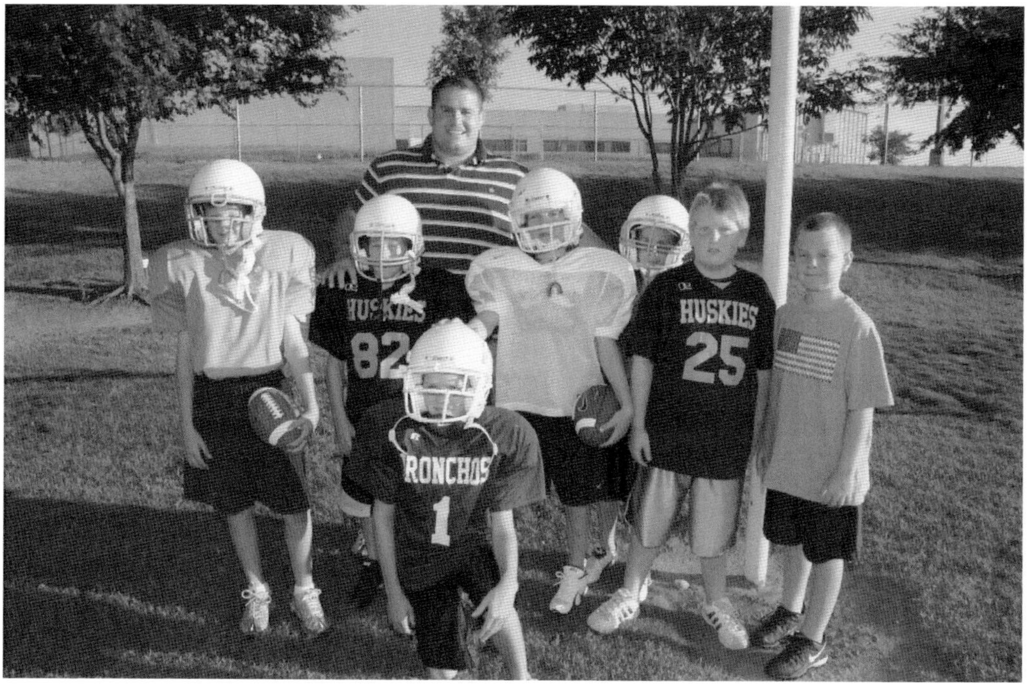

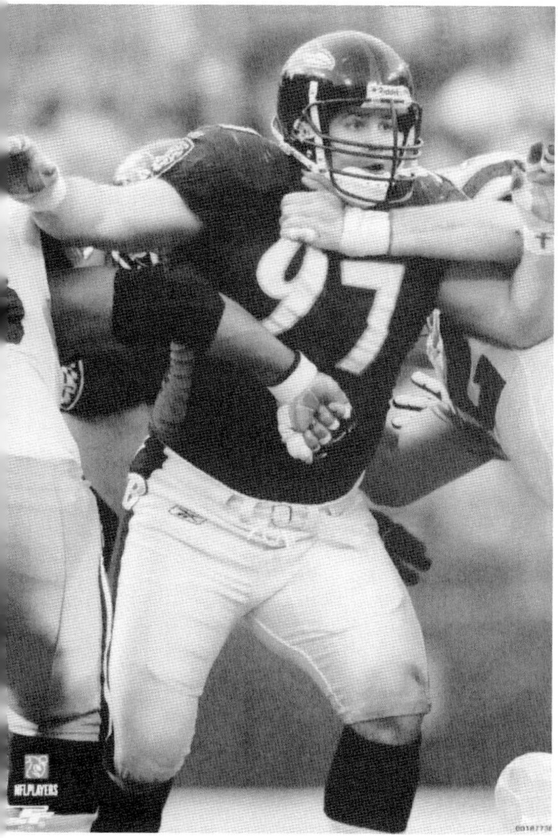

Kelly Gregg

Gregg starred at not one but two Edmond schools before playing at Oklahoma University and then putting together a stellar career in the NFL as a nose tackle. Edmond North High School retired Gregg's number 71 jersey in 2012. Before attending North as a senior, he was an Edmond Memorial Bulldog and helped lead the team to the state finals his junior year. He had time to be a three-time state champion heavyweight wrestler while in high school as well. Gregg played in 153 NFL games and was considered small at 6 feet and 300 pounds. He had a longer NFL career than any other player from Oklahoma, his uncle Bob Gregg said, spending most of his 13-year career with the Baltimore Ravens. Gregg is retired and raising his three sons in Edmond. He loves to fish and there is a pond in his front yard stocked with fish. His father, Terry Gregg, a longtime Edmond police officer, had taken him fishing growing up, and Gregg told the *Baltimore Sun*, "I love to fish with my boys." Terry Gregg died in 2004. Kelly Gregg told the *Oklahoman*, "I can't think of a better place to raise my family than here in Edmond." He still shows up at his old stomping grounds at Sequoyah Middle School to visit with coaches and players. Rich Bollenbach, who was his high school wrestling coach, told the *Oklahoman*, "Anybody that ever doubted him, the best thing that could happen was him finding out. He loved proving people wrong." (Both, courtesy Kelly Gregg.)

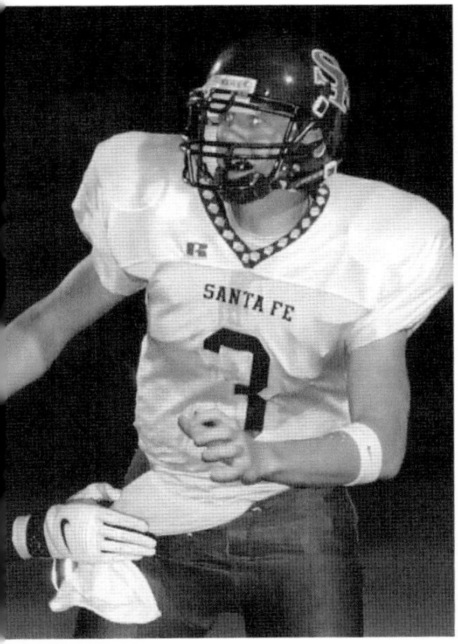

Brandon Weeden

As quarterback, Weeden led Santa Fe High School to the state football semifinals in the school's first-ever playoff appearance in 2001. He was also a star baseball player, drafted by the New York Yankees as their first pick in the draft in 2002. After several years in the minor leagues, Weeden decided to give up baseball and move back to Edmond. He then enrolled at Oklahoma State University in Stillwater, where he took up his first love, football. As a walk-on and older than most college students, he eventually became starting quarterback for the Cowboys, leading them to an 11-1 season and a bowl game win in 2011. OSU football coach Mike Gundy called Weeden the best quarterback in school history. Weeden set many records at OSU for passing and offense, many of which surpassed records set by Gundy. He was drafted by the Cleveland Browns in the 2012 draft, the oldest player ever taken in the first round at 28. He beat out Colt McCoy for the Browns starting job. A star off the field as well, Weeden set up the "Swing From the Heart" Brandon Weeden Golf Challenge. Funds go to the Children's Hospital Foundation. (Courtesy the *Oklahoman* archives.)

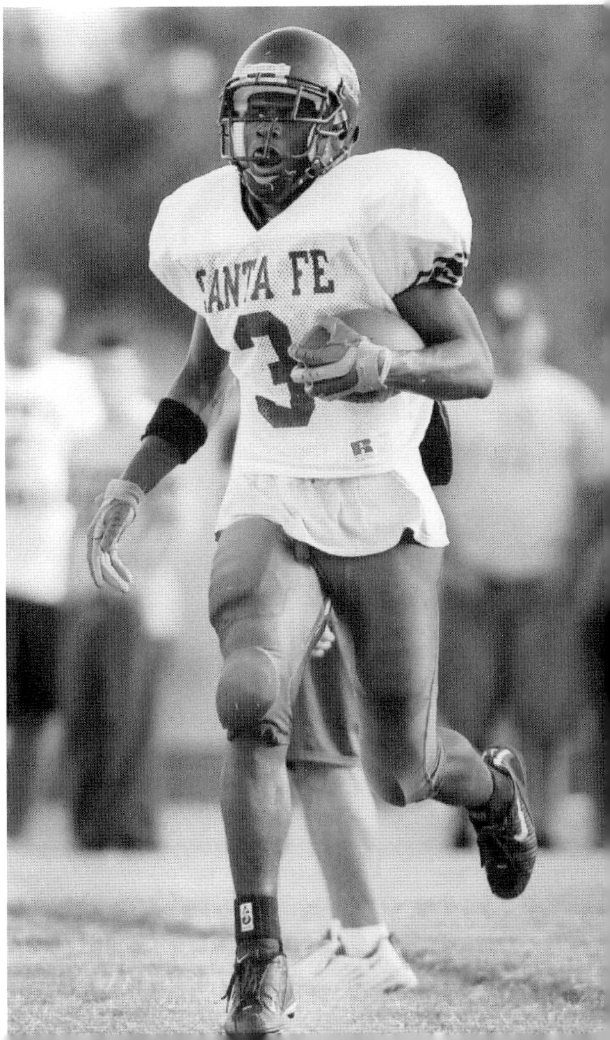

Reggie Smith

Smith was a two-way star at Edmond Santa Fe High School before his days as an defensive back in the NFL. His coach at Santa Fe, Dan Cocannouer, called him "the best all-around player I've ever coached." He was the *Oklahoman*'s Player of the Year as a junior and Defensive Player of the Year in 2004 as a senior. He racked up more than 1,500 yards on offense and had 6 interceptions his senior year and 28 in total over his four years at Santa Fe. After a standout college career as a University of Oklahoma Sooner, Smith was drafted in the third round of the 2008 draft by the San Francisco 49ers. After playing four years with the 49ers, he signed with the Carolina Panthers and was cut in 2012. Smith signed with the Oakland Raiders in 2013. For several years, he has hosted the Reggie Smith Foundation Charity Weekend football camp at Santa Fe. He formed the foundation during his second year as a professional. (Courtesy the *Oklahoman* archives.)

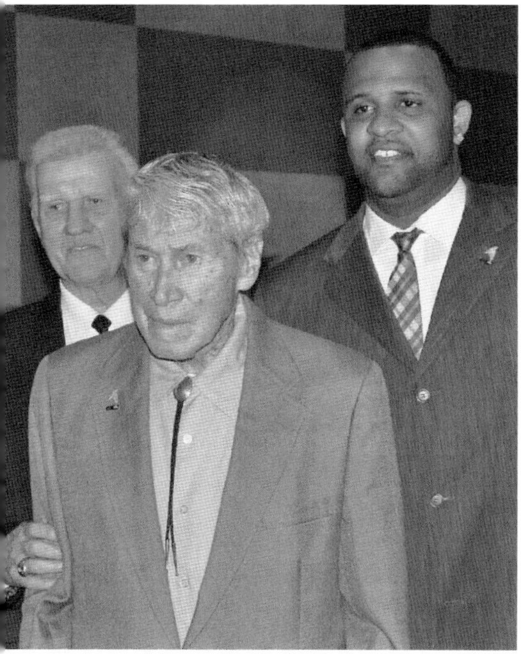

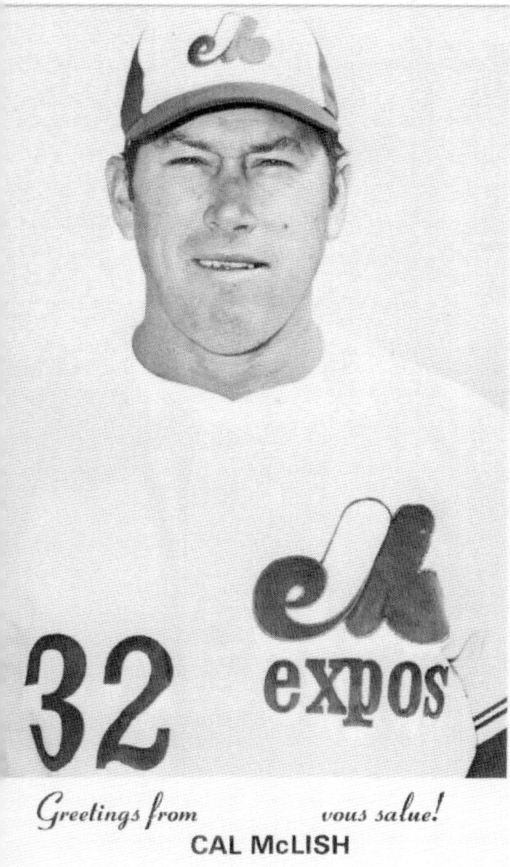

Cal McLish

He did not have the longest home run or longest winning streak, but he has the longest name in major-league baseball history. He was Calvin Coolidge Julius Caesar Tuskahoma McLish. In 1925, his father chose the name after McLish's mother told John McLish he could name his son. A member of the Oklahoma Sports Hall of Fame, McLish spent 15 years pitching in the major leagues and almost 50 years more as a coach and instructor. Richard Hendricks, director of the Oklahoma Sports Museum in Guthrie, said McLish "was a great teacher of the game." McLish told him, "I want to be known for what I did to teach baseball." McLish died in 2010 at the age of 84. Originally signed by the Brooklyn Dodgers, McLish broke into the majors at age 18 in 1944, spending a season with the Dodgers before serving in the US Army in 1944–1945 at the end of World War II. McLish, who lived in Edmond since 1960, told the *Edmond Sun*, "We were on the front lines the whole time I was there. . . . Then when the war was over, we had to go up in the mountains and root out machine gun nests. I guess the Germans didn't know the war was over." Anadarko native McLish had a 92-92 career win-loss mark and set a major-league record with 16 consecutive road wins (since surpassed by Greg Maddux) over the 1958–1959 season. He also played for the Pirates, Cubs, Indians, Reds, and White Sox, ending his career in 1964 with the Phillies. In 1959, he won a career-high 19 games and made the All-Star team, earning the save for the American League. One of his nicknames was "Bus," as his father reportedly stated upon Cal's birth, "he's as big as a bus!" "It's amazing what he was able to accomplish," former Edmond Memorial athletic director Mike de la Garza told the *Oklahoman*. De la Garza got to know McLish, playing golf with him at Kickingbird in Edmond. De la Garza said during the hall of fame induction ceremony for McLish, "He was the most genuine, humble guy that I've ever met that had the opportunity to be the exact opposite." (Above, courtesy David Fisk; below, courtesy Oklahoma Sports Museum.)

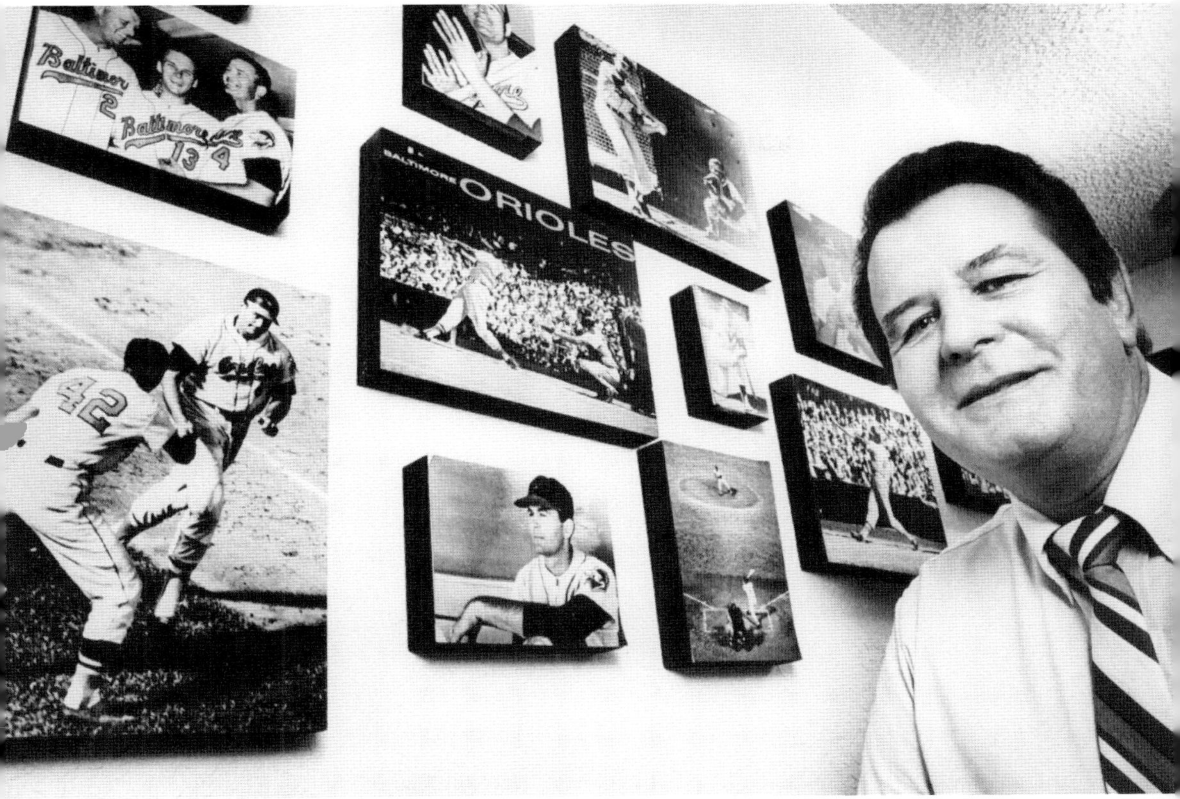

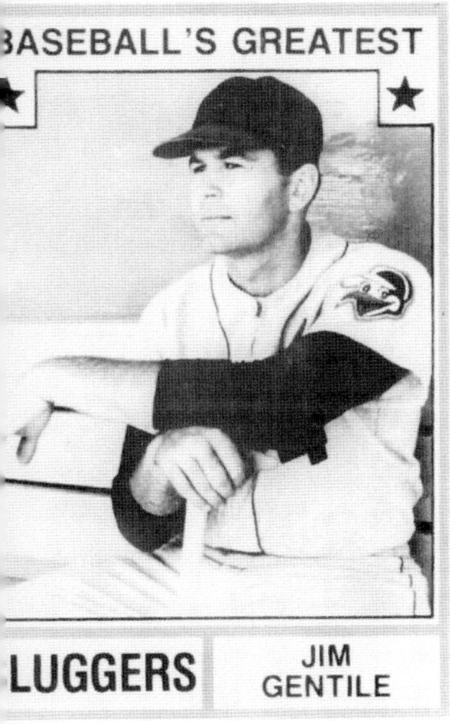

Jim Gentile

Big "Diamond Jim" was a three-time All-Star and major-league slugging first baseman for nine years. He posted a career year in 1961, overshadowed by the home run race between Roger Maris and Mickey Mantle. Gentile knocked out 46 homers that season and drove in 141 runs to share the RBI crown. He slammed five grand slams that season and finished third in the Most Valuable Player balloting behind Maris and Mantle. He married an Oklahoma woman who was an airline stewardess and has lived in Edmond more than 33 years. In 1988, Gentile was named to the Oklahoma City 89ers Hall of Fame, mostly because of the recognition he brought them even though he played just 30 games in OKC. He was a dominant slugger for several years, finishing with 179 home runs during his MLB career and another 208 minor-league homers. Known for his temper, he starred with the Orioles and also played in Houston, Kansas City, Cleveland, and originally with the Dodgers. Gentile told *Edmond Outlook* magazine "I had a hot temper. Not at others though—at myself." His nickname "Diamond Jim" came from Dodger catcher and hall of famer Roy Campanella, who called Gentile a "diamond in the rough." (Above, courtesy the *Oklahoman* archives; left, courtesy Oklahoma Sports Museum.)

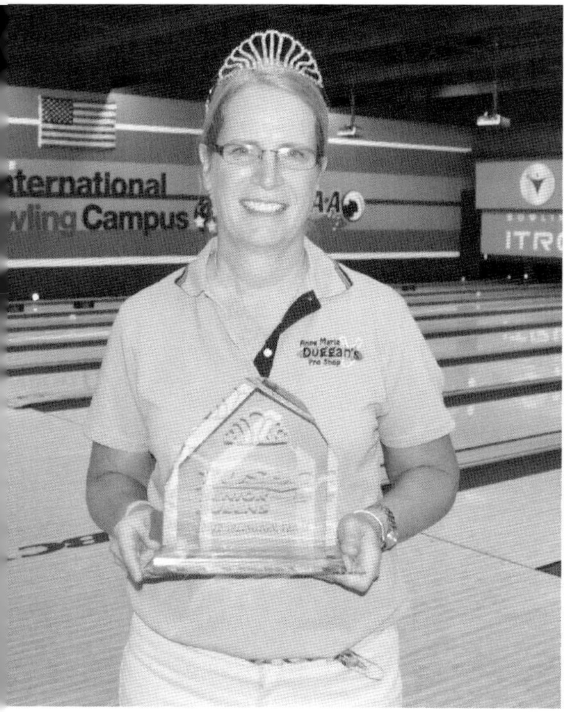

Anne Marie Duggan

For more than 30 years, Duggan made her mark with her bowling prowess on lanes across the country. Still going strong at age 50, Duggan, a member of two halls of fame, captured yet another title by winning the 2012 US Bowling Congress Senior Queens Tournament in Arlington, Texas. She defeated fellow hall of famer Dana Miller-Mackie in the final game of the stepladder finals to nail down the crown. In between tournaments, Duggan can be found taking orders and drilling balls at her pro shop in AMF Lanes in Edmond. Duggan told Bowl.com, "It was really fun to win something again." She has won 15 national and 25 regional titles on the women's professional tour. Duggan is a member of the USBC (US Bowling Congress) and Professional Women's Bowling Association (PWBA) Halls of Fame and was the 1994 PWBA Player of the Year. (Courtesy the US Bowling Congress.)

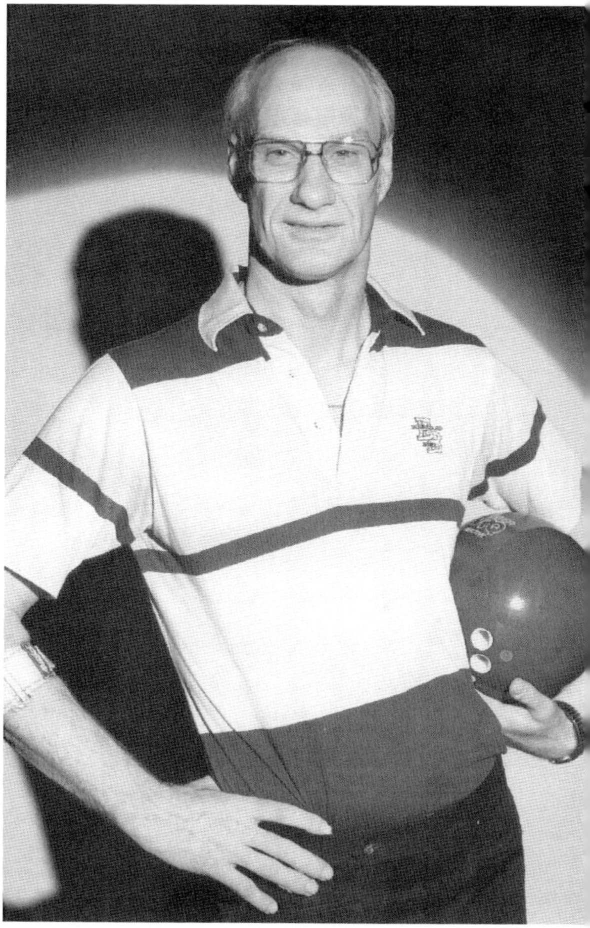

Gary Dickinson

Named one of the top 50 bowlers of all time by the Professional Bowlers Association (PBA) during the organization's 50th anniversary, Dickinson has won many titles on the PBA and PBA Senior Tour. Dickinson was among the steadiest performers on the pro tour. His breakthrough came in 1971, when he won the ABC Tournament Classic all-events title and finished third in two other events. Dickinson had one of his best years in 1983, when he won the US Open and earned $60,000. He continued strong in 1997, winning the ABC Senior Masters, which he again won in 2004. He was the recipient of the PBA's Steve Nagy Sportsmanship Award in 1972 and 1973. He is still a force on the PBA's Senior Tour, where he ranks second all-time with 12 titles. He has been a PBA Senior Player of the Year three times. The Texas native, who has made Edmond his home for many years, was inducted into the PBA Hall of Fame in 1988. He has won more than $1.3 million as a pro bowler, which ranks him as one of the top 50 professional bowling money earners of all-time. (Courtesy Oklahoma Sports Museum.)

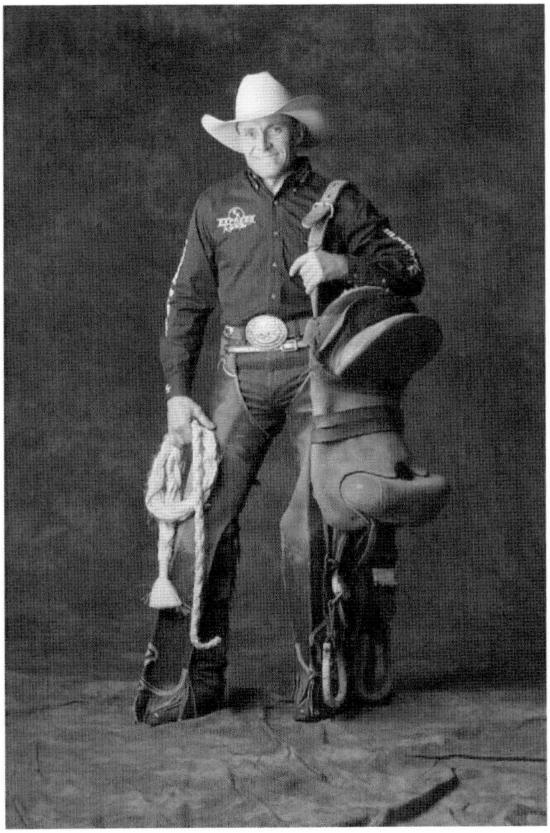

Billy Etbauer

Retired Professional Rodeo Hall of Famer Etbauer is busy raising quarter horses these days at his Performance Horses Stables on 440 acres in northwest Edmond. The Professional Rodeo Hall of Fame inducted the saddle-bronc rider in 2012. One of the most popular cowboys of his generation, Etbauer is known for his "go-for-broke" style. He met his wife, Hollie, at the Lazy E Arena during the Ram Prairie Circuit Finals Rodeo. He is a five-time world champion saddle-bronc rider. (Courtesy Express Ranch.)

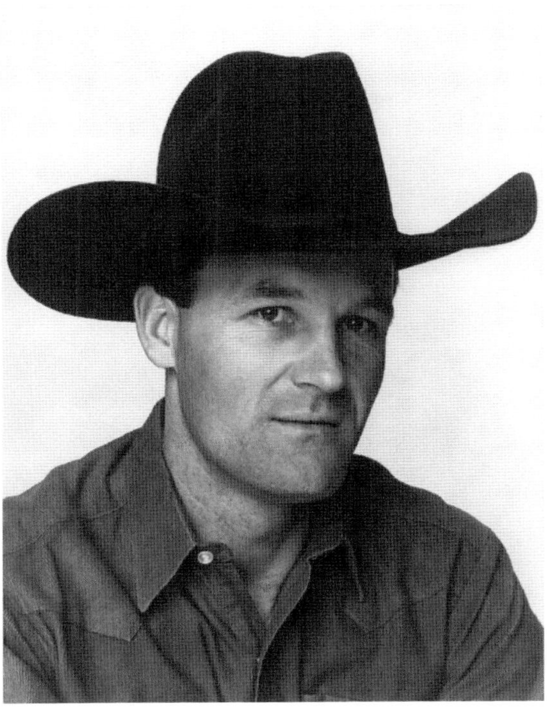

Dan Dailey

All-around cowboy Dailey was once called "the best secret in rodeo." He lives in Florida now, but he called Edmond home for many years during the height of his career. He holds 29 International Professional Rodeo championships, including 17 all-around titles. He once told a reporter, "What really keeps you going is winning." Dailey proved that right as perhaps the top bulldogger ever. He told the Associated Press, "Sometimes I think they don't make enough rodeos for me to get to." (Courtesy Edmond Historical Society Photographic Collection.)

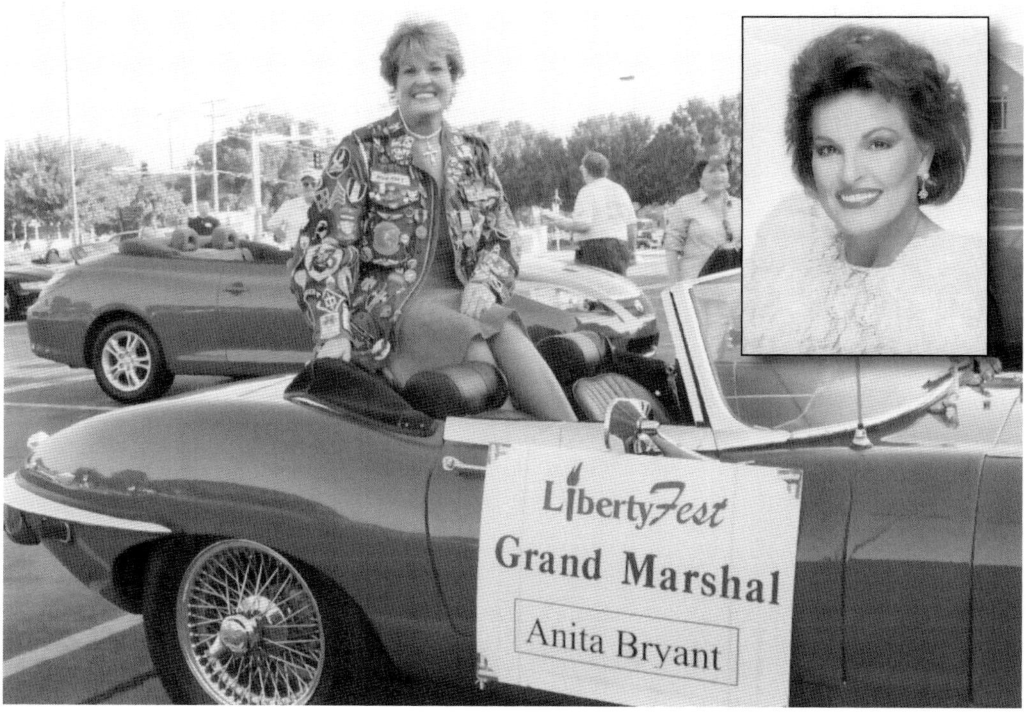

Anita Bryant

Bryant, a former Miss Oklahoma, was Pres. Lyndon Johnson's favorite singer. Her final performance for LBJ was an a cappella version of "The Battle Hymn of the Republic" at his funeral. When she was 19, Bryant skyrocketed to national fame in 1959 as second runner-up in the Miss America beauty pageant. She enjoyed a career as a pop singer, placing 11 songs in the US Hot 100 during the 1950s and 1960s. Her biggest hits were "Till There was You" and "Paper Roses." She travelled seven times on Bob Hope's tours to entertain troops. She sang at the 1971 and 1976 Super Bowls. A champion of traditional family values and outspoken critic of homosexuality, Bryant, now in her 70s, lives in Edmond with husband Charlie Dry and runs Anita Bryant Ministries in Oklahoma City. Dry is in the Oklahoma Aviation and Space Hall of Fame. He enjoyed a long and illustrious career at NASA. He was the senior systems engineer on the Apollo command module. Dry was also selected as a NASA astronaut test crewman, where he tested the lunar surface probes that Neil Armstrong and Buzz Aldrin used to penetrate the surface of the moon. Bryant began singing at age two and at age 12 starred in the *Anita Bryant Show* on WKY radio in Oklahoma City. She considers her most important role to be that of mother and grandmother. She says her secret to life is prayer. (All, courtesy Anita Bryant.)

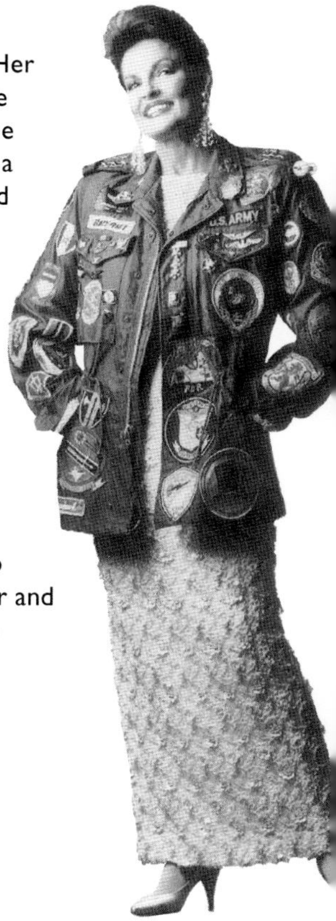

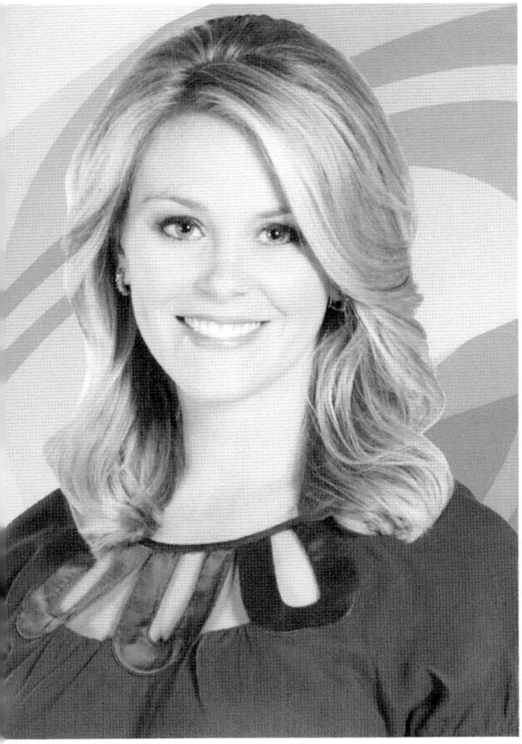

Lauren Nelson
Nelson was a student at the University of Central Oklahoma when she was crowned Miss America in 2007 at age 20. She was the sixth Oklahoma woman to win the crown. In 2008, she was named one of the "Ten Outstanding Young Americans" by the US Jaycees. She launched a nationwide platform of Internet safety, Be NetSmart—Protecting Kids Online. Nelson teamed up with *America's Most Wanted* host John Walsh to help catch potential child predators and testified before Congress about Internet safety. Since 2010, she has cohosted the news at KWTV's News 9 in Oklahoma City. Nelson, an accomplished singer and performer, was in several theater productions while at UCO and costarred with Shirley Jones and Patrick Cassidy in *Carousel*. She and her husband lead worship services for youth at Edmond's First Baptist Church. (Courtesy KWTV.)

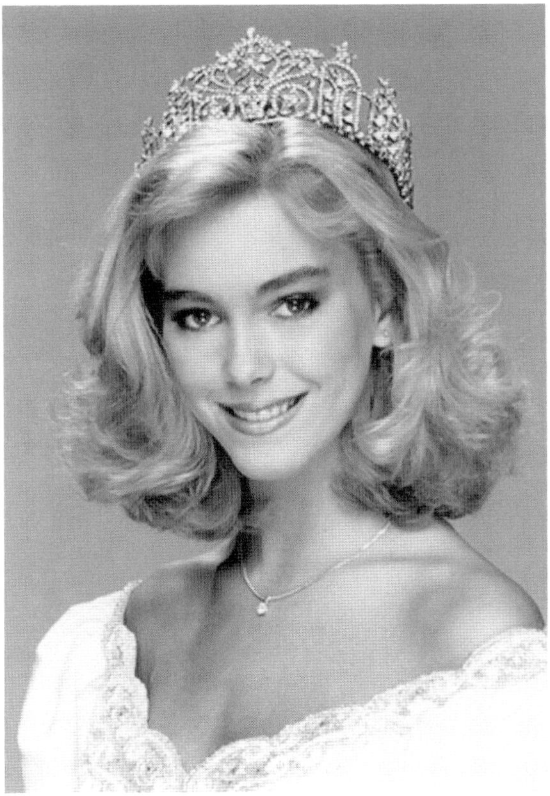

Allison Brown
Brown was a 17-year-old senior at Edmond's Memorial High School in 1986 when she was crowned Miss Teen USA. Brown swept the contest, winning the interview, swimsuit, and evening gown competitions. Brown said that she and "the love of her life" Marin Starr now own an award-winning bed-and-breakfast in Ohio. She said after winning Miss Teen USA she moved to Los Angeles and appeared in some TV shows and commercials, including a spot as Sarah Horton on *Days of Our Lives*. She realized acting wasn't for her, so she went to UCLA, where she graduated before eventually moving to Ohio about 2005. (Courtesy Allison Brown.)

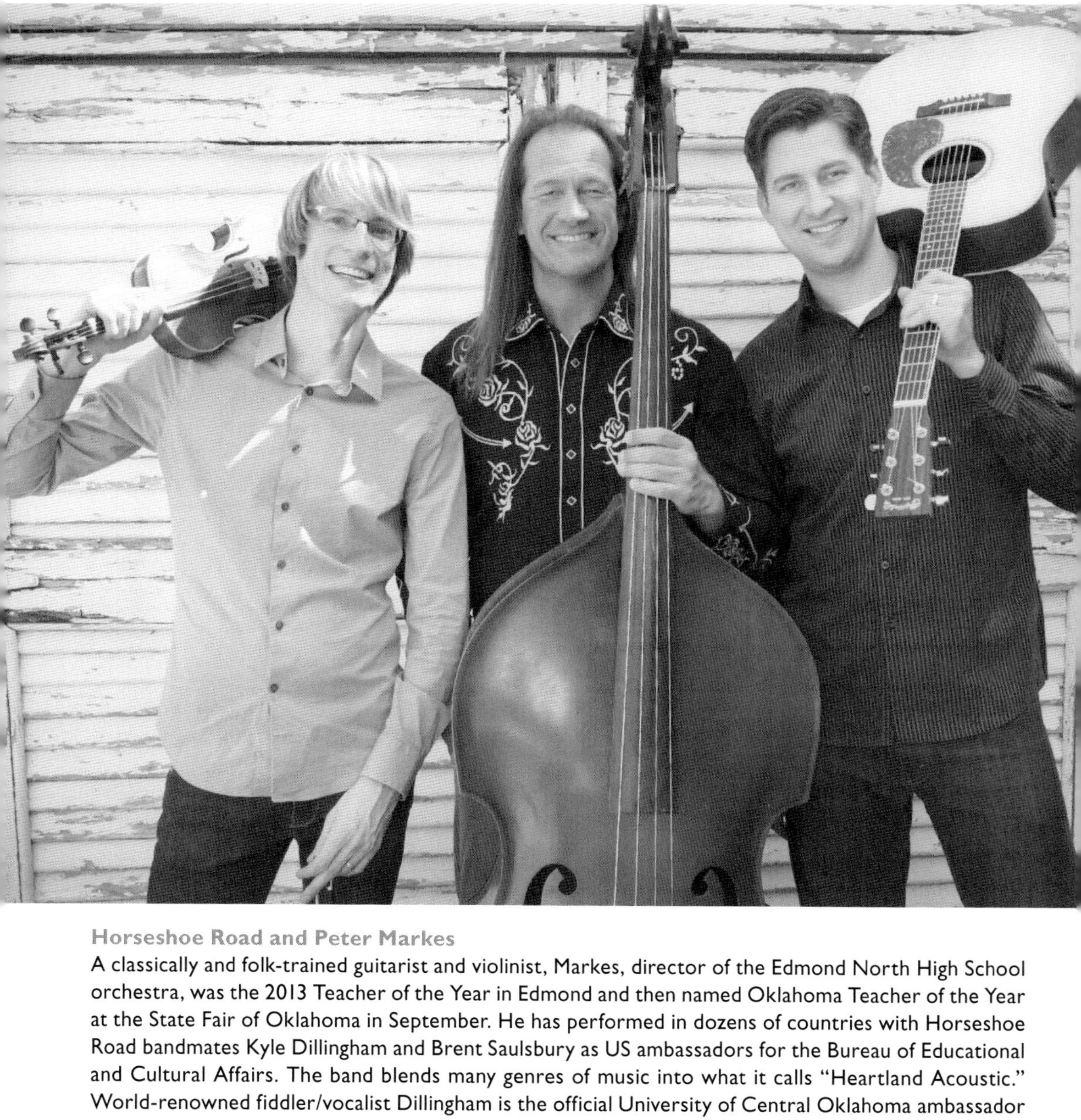

Horseshoe Road and Peter Markes
A classically and folk-trained guitarist and violinist, Markes, director of the Edmond North High School orchestra, was the 2013 Teacher of the Year in Edmond and then named Oklahoma Teacher of the Year at the State Fair of Oklahoma in September. He has performed in dozens of countries with Horseshoe Road bandmates Kyle Dillingham and Brent Saulsbury as US ambassadors for the Bureau of Educational and Cultural Affairs. The band blends many genres of music into what it calls "Heartland Acoustic." World-renowned fiddler/vocalist Dillingham is the official University of Central Oklahoma ambassador for music, and Saulsbury is the upright bass player, saxophonist, and vocalist. Markes is also conductor for the Oklahoma Youth Philharmonic. Dillingham received the governor's Arts Award in 2009. Saulsbury has been teaching and performing music for many years. Horseshoe Road is, from left to right, Dillingham, Saulsbury, and Markes. (Courtesy Horseshoe Road.)

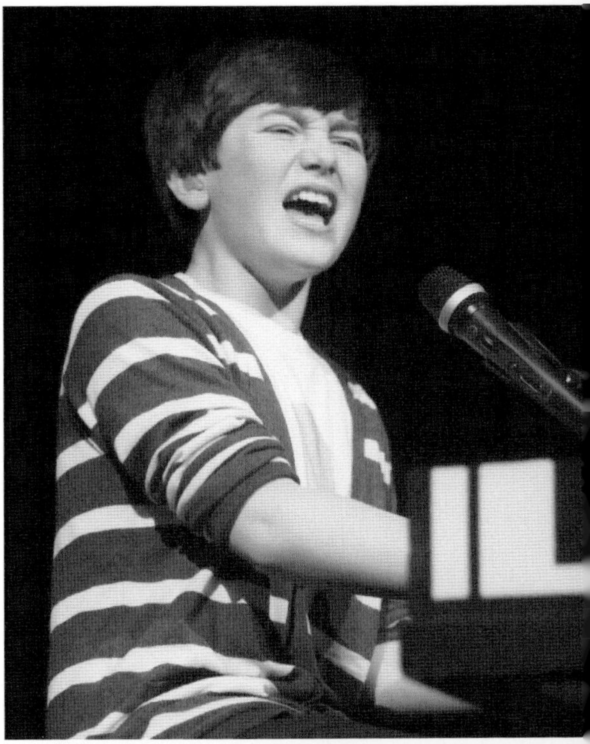

Greyson Chance

At age 12, Chance was sitting in his sixth-grade class at Edmond's Cheyenne Middle School one day only to earn instant stardom the next. In 2010, Chance became an internet sensation overnight because of a video he uploaded with his cover of a Lady Gaga song. He has had a meteoric rise to music stardom as a teenager, helped by an appearance on the *Ellen* show. He released a single in 2010, followed by an album, *Hold on 'Til the Night*, in 2011. Oklahoma Historical Society executive director Bob Blackburn said Chance will be a featured artist in the new Oklahoma Museum of Pop Culture in Tulsa. (Courtesy the *Oklahoman* archives.)

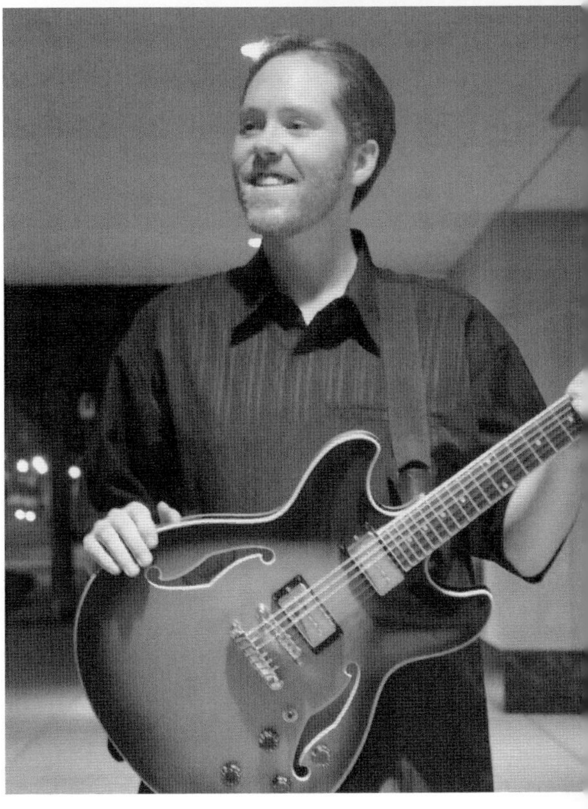

Garrett "Big G" Jacobson

Big G, as he has been called since he was a teen, started playing guitar at 10 and by age 12 was playing on stage with Oklahoma blues legend D.C. Minner. After three years of playing with Minner's band, Jacobson formed his own band in 1998 and recorded his first record, *Rhythm Attack*. Firmly rooted in the blues, Big G has been a mainstay at the Edmond Jazz and Blues Festival. A University of Central Oklahoma graduate, he has performed regularly at the UCO Jazz Lab since it opened in 2002. In 2013, he moved to Chicago and formed the Garrett Jacobson Trio. His CD *In Person* captures the dynamic energy of his live show. Also a jazz organist, he plays various jazz venues in between blues dates. (Courtesy Garrett Jacobson.)

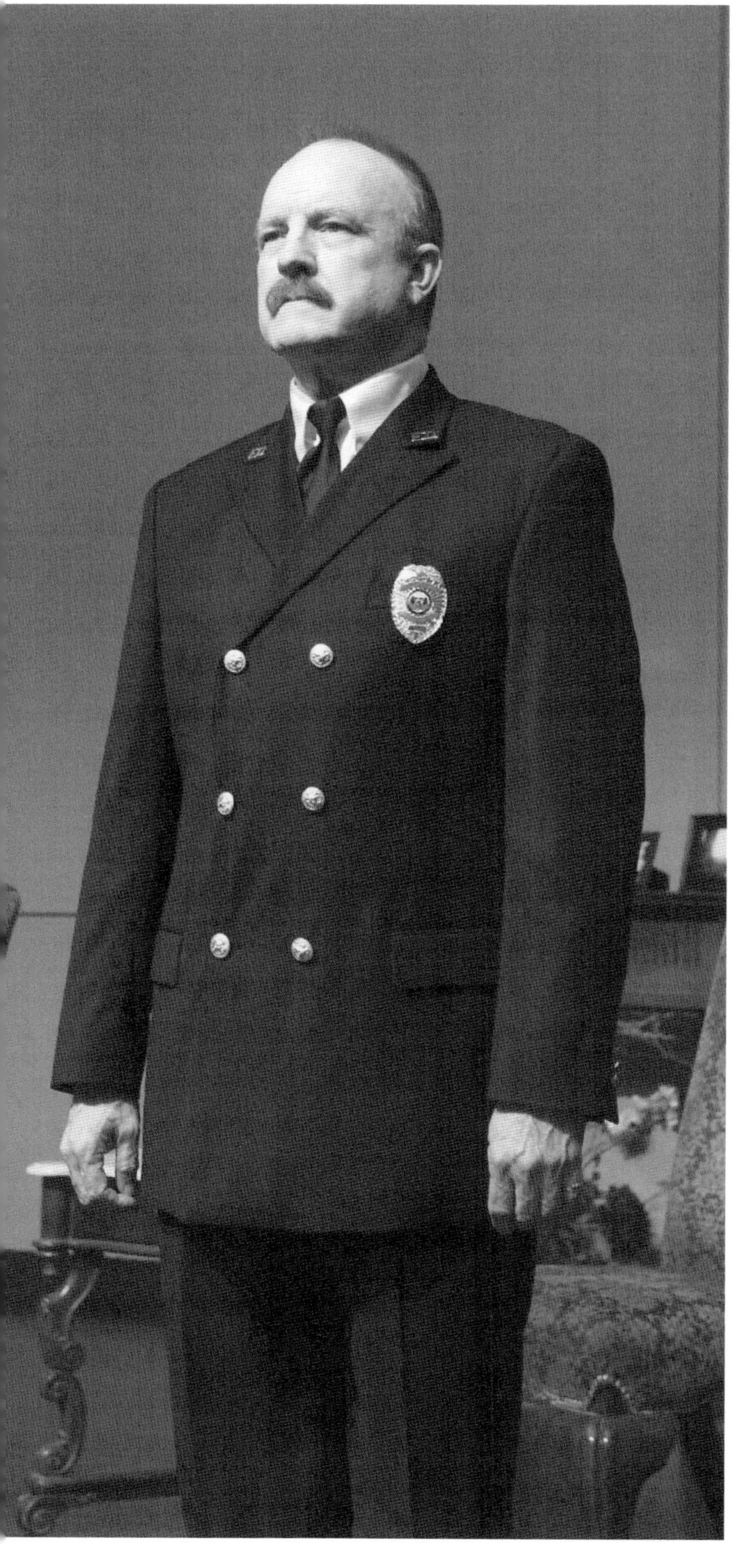

Jim Beaver

Beaver has come a long ways since his days at Central State University, where he earned his degree in 1975. A familiar face on television and in the movies, he had major roles in *Deadwood*, *Supernatural*, and *Justified*. As a teenager, he developed a fascination with movies and actors and began to imagine life as a writer of film history. Beaver joined the Marines after high school and was a radio operator in Vietnam. He returned to the states in 1971 and entered Oklahoma Christian University, where he became interested in theater. He made his theatrical debut in *The Miracle Worker*. He transferred to Central State University, where he was in several plays. He made his professional debut in an adaptation of Somerset Maugham's *Rain* at the Oklahoma Theatre Center in 1972. He worked in Dallas and New York before going to Los Angeles, where a chance meeting led to a starring role in *In Country* with Bruce Willis. Beaver married actress Cecily Adams, the daughter of Don Adams, legendary star of TV's *Get Smart*. He landed a role on the HBO drama *Deadwood*. Cecily had fans from her role on *Star Trek: Deep Space Nine* and was a casting director. In 2003, Cecily learned she had inoperable lung cancer and died four months later. Beaver began writing emails to keep family and friends current about her condition. The emails became a book, *Life's That Way: A Memoir*, Beaver's chronicle of the tragic year his wife died. In 2011, Beaver returned to Edmond to star in UCO's *The Guys*, a play about a fire captain who lost eight men in the collapse of the World Trade Center on September 11, 2001. (Courtesy UCO College of Fine Arts and Design.)

CHAPTER FOUR

Heroes, Lawmen, and Firefighters

Since 1903, when John Sumner was the first captain, Edmond firefighters have risked their lives countless times to save lives and property. In all those years, only one firefighter has lost his life. Steve Begley died in 1989 while on a recovery dive in an Oklahoma lake. During the 1930s, fire chief Lothar Smith created a fireman training program at Oklahoma State University and initiated building inspections in Edmond. Chiefs Dwight Maker and Gil Harryman helped build the department to the innovative and top-notch unit it is today. With five modern stations and a sixth in the works, the Edmond Fire Department is more than ready to serve local residents.

In 1995, when the Murrah Federal Building was blown up in Oklahoma City, 18 victims were from Edmond, including secret service agents Donald Leonard and Alan Whicher. Many Edmond firefighters, lawmen, and volunteers helped with rescue and recovery efforts. One was police detective Rockie Yardley, whose team left spray-painted words on the side of the Journal-Record Building, demanding justice for the victims

Before that terrible event, Edmond was the site of another tragedy in 1986, when an angry postal worker shot and killed 14 fellow employees at the downtown post office. The term "going postal" has been said to stem from this deadly day. A statue was erected next to the post office to memorialize the slain workers.

Police chief Bob Ricks came to Edmond from the FBI, where he gained fame during the Waco standoff at the Branch Davidian compound. He was also in charge of the FBI investigation of the Murrah blast. Dwight Adams, former top FBI forensics man, was brought in to direct the University of Central Oklahoma's new Forensic Science Institute.

Many war heroes were from Edmond or called Edmond home. Russell Dougherty was an air corps bomber pilot in World War II and the first Edmond High School graduate killed during the war. Claude Scoggins Jr. was one of the first paratroopers to land in France during the D-Day invasion in 1944, and Frederick Ransbottom was a Vietnam soldier killed in 1968, his fate unknown for 39 years. Later, 45th Infantry Combat Team member 2nd Lt. Jered Ewy was killed while helping disarm a roadside bomb in Afghanistan.

These stories represent just a few of the countless firefighters, heroes, and lawmen connected to Edmond's history.

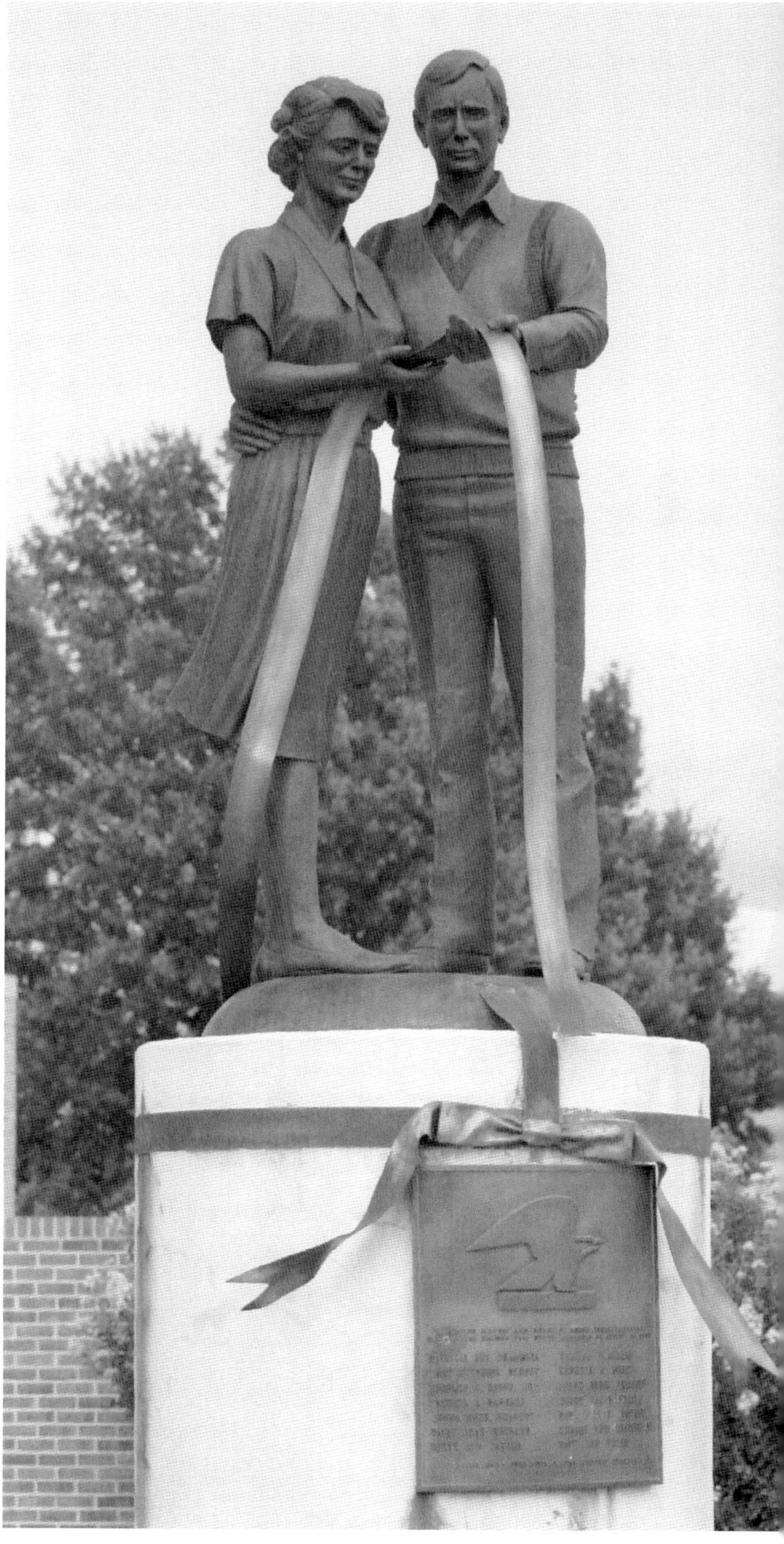

Post Office Shooting Victims
August 20, 1986, began as a routine day at Edmond's downtown post office. Hours later, it was anything but normal as 14 Edmond postal employees lay dead, slain by coworker Patrick Sherrill, who took his own life. The phrase "going postal" became an American expression after the tragedy. A statue sculpted by Rich Muno stands to the south of the post office as a reminder of the incident and honoring the 14 victims slain that hot summer day. It features a life-size man and woman holding a ribbon. The *Oklahoman* published an extra edition that day, the first since the Kennedy assassination. The victims were as follows: Patricia Ann Chambers, 41; Judy Stephens Denny, 41; Richard C. Fraser Jr., 38; Patricia A. Gabbard, 47; Jonna Gragert Hamilton, 30; Patty Jean Husband, 48; Betty Ann Jarred, 34; William F. Miller, 30; Kenneth W. Morey, 49; Leroy Orrin Phillips, 42; Jerry Ralph Pyle, 51; Paul Michael Rockne, 33; Thomas Wade Shader Jr., 31; and Pam Lou Welch, 27. They were supervisors, clerks, and carriers. Six other employees were wounded that day but survived. (Courtesy David Fisk.)

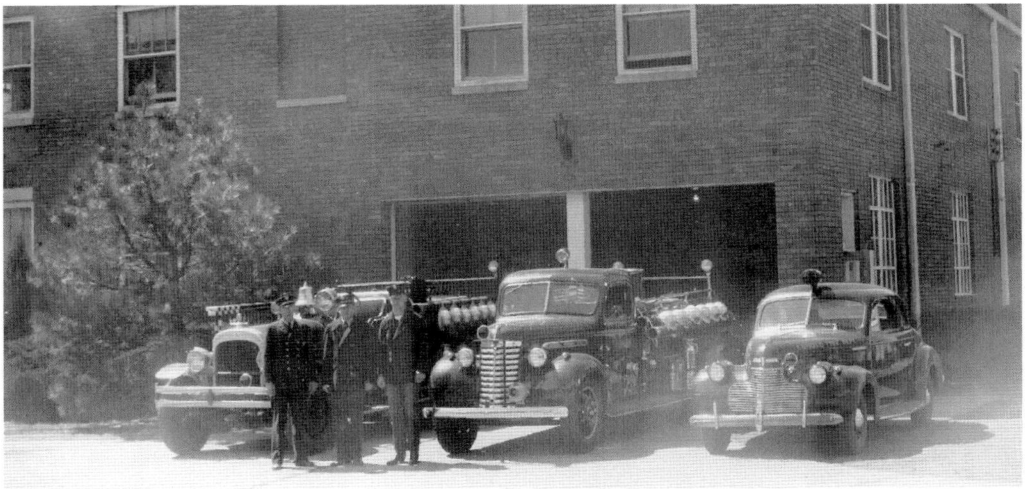

John Sumner

The first Edmond Fire Company was organized in 1903. Sumner, who had served as city marshal and cemetery superintendent, became the first company captain. The fire department had one aerial-ladder truck in 1903, which could carry a hose nozzle to a six-floor building, but still maintained the use of "fire brigade buckets" that were handed from person to person to bring water to the emergency. Early helmets were covered in leather to stand the heat of the blaze. Beginning in 1904, the first Edmond fire station was on Broadway between First and Second Streets. During those early days, a fire bell, called "Diane," sounded the alarm for the many volunteers in the area to come running. In 1905, after two houses had burned to the ground, the city council issued an ordinance that all occupants of lots on Broadway were to keep a barrel of water and one peck of salt on hand in case of a fire emergency. In 1950, the fire department consisted of Chief Lothar Smith, pictured above, four paid firemen, six volunteers, and six part-time student volunteers. Two triple combination pumpers with up to 600-gallon tank capacity and the chief's car, considered state-of-the-art, were the extent of their equipment at the time. (Courtesy Edmond Historical Society Photographic Collection.)

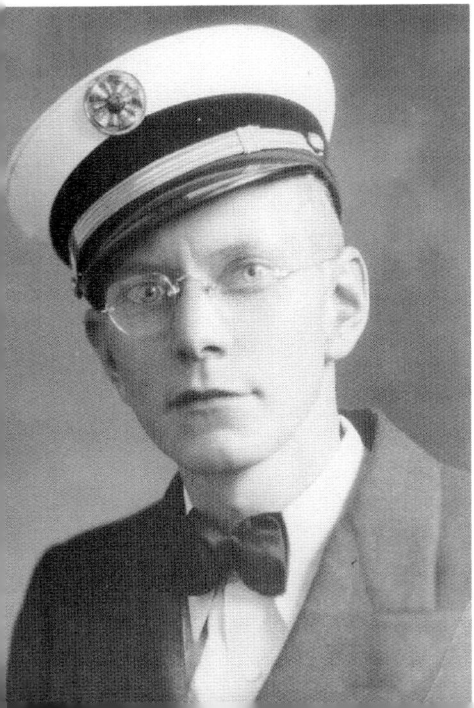

Lothar Smith

Smith joined the Edmond Fire Department while he was a student at Central State College and served as assistant chief. Following in fire chief Charles Steen's footsteps, Smith became chief in 1934. His leadership helped shape the future of the Edmond department. He helped establish a fireman training program at Oklahoma A&M, where a building for the program was constructed. Called the "West Point of firemanship," the school offered a two-year training course to teach young men firefighting skills. With the help of citizens, the department bought a resuscitator and inhalator in 1939, which in the first five years were used on 40 calls, resulting in 20 successful revivals. He was responsible for inaugurating a fire prevention program with building inspections. During his tenure, many improvements were made in the living conditions of firefighters. Edmond was able to boast one of the best fire departments for towns under 10,000. He retired as chief in 1950. (Courtesy Edmond Historical Society Photographic Collection.)

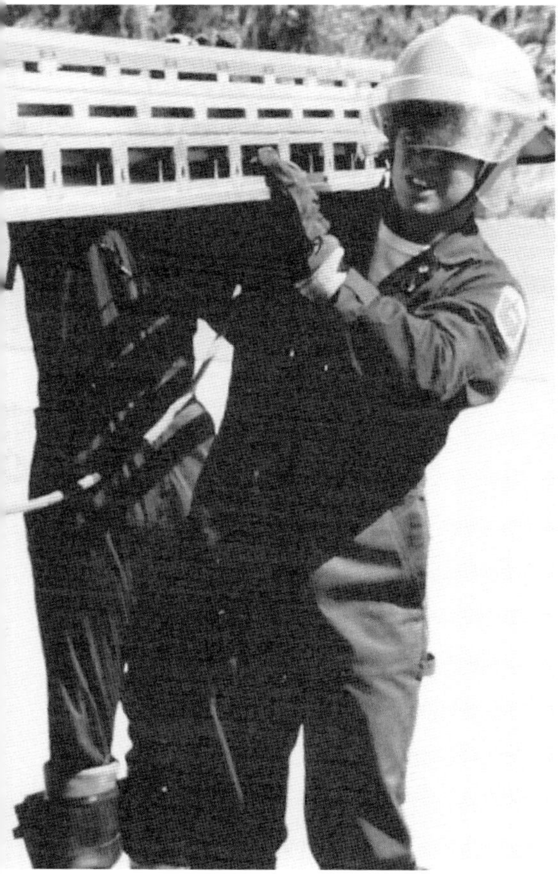

Steve Begley

The only Edmond firefighter to ever die in the line of duty, Begley drowned during a rescue diving mission at Keystone Lake near Tulsa in 1989. His name is on the Oklahoma State Fallen and Living Firefighter's memorial at the Firefighters Museum in Oklahoma City. Begley was 28 and had just been told of a promotion days before the accident. Begley's death occurred when he and other Edmond firefighters were searching with the lake patrol for the body of a man who had gone missing while parasailing several weeks earlier. The body was found. Begley had been a member of the scuba rescue team for more than two years. Fire chief Dwight Maker said, "He was one of our best." (Courtesy Kyle Begley.)

Dwight Maker

Maker became fire chief in Edmond in 1993 after working his way up the ranks since beginning his career as a firefighter in 1972, when there were just 19 people in the fire department. He served in numerous capacities, including driver, captain, battalion chief, and deputy chief. Maker was largely responsible for getting Fire Station Number 4 open in the 1990s on I-35 south of Fifteenth Street, greatly improving the department's ability to serve areas of East Edmond, where there were several housing additions without fire hydrants. The mural pictured is on the wall as one enters the station and was created by two Edmond firefighters stationed there. According to then city manager Leonard Martin, when Maker became chief, he put up a sign that said "head coach" and took down the "fire chief" sign. A retired firefighter's wife once said of Maker, "He always made sure his men were taken care of and they know he stands behind his men." Maker was chief until he retired in 2001, when Gil Harryman took the reins. (Courtesy David Fisk.)

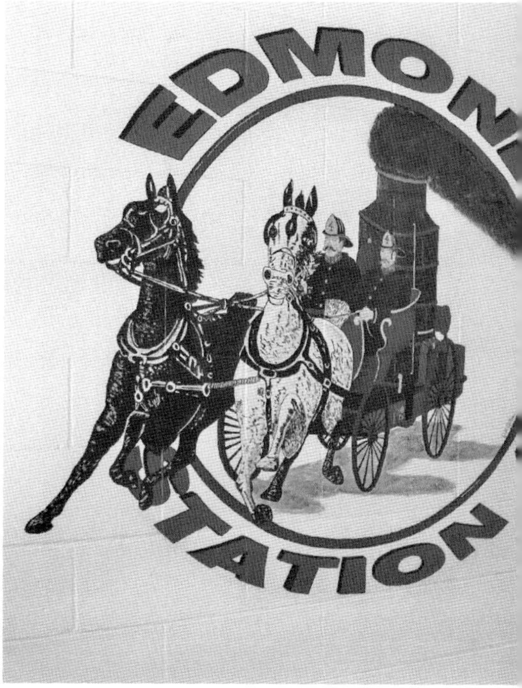

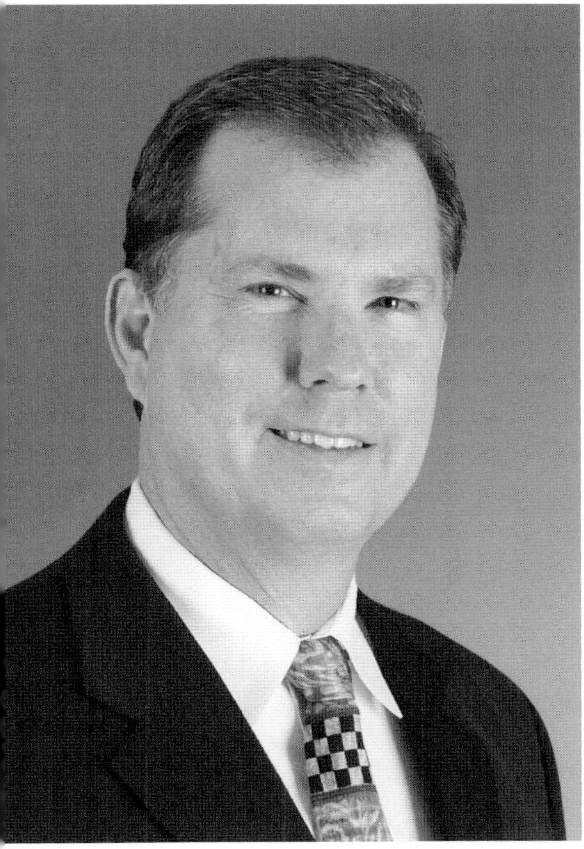

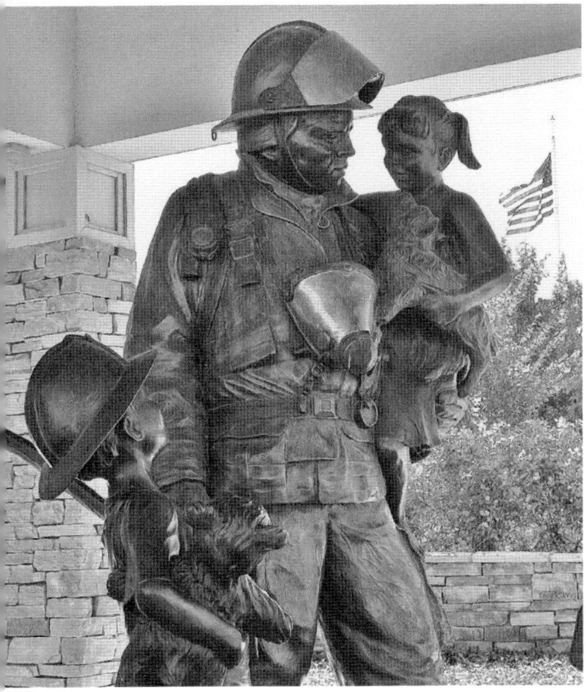

Gil Harryman

When Harryman became an Edmond firefighter in 1977, there were 30 people in the department. When he retired 35 years later, he was fire chief and commanded more than 120 firefighters. He stepped down in 2012. Called forward thinking by Mayor Charles Lamb, Harryman was responsible for the opening of Edmond's fifth station and the new administrative, fire prevention, and training facility on Covell Road. The Children's Safety Village was created under his watch next to the administrative complex. This is where children can learn about safety in a hands-on way. Land for a sixth fire station was purchased by the city under his leadership. During his 11 years as chief, he hired the majority of firefighters now in the department. He began his career as a firefighter, became a driver, then a lieutenant, and in 1982 became a captain. He served as a training officer, battalion chief, and then assistant fire chief before taking the reins as chief in 2001. His men were on hand after the Murrah bombing and did a top-to-bottom search of the Journal Record Building. Working out of the Edmond emergency operations center, Harryman helped Edmond workers coordinate agencies calling in to help Oklahoma City. Pictured below is the *Reunion* sculpture of a fireman holding a young girl who has a puppy in her arms. The young boy standing with them is wearing a fireman's hat and is holding a stuffed toy. It is located at the entrance to the Edmond Fire Department Training Center, which was Harryman's project. (Above, courtesy the Harryman family; below, courtesy David Fisk.)

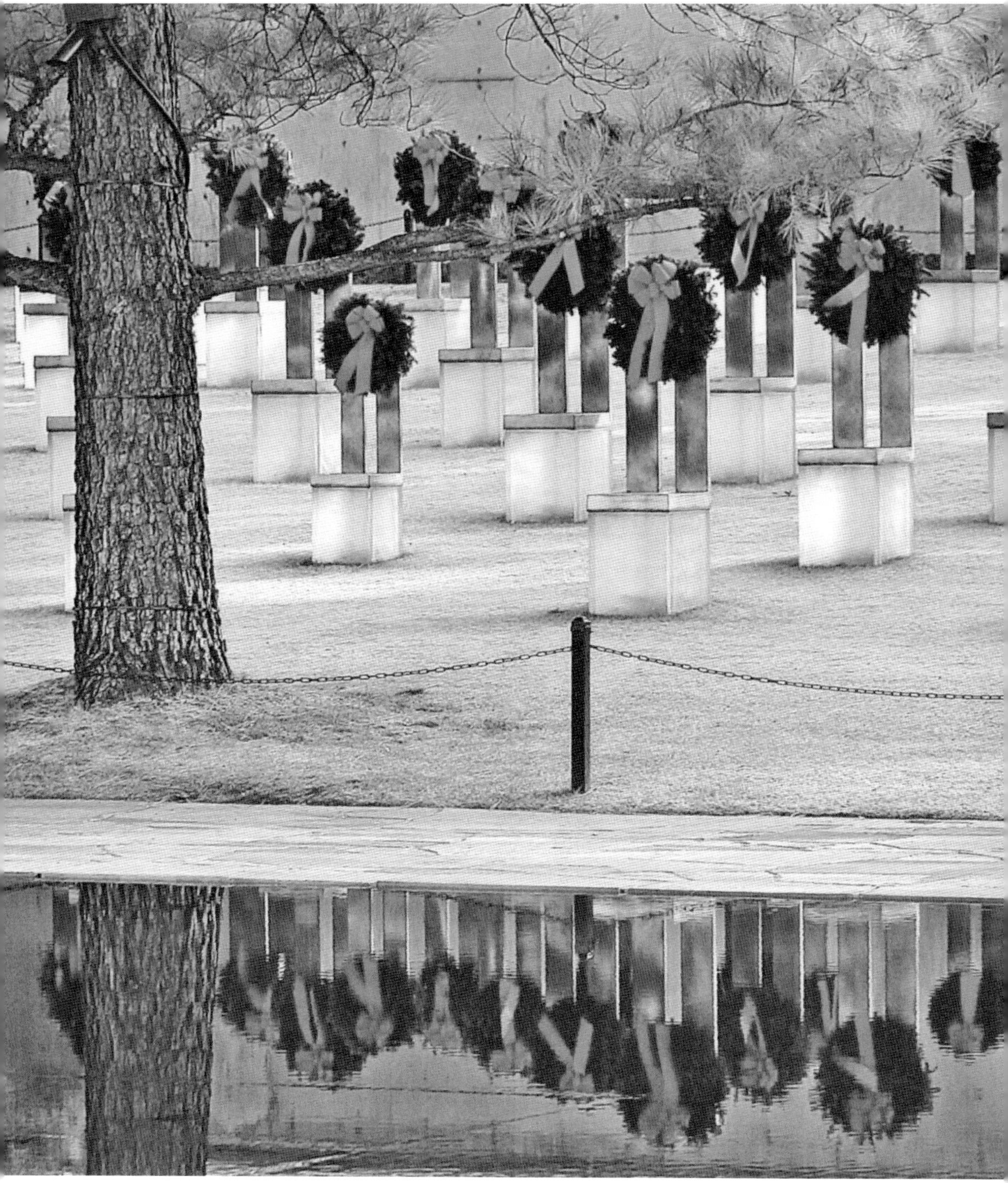

Murrah Bombing Victims

On April 19, 1995, 168 people lost their lives when the Alfred P. Murrah Federal Building in Oklahoma City was blown up. Eighteen victims were from Edmond, and their names are listed on a memorial that overlooks a creek and wooded area near walking trails in Mitch Park. Shown above is the National Bombing Memorial Park at the building site in downtown Oklahoma City. The Edmond victims were Diane E.

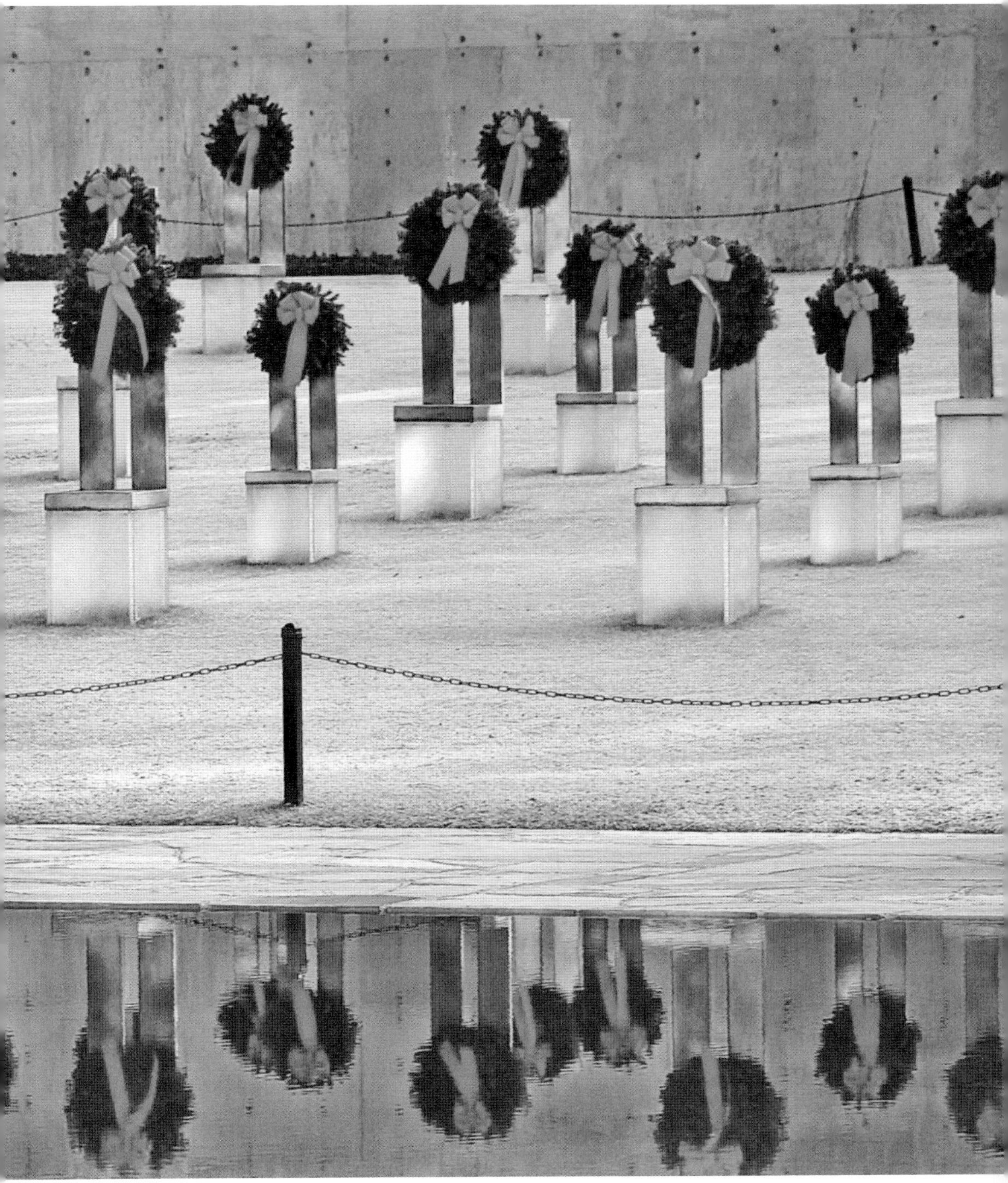

Althouse, 45; Paul Broxterman, 43; Robert Chipman, 51; Sgt. Benjamin Davis, 29; Carol "Chip" Fields, 48; Ethel Griffin, 55; Christi Jenkins, 33; Donald Ray Leonard, 50; James McCarthy, 53; Kenneth McCullough, 36; Pat "Trish" Nix, 47; Antonio Reyes, 55; Johnny Wade, 45; David Jack Walker, 54; Jules Valdez, 51; Michael Weaver, 45; Alan Whicher 40; and Ronota Woodbridge, 31. (Courtesy David Fisk.)

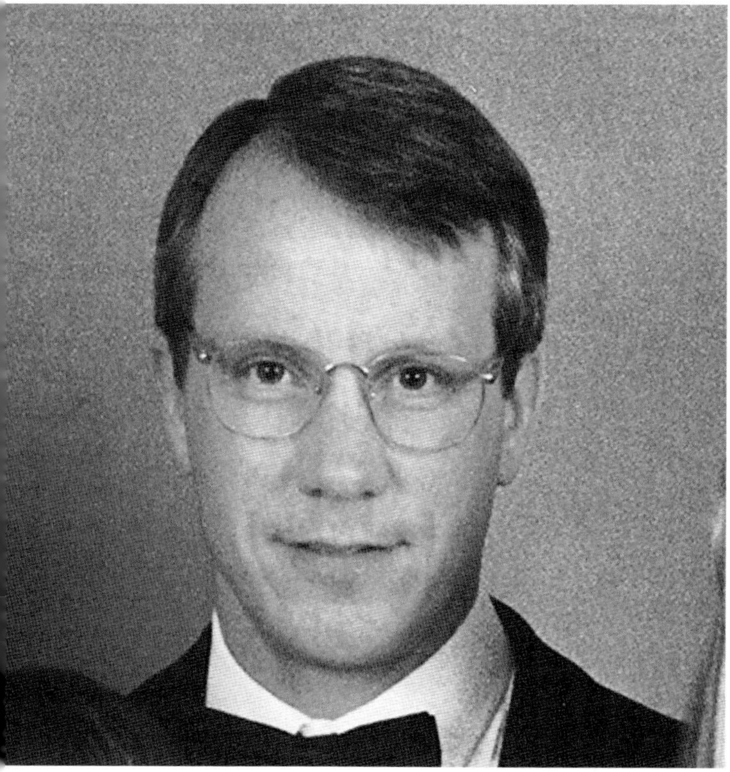

Alan Gerald Whicher
A Secret Service agent for 19 years, Whicher was in his new office in the Alfred P. Murrah Federal Building in Oklahoma City when it was destroyed on April 19, 1995. He was assistant special agent in charge when he died. Whicher had moved to Edmond with his family just nine months before from Washington, DC, where he had helped protect the president. They lived in the Old Town addition, where a pond was dedicated in his honor. Pres. Bill Clinton remembered the former member of his protective detail at his funeral service in Maryland, saying Whicher "was the kind of man every parent wants his or her son to be." (Courtesy the Oklahoma City National Museum and Memorial.)

Donald Ray Leonard
Secret Service agent Leonard never got a chance to enjoy his retirement, which was just a few months away when he was killed in the Alfred P. Murrah Federal Building bombing. After more than 20 years, Edmond resident Leonard was looking forward to more time on the golf course and traveling with his family. His brother said Leonard served on presidential details during the Nixon and Ford presidencies. He worked for the Oklahoma City Police Department while working on his degree at Central State University. He joined the Secret Service in 1970 and had been at the Oklahoma City office since 1990. (Courtesy the Oklahoma City National Museum and Memorial.)

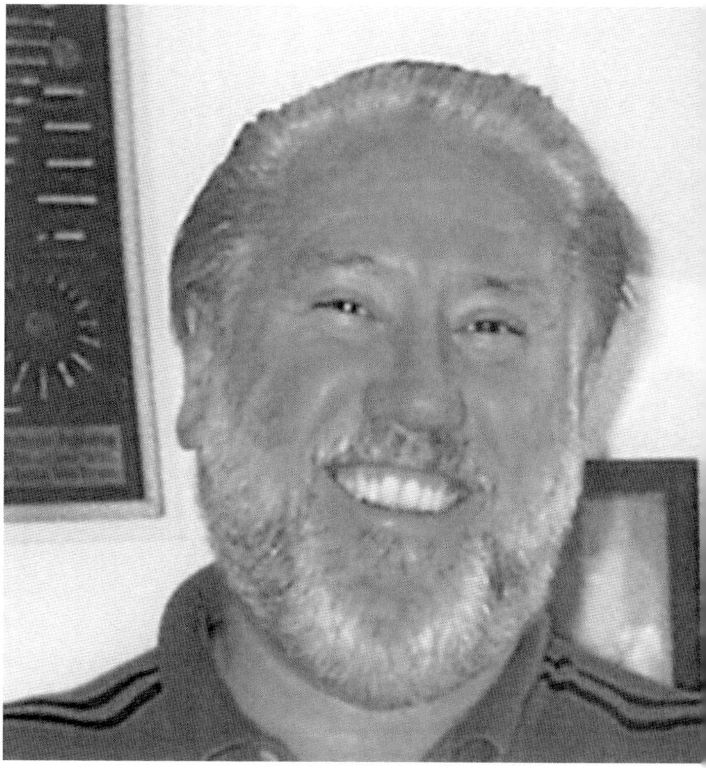

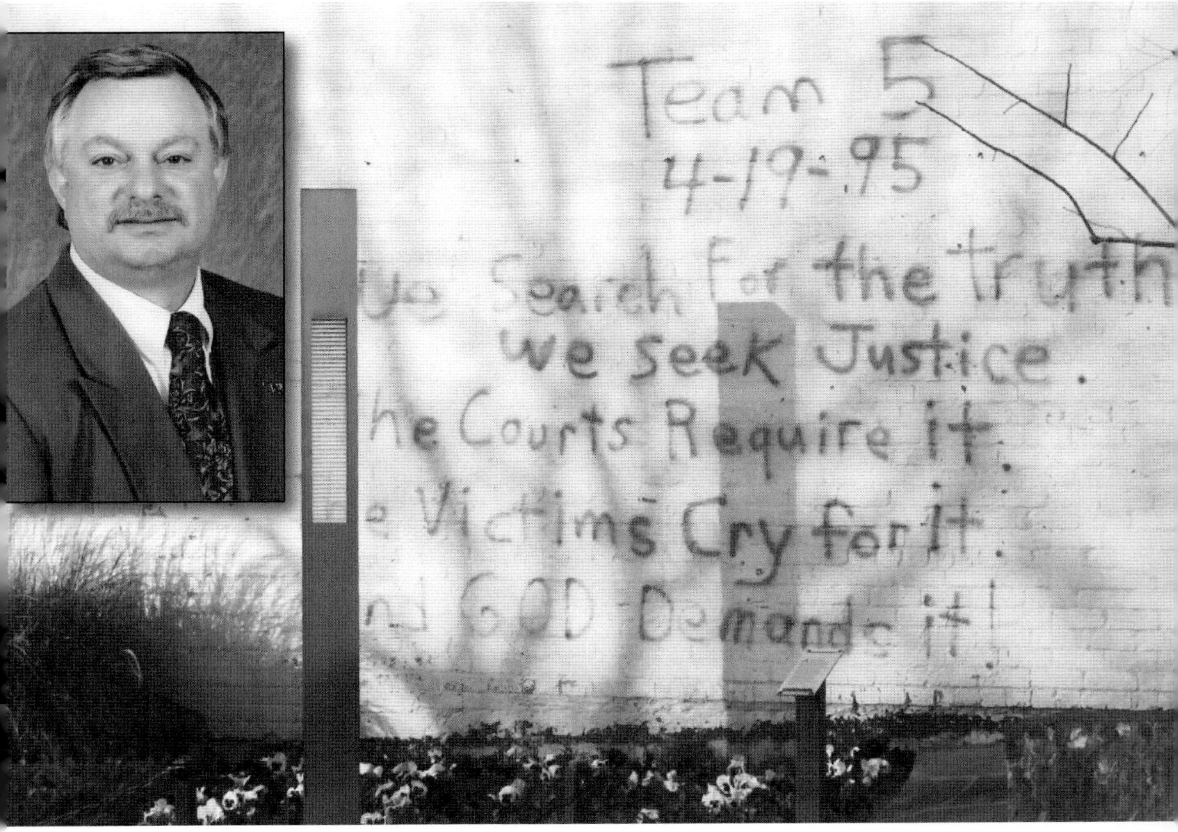

Rockie Yardley

In his more than 30 years with the Edmond Police department, Yardley has been involved in many phases of law enforcement, including investigation of the 1986 post office shootings. In 1995, when the Murrah Federal Building was bombed in Oklahoma City, Yardley was a first responder and one of many heroes. In 2009, Yardley spoke about his emotions and encounters with victims during a Stories of Hope program at the Oklahoma City National Memorial. He described the "utter chaos" when he arrived at the scene 30 minutes after the bomb exploded. Victims and responders were everywhere. He spent time in the area where many of the day care children's bodies were recovered. Yardley helped recover bodies before and after the building was imploded. While working in the rubble, Yardley and his rescue and recovery team members spray painted their heart-felt words on the wall of the Journal Record building (above), now the south wall of the Memorial Museum. It reads, "Team 5, 4-19-95. We search for the truth. We seek justice. The courts require it. The victims cry for it. And God demands it!" The words remain today. He and other investigators refused to go to the memorial service with Pres. Bill Clinton four days after the blast; they still had work to do. A month later, when the building was imploded, they recovered the bodies of the remaining three victims whose location they had marked. Detective Yardley was awarded the Medal of Valor from the Edmond Police Department and Exceptional Service Award for 1995 from the Oklahoma Association of Chiefs of Police. (Courtesy David Fisk; inset, courtesy Edmond Police Department.)

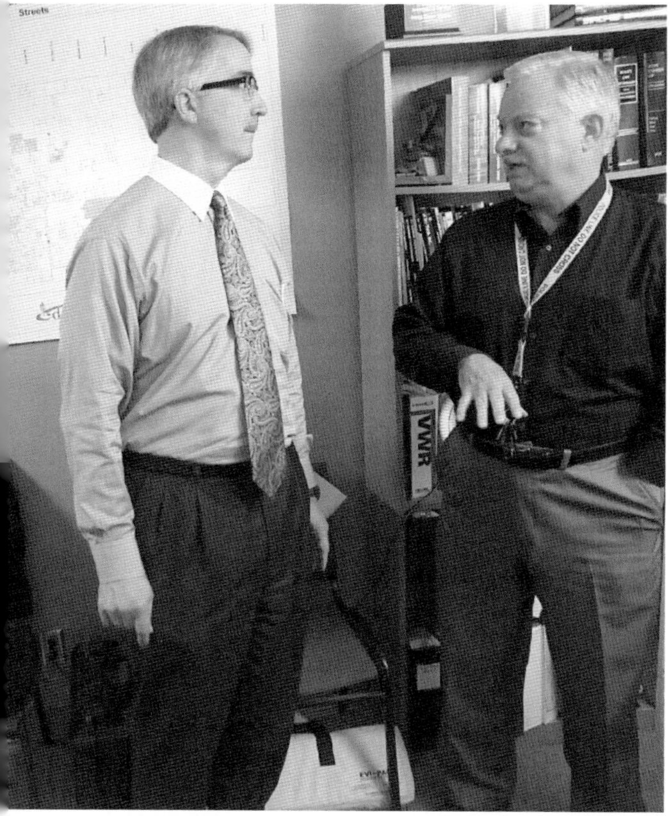

Dwight Adams

Adams is director of the University of Central Oklahoma W. Roger Webb Forensic Science Institute. Adams came to UCO after a 23-year career with the FBI, where he was director of the FBI Crime Laboratory in Quantico, Virginia. While with the FBI, Adams helped develop DNA techniques first used in 1988. Pictured at left with Edmond detective Rockie Yardley, right, Adams graduated from UCO in 1977 and has a doctorate from the University of Oklahoma in botany. He returned to his alma mater in 2006 to be the first director of the Forensic Science Institute. He created a dual-degree academic program and oversaw construction of the 30,000-aquare-foot facility. Considered an outstanding professor, he learns his students' first names and greets his students by name as they enter the classroom on their first day. In 2012, Adams won the Oklahoma State Bureau of Investigation Director's Award for Law Enforcement. (Left, courtesy the *Oklahoman* archives; below, courtesy David Fisk.)

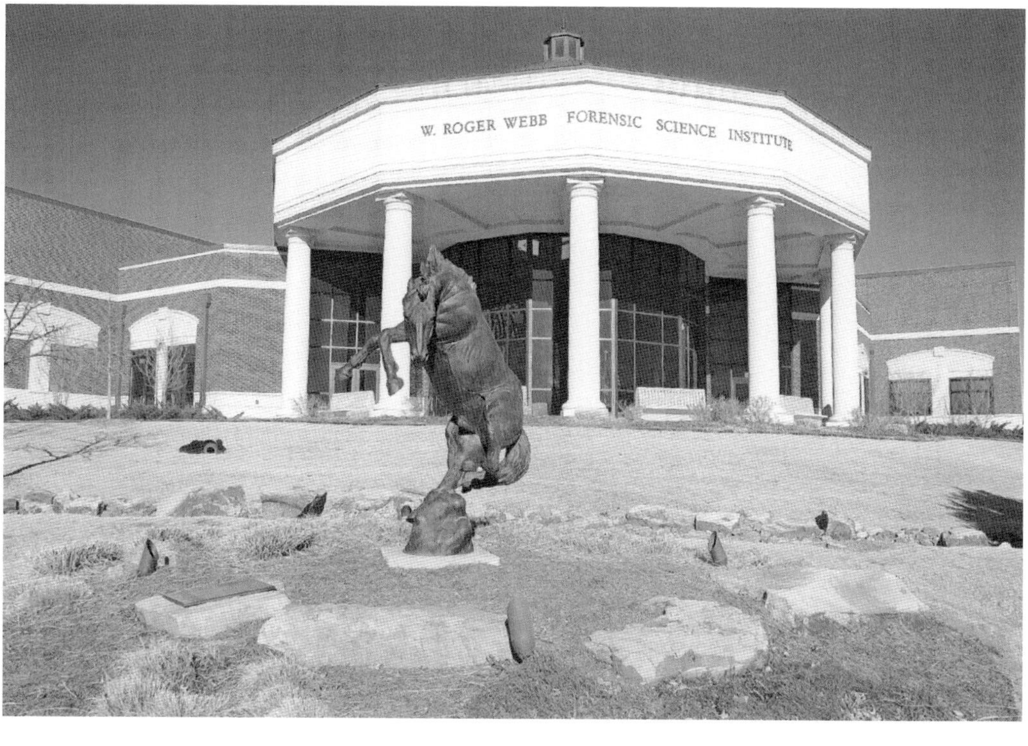

Bob Ricks

It is appropriate that Ricks's favorite movie is *High Noon*. During a long career in law enforcement, Ricks has been at the forefront of some pretty intense and historic cases. In 1993, Ricks was special agent in charge of the FBI's Oklahoma City field office. When the Bureau of Alcohol, Tobacco, and Firearms launched a raid on the Branch Davidian compound in Waco, Ricks was named one of the assistant special agents in charge. He served as spokesman during the siege. Ricks told the media, "We are going to get them . . . to bring them before the bar of justice for the murder of our agents."

Two years later, in 1995, Ricks was in charge of the FBI in Oklahoma City when Timothy McVeigh blew up the Alfred P. Murrah Federal Building—168 people were killed and hundreds injured. As the official FBI incident commander, he worked with Oklahoma governor Frank Keating and senior FBI and Justice Department officials in response to the attack. He retired from the FBI soon after that and took over as director of safety and security for Governor Keating. In this job, he oversaw all state law enforcement agencies, including the Oklahoma Highway Patrol. In 2003, he became police chief of Edmond. One of the first things he did was revise the official police slogan to "trustworthy service." Ricks told the *Edmond Sun* that the most rewarding part of his time in Edmond had been seeing the growth in the members of the agency. He established Edmond's first in-house police academy, made sure crime rates stayed low, and saw his vision for a new downtown $33.9-million public safety center complex move forward. Edmond remains one of Oklahoma's, and America's, safest cities. (Courtesy Edmond Police Department.)

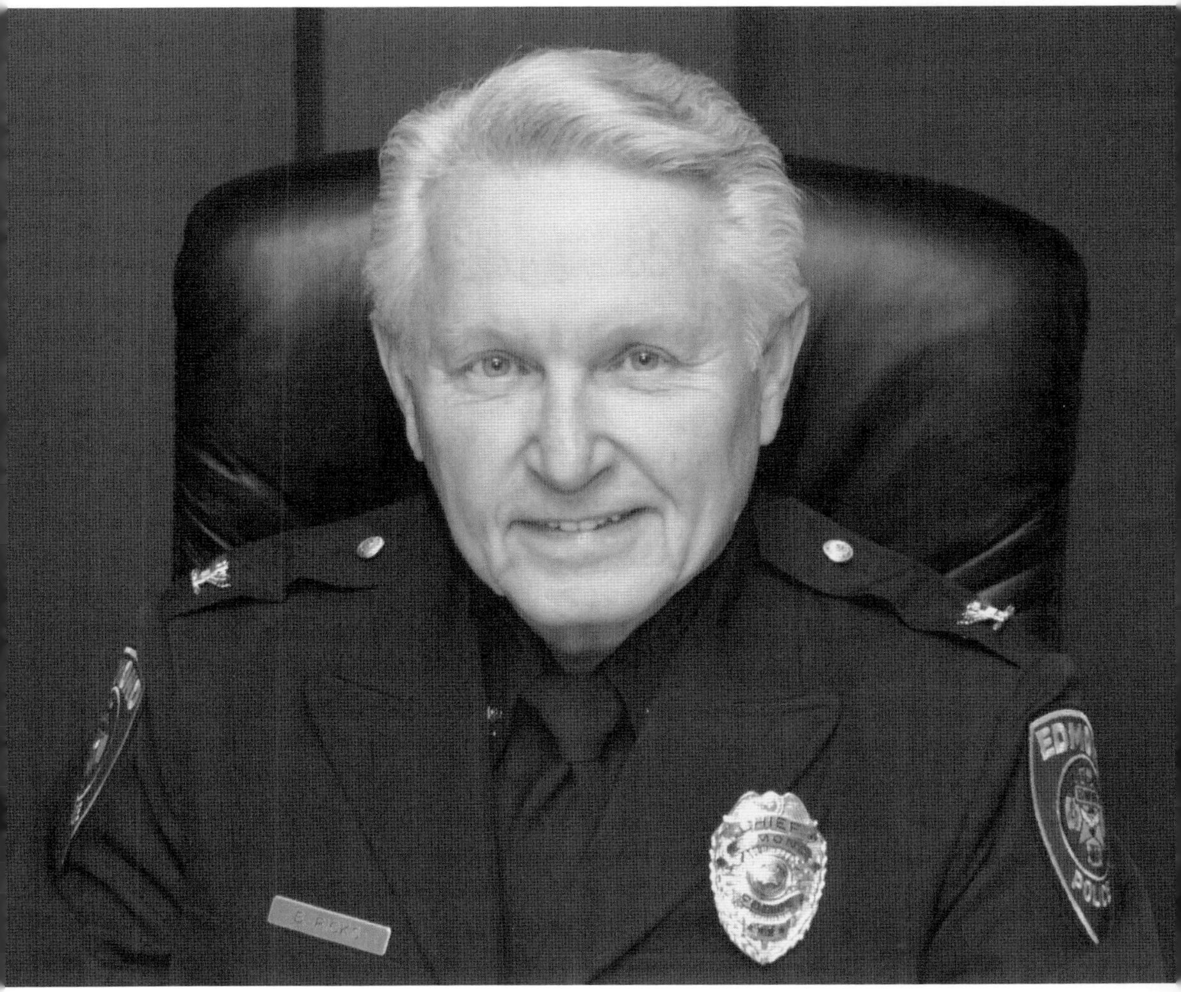

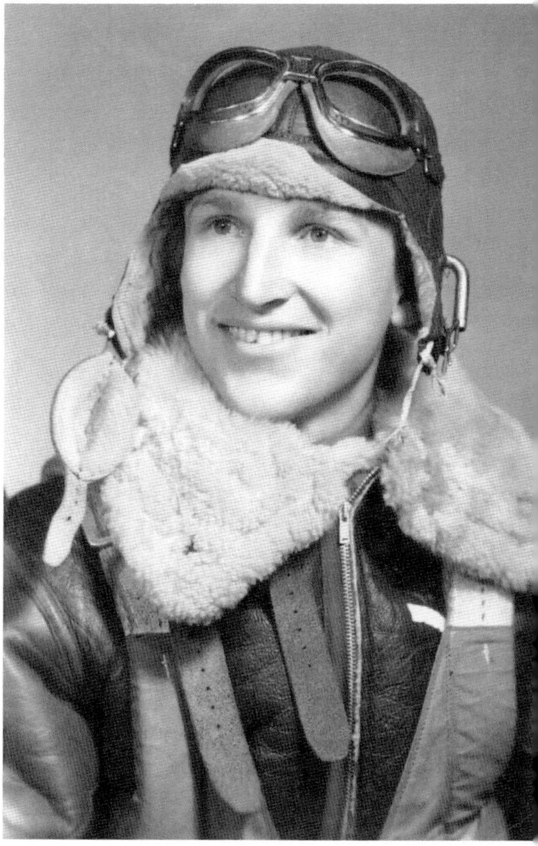

Russell Dougherty

Dougherty was the first graduate of Edmond High School killed during World War II. A life-size statue sits in front of Russell Dougherty Elementary School on Boulevard Avenue. He was stationed on Quadalcanal in April 1943 when he and his crew crashed in their B-24 over the Solomon Islands. An Edmond native, Dougherty was 24 when he died. He was an Air Corps bomber pilot flying with the 307th Bomb Group, known as the "Lone Rangers." He was awarded the Air Medal with three oak leaf clusters for missions in the Pacific theater. Dougherty grew up in a farmhouse at what is now the corner of 150th Street and Pennsylvania Avenue. (Right, courtesy Edmond Historical Society Photographic Collection; below, courtesy David Fisk.)

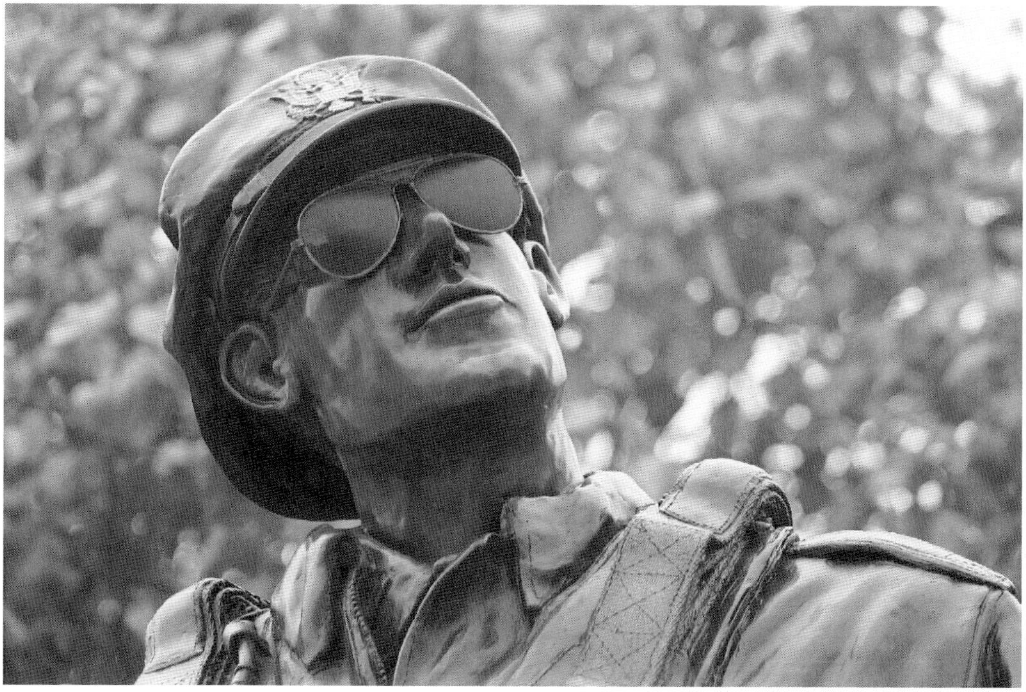

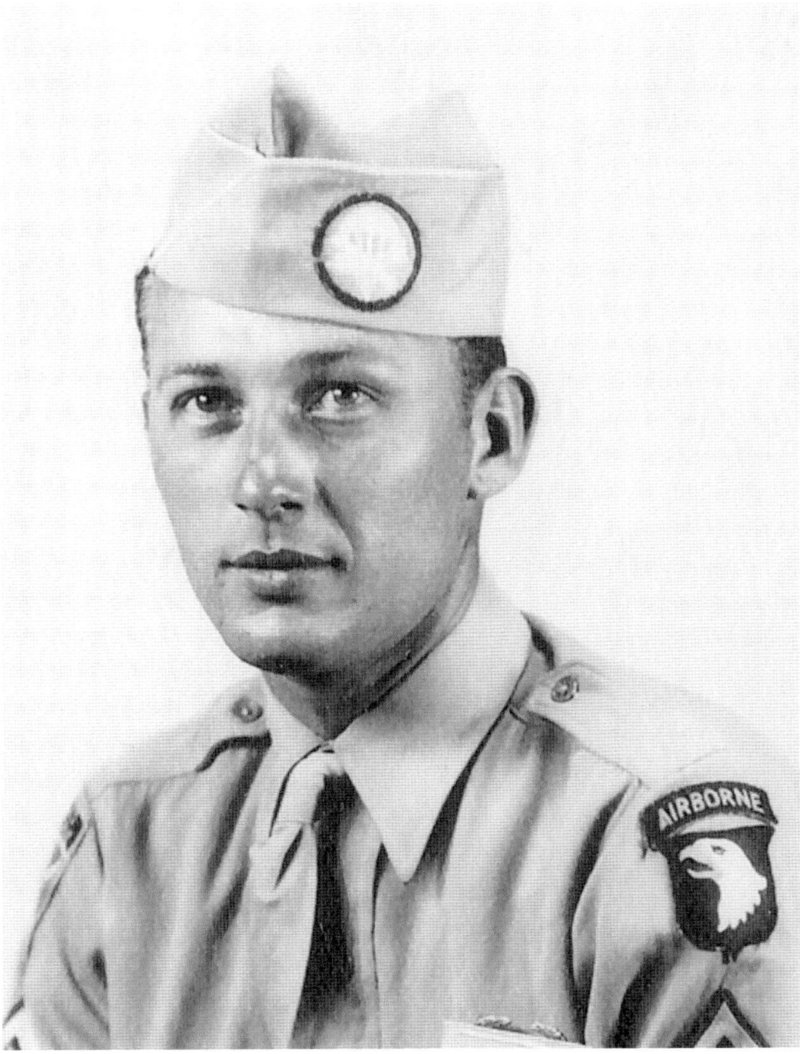

Claude Scoggins Jr.
Company C was not made famous in a television series like Company E in *Band of Brothers*, but Scoggin's Company C was its own band of brothers. Scoggins, who lived in Edmond 50 years, took part in the Normandy invasion and the Battle of the Bulge and helped liberate Hitler's Eagle's Nest as a part of the US 101st Airborne Division, 506th Parachute Infantry Regiment during World War II. Scoggins died at age 90 in 2013, but *Edmond Life and Leisure* writer Steve Gust told his story in a 2007 newspaper article. Before the war, he joined the Marines as a teenager from Pauls Valley but was discharged because of an eye injury. Not to be discouraged, Scoggins went to Canada, where he served in the Canadian Army's Essex Scottish Regiment. He made it to Europe and transferred to the American 101st Airborne Paratroopers in England. As a young man, he wanted to get into combat, and he soon got his wish. His unit of paratroopers was one of the first to land in France during the D-Day invasion in 1944. His company went into the historic battle with 140 men, and Scoggins said only 34 walked away. He was awarded three Purple Hearts and two Bronze Stars. Scoggins said of the liberation of Hitler's Eagle's Nest, "Yeah, Easy Company [E] was there, but we [Company C] were there first." He went to the University of Oklahoma after the war and became a petroleum engineer. He moved with his family to Edmond in 1963 and had one of the first homes in Smiling Hills, which was "in the country" at the time, recalls his son Jeff. (Courtesy the Scoggins family.)

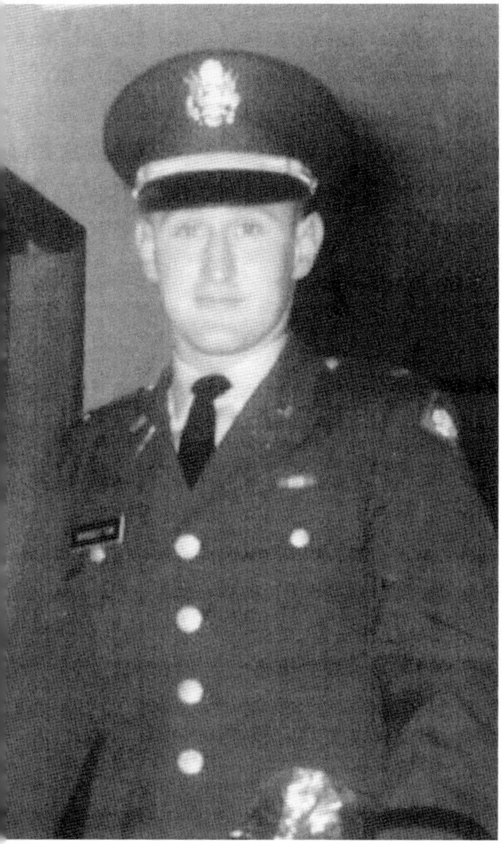

Fredrick Joel Ransbottom

Ransbottom died in battle in 1968 in Vietnam, but it was almost 39 years before his remains were returned home to Edmond. In early 2007, his flag-draped coffin arrived at Will Rogers Airport and was greeted by the governor's National Guard honor guard. First Lieutenant Ransbottom was 22 when he was killed. He had been listed as a possible prisoner of war for years and later as missing in action. His platoon had been conducting reconnaissance along the Ho Chi Minh Trail east of the Laotian border when they were attacked and overrun. His remains were found in 2006 when a joint POW/MIA accounting command mission went to the outpost, where they also uncovered artifacts where he and his men were last known to be. His dog tags and wallet with his ID along with his Putnam City High School ring were recovered. He was posthumously awarded a Silver Star and had been promoted to major while he was MIA. He was buried with full military honors following his funeral at Henderson Hills Baptist Church. Rev. Dennis Newkirk said Ransbottom "was a unique man, not just a statistic. He chose to give his life for friends, family, and country. Today, we say welcome back Fred." He is buried in Memorial Park Cemetery. In 2012, a silver Missing in Action bracelet, worn by Mary Milley for 39 years until she died, was given to his mother, Laverne Ransbottom of Edmond. In 2013, he was inducted into the Oklahoma Military Hall of Fame. (Left, courtesy Oklahoma Military Hall of Fame; below, courtesy David Fisk.)

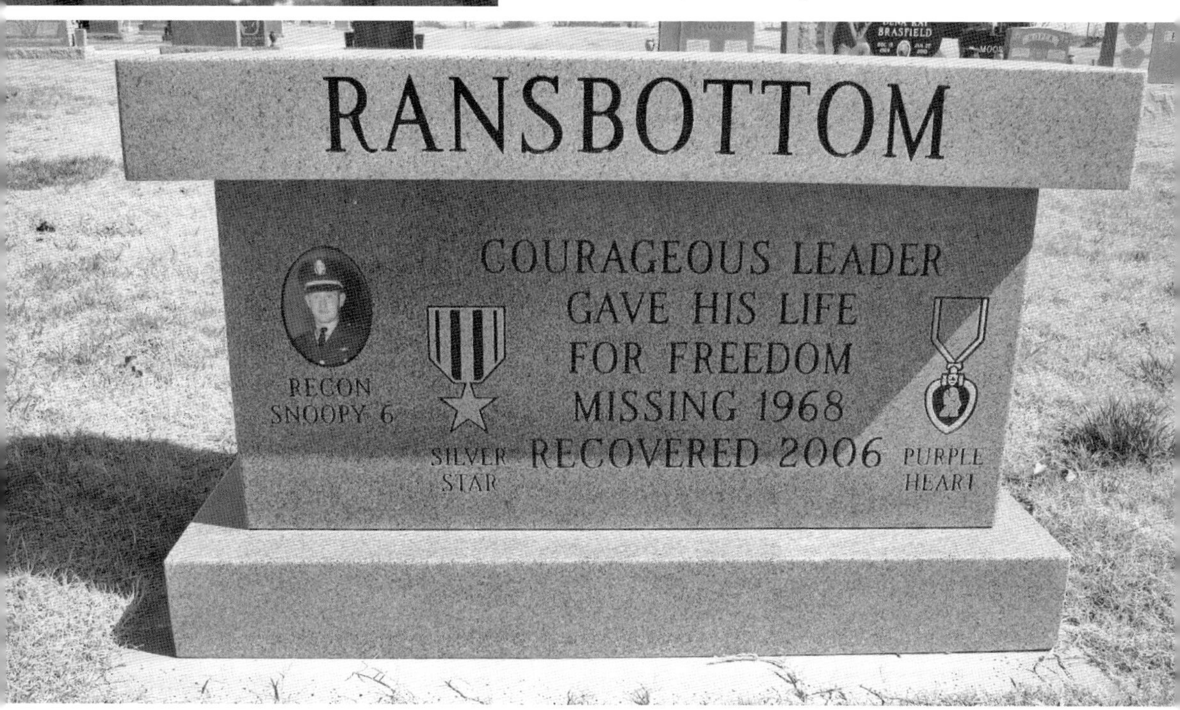

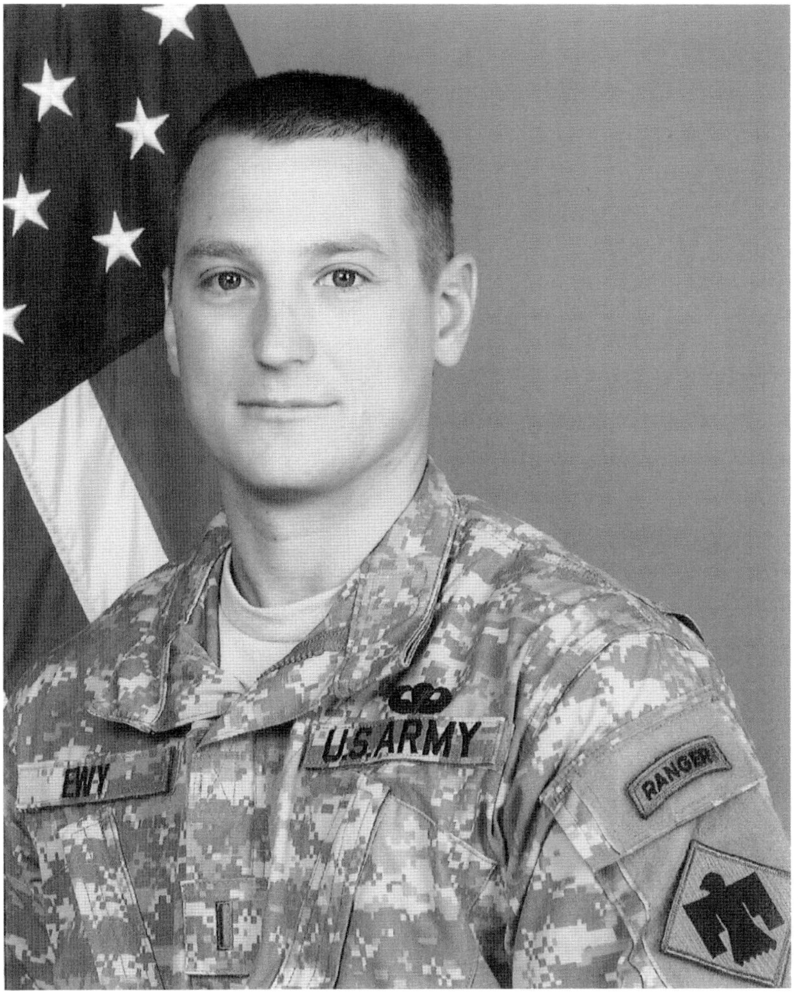

Jered W. Ewy

Second Lieutenant Ewy was the first Oklahoma Guardsman killed during the 45th Infantry Brigade Combat Team's deployment to Afghanistan in 2011. Ewy had just become a father in June to a girl, Kyla. He was killed on July 29, 2011, after returning from paternity leave. Ewy had been an Army Ranger since 1998 and served three tours of duty before leaving the Rangers to join the National Guard in 2003 so he could attend the University of Central Oklahoma, where he earned a criminal justice degree. As a Ranger, he was one of the first troops on the ground in Afghanistan in 2001. Ewy was killed while disarming a roadside bomb. He was a member of Company B, 1st Battalion, 279th infantry of the famous Thunderbird 45th Infantry unit. Ewy, 33, was a gymnastics coach at Oklahoma Gold in Edmond, where he met his wife, Megan, whom he married in 2009. He graduated from Officer Candidate School in 2011 as a second lieutenant. In a story in the *Oklahoman*, Ewy was remembered as a friendly family man who instilled discipline as he taught. One friend said, "He was one of those people that you didn't have to know him a long time for him to leave a lasting impression." He loved snakes and was a big hit with kids when he brought his reptiles to birthday parties. More than 1,500 people came to his funeral at Henderson Hills Baptist Church. An endowed military scholarship was established at UCO by Megan, also a UCO alum. She said, "Jered was a big advocate of the military and going to college." Ewy's sister, Penny Clark, told the *Moore American* that he was "a very skilled and great soldier. He was quiet and a very humble man." (Courtesy UCO Development Office.)

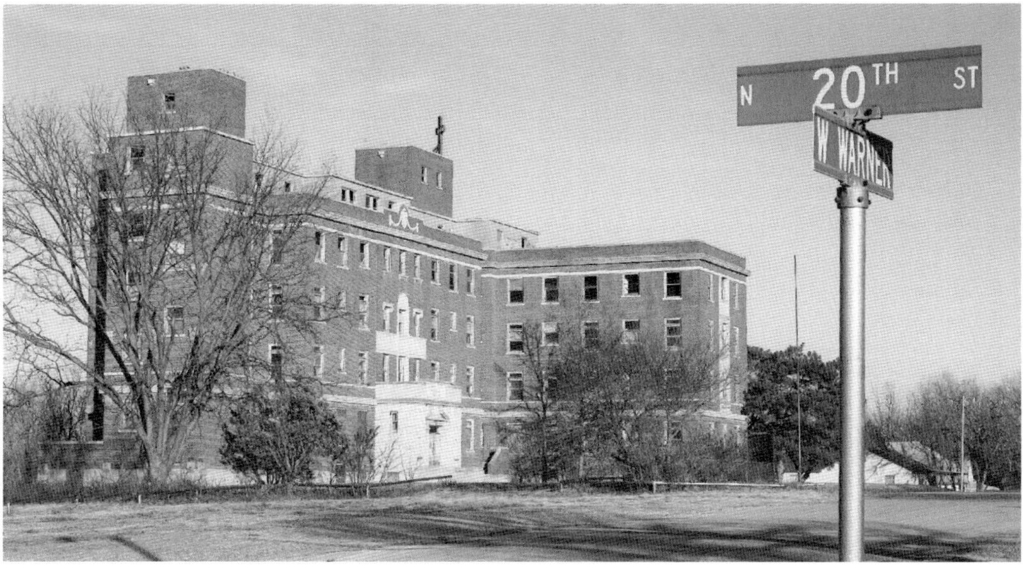

Karen Silkwood

Silkwood was a whistleblower made famous in the movie *Silkwood* by actress Meryl Streep. She lived in Edmond, near Central State University on Washington Street, not in Crescent as the movie depicted. She worked at the now closed Kerr-McGee Nuclear Plant on Highway 74 south of Crescent, where she became contaminated with radioactive particles. Her apartment was scrubbed down after by Kerr-McGee, and health department investigators found it totally contaminated. She died under mysterious circumstances a few days later in a one-car crash near where Highways 33 and 74 intersect, and her body was taken to Logan County Hospital, above. She had been on her way to Crescent to meet with a *New York Times* reporter with alleged safety violations at the Kerr-McGee plant. Years later, her family sued Kerr-McGee. (Both, courtesy David Fisk.)

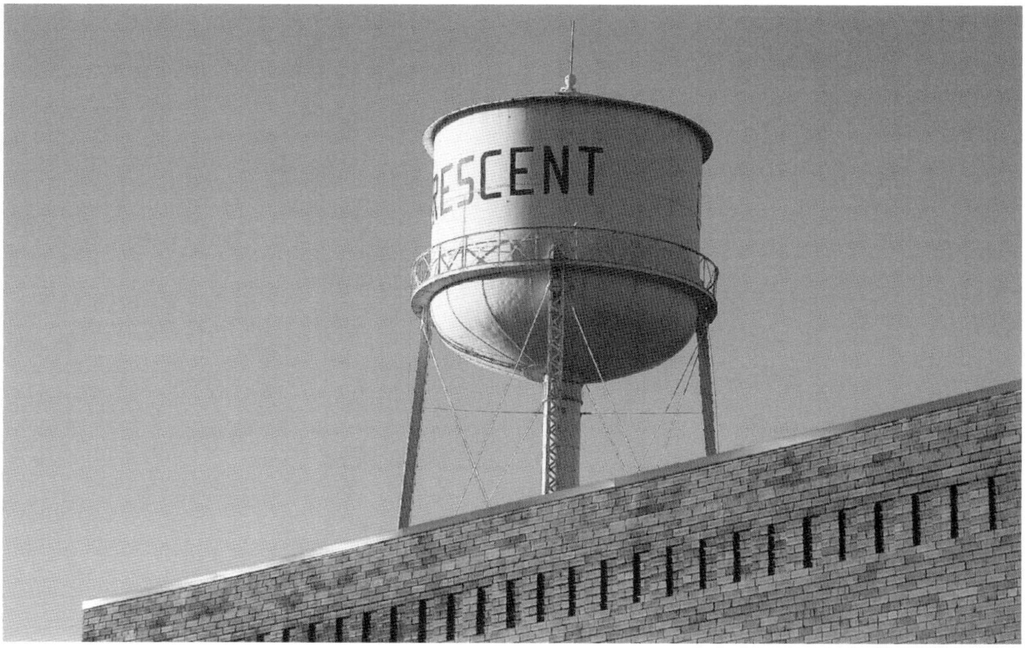

CHAPTER FIVE

Getting Down to Business

Since that first hectic day in April 1889, Edmond has had its share of entrepreneurs and business leaders. In early mill operator Isaac Rodkey, developer Henry Clegern, dry cleaning man Everett Bryant, retailer Mark Neighbors, newspaperman Ray Hibbard, and more, the spirit of working hard has been present. And then there is Hoot Gibson, who goes to work at age 90 in McCall's, the men's clothier he founded in the early 1950s.

Restaurants had their heyday, starting in the 1930s with the Wide-A-Wake Café, run by Crawford and Cleo Noe, and Royce's Café, owned by former newspaperman Royce Adamson. These diners were conveniently located at the American crossroads of Route 66 and US Highway 77. Around-the-Corner restaurant (see the Neighbors chapter) was a popular gathering spot for politicians and business leaders that was run for years by Charlotte Worsham until her death in 2013.

Morey Baggerley's funeral home is still doing business even though it is no longer family owned. Not to be forgotten are well-know businesses like Fred Snyder's hardware store, now gone; the state's oldest newspaper, the *Edmond Sun*; and the historic Van's Bakery. Other businesses included Ray Devereaux's defunct jewelry store and the still active Farmer's Grain, founded 100 years ago and still operated by the Suenram family.

Today, Edmond has hundreds of small businesses supported by an aggressive chamber of commerce; a few larger ones like Adfitech, Petra Industries, and Midcon Datal and of course a few big-box stores like Home Depot, Lowe's, Wal-Mart, and the Sam's on the I-35 frontage road. Two new hospitals have opened in the past few years, giving Edmond three medical centers instead of one. Homes are being built at a fast pace with no end in sight.

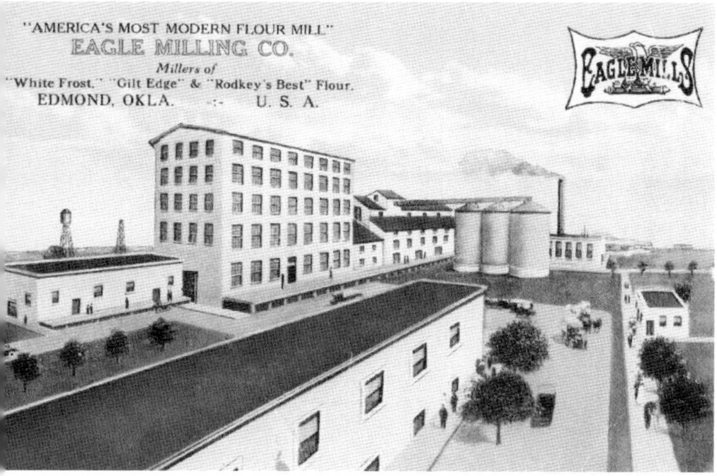

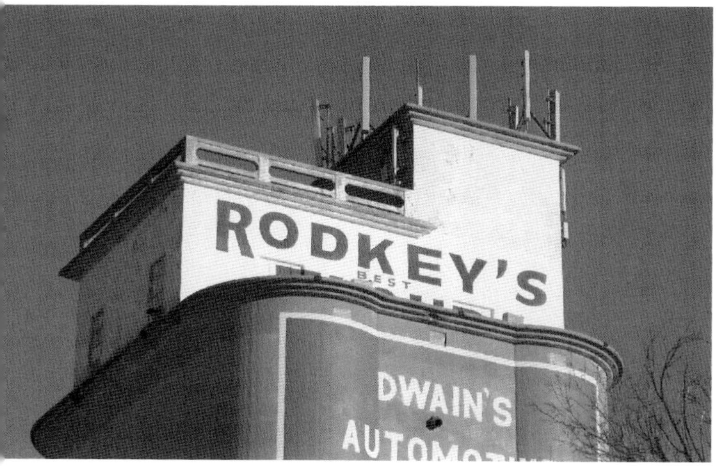

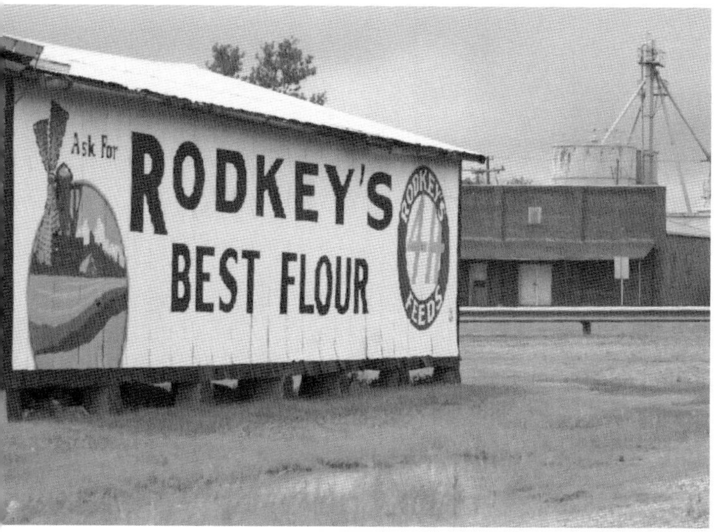

Isaac Wesley Rodkey

During the early years of Edmond, Rodkey Flour Mill was one of the largest employers and more successful businesses. Isaac Wesley Rodkey was born in Maryland to a German immigrant farm family in 1864. Rodkey moved to Kansas in 1881 to learn the flour milling business. He met his wife, Alice Kate Rank, in 1888. In 1894, the Rodkey family moved to Oklahoma City, where Isaac became a partner in Acme Mill. The family moved to Edmond three years later. He and his new partner, George Farrar, bought a mill and renamed it Eagle Flouring Mill. In 1911, Rodkey bought out Farrar and sold one-half interest in the mill to his eldest son, Earl. The flour mill was closed in 1972. In 1922, Isaac bought a large brick home on Jackson Street and sold the family's Campbell Street home to his youngest son, Don, who lived there with his wife until 1960. The home went through a series of ownerships until an Edmond businessman donated it to the City of Edmond. The city relocated the home to Stephenson Park in 2007. (Top, courtesy Edmond Historical Society Photographic Collection; middle and below, courtesy David Fisk.)

Emil Suenram

The Suenram family has been involved in the operation of Farmer's Grain, which is the oldest Edmond business to be in the same location—102 West First Street—for generations. In 1924, Emil H. Suenram took over as manager of the business, which was started in 1890 by a group of local farmers. It was known in the early years as Edmond Grain Company, until it went bankrupt in 1920. Suenram, pictured at right with a young customer, managed the business for 41 years until his death in 1966. Over the years, the Suenram family bought a majority of the stock. Emil's grandchildren Chris Suenram and Cindy Roof run the store now. Their parents, Charles and Donna Suenram, are primary owners. Another sister, Joy, is a stockholder. The focus of the business has shifted from supplying farmers to supplying local residents with plants and gardening materials. (Both, courtesy Farmer's Grain.)

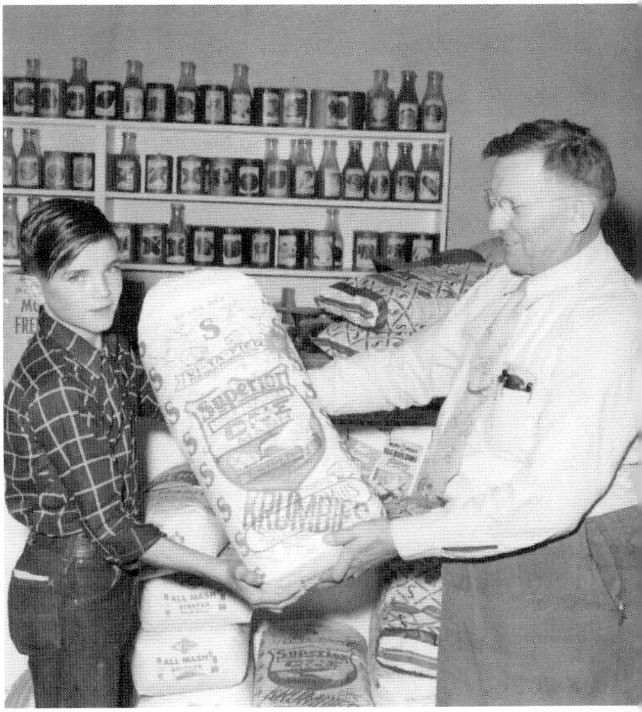

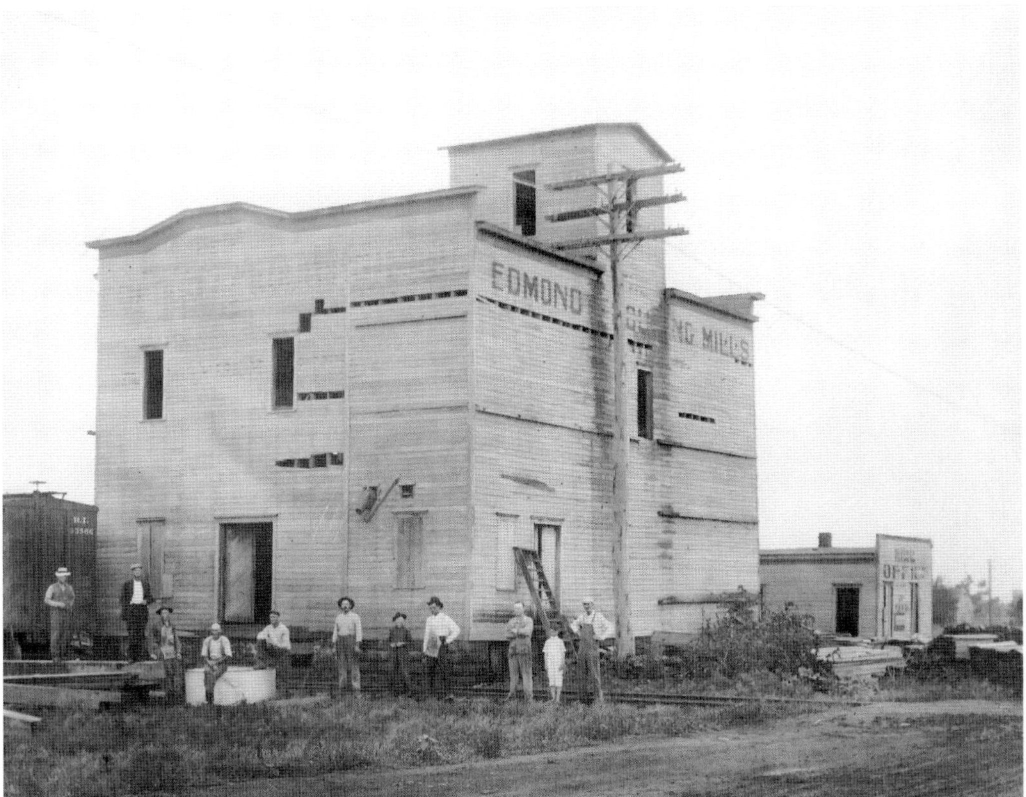

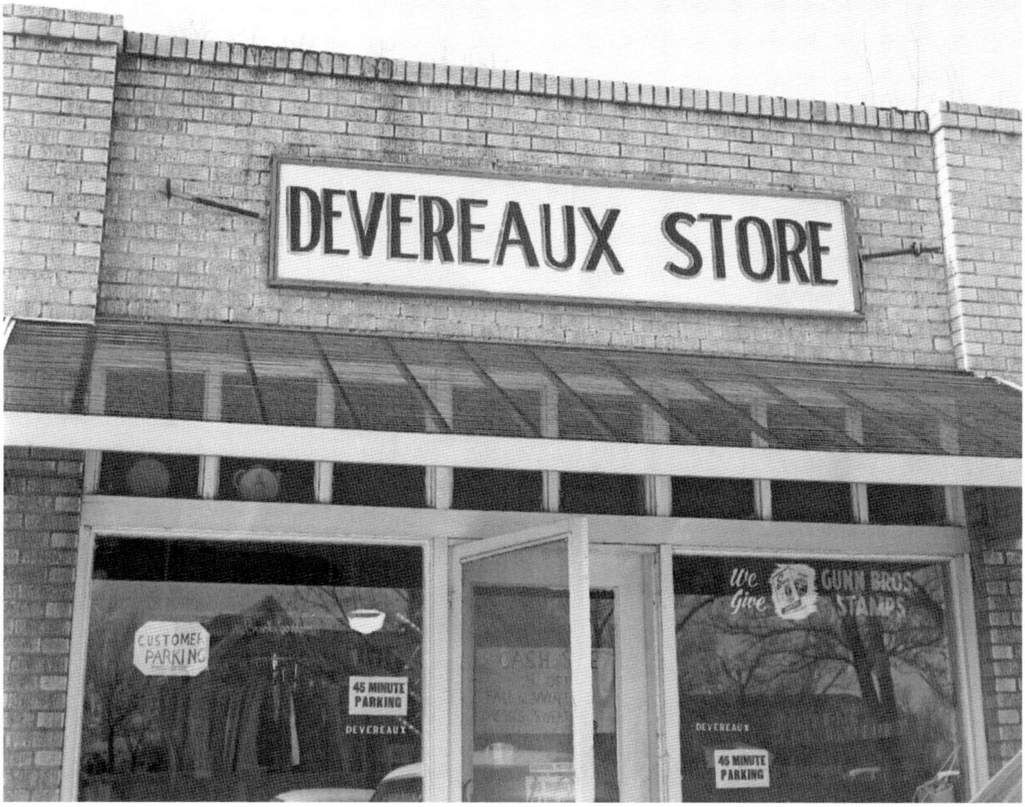

Ray Devereaux

In 1914, Devereaux hitched his pony to a "pony cart" and trekked from Missouri to Edmond, sleeping under his cart on the 10-day trip. His brother, Sol, operated a drugstore in downtown Edmond, and after going to school to be a jeweler, Devereaux opened a jewelry store in a corner of the drugstore. He moved to another location a year later and operated Devereaux Jewelry until 1969, when he sold the store to Paul Lawrence; it is no longer in business. He was known as a Christian gentleman and was a philanthropist, making gifts to Oklahoma Baptist University and many youth causes. When he was nominated for the Edmond Historical Society's Roll of Honor, it was acknowledged he had "a lifetime love for young people." Minister Alan Day said he "greatly distinguished himself among our great citizens." (Above, courtesy UCO Library, Archives/Special Collections; right, courtesy Karen Moore Photography.)

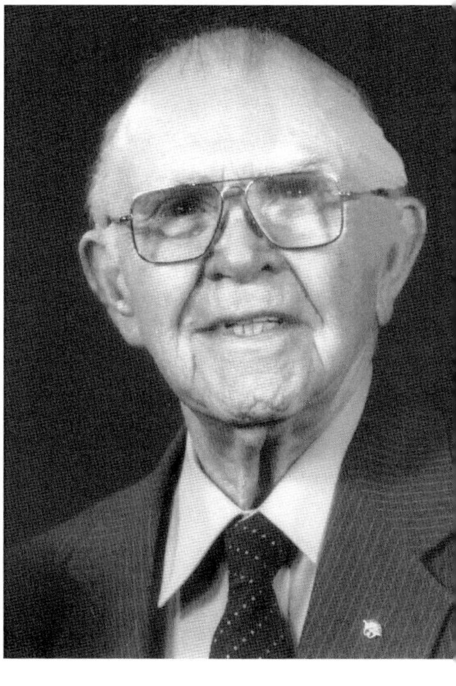

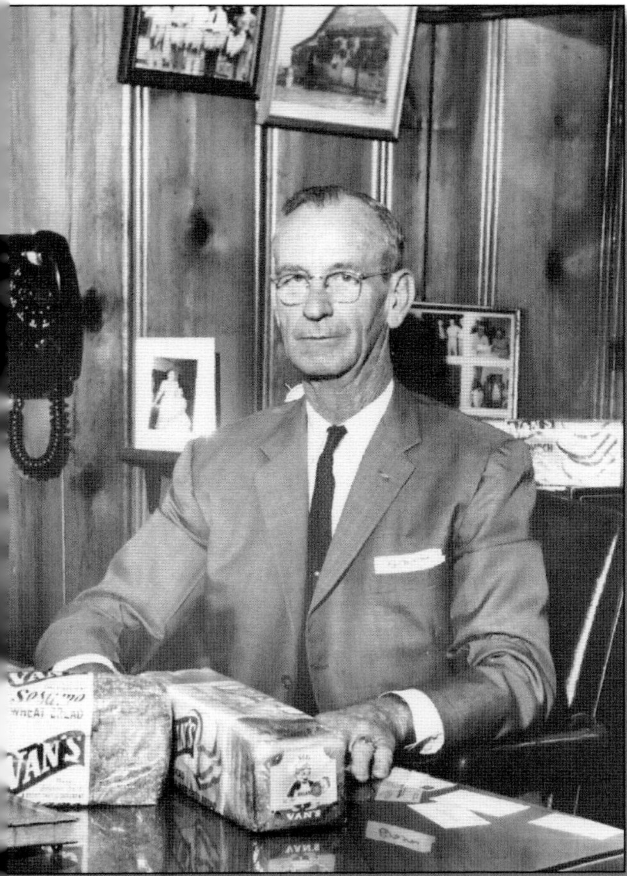

Everett Howard Van Antwerp

In the days when Edmond had a hometown bakery, one resident recalled that the "whole town smelled like fresh-baked bread." Van's Bakery at the northeast corner of Second Street and Broadway was the reason. Van's was an Edmond landmark and an outstanding independent bakery in Oklahoma. Opened in 1915 by George Van Antwerp and his brother, Irvin, the building had a café and confectionery. After George's son Everett left the military after World War I, he bought out his father's and uncle's shares of the business. The bakery was named for Everett, called "Van" by his friends. After 44 years, Van Antwerp shut it down in 1965. The Independent Baking Council touted the bakery's famous potato bread as "blue ribbon for excellence of freshness, flavor and quality." The bakery employed almost 50 people at the height of its existence, including many college students. Van Antwerp was known to loan money to his student employees to help pay for their college. (Both, courtesy Edmond Historical Society Photographic Collection.)

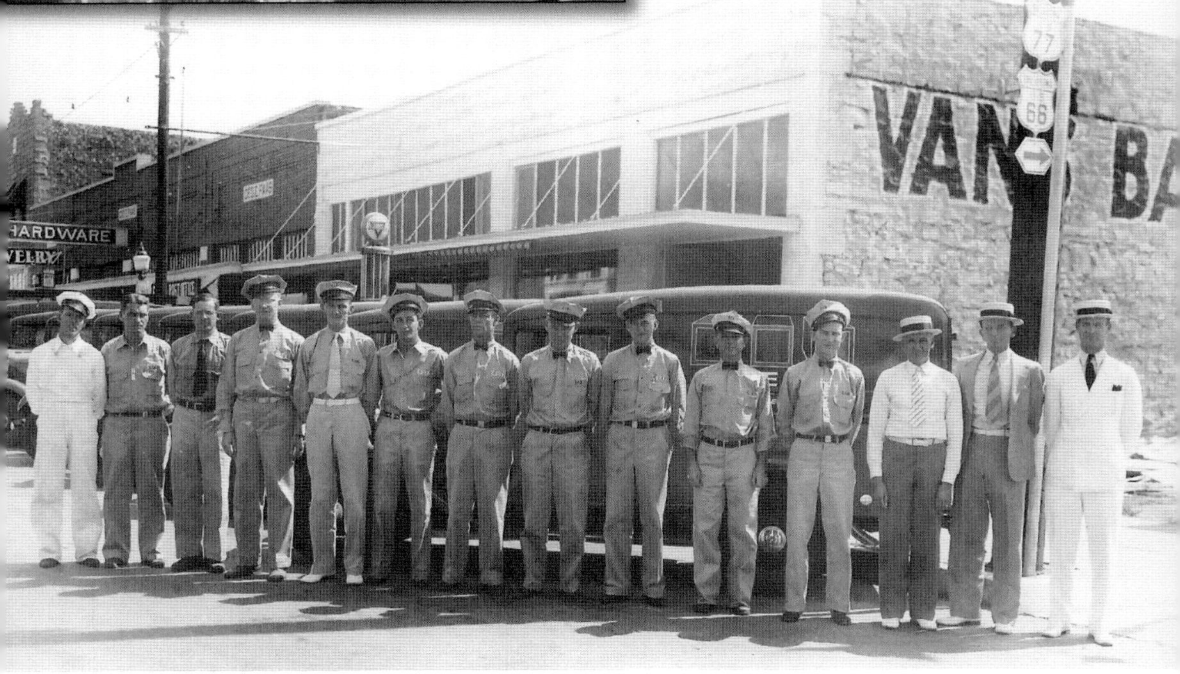

Crawford H. Spearman Sr. (BELOW AND OPPOSITE PAGE)
Until his death in 1998 at age 101, Spearman was the oldest living firefighter in the United States. A volunteer firefighter for 25 years, he finally got a badge in 1997 from Chief Dwight Maker. His son C.H. Spearman Jr. said the fire department "was his big love." Crawford was truly a man for all seasons, at home on the golf course or running the Gem and Broncho Theaters with his dad, W.Z. "Pops" Spearman. The year 1926 proved to be a good one for 29-year-old Crawford, who sank the first-ever hole-in-one on an Edmond golf course. Called Reynolds's Pasture, the course was on a patch of land near Broadway and Boulevard between Ninth and Fifteenth Streets. He didn't score another hole-in-one until 1949 at Lincoln Park Golf Course in Oklahoma City. He came to Edmond in 1917 after serving in the Army during World War I. He helped his dad with the newly opened Gem Theater. They bought two nearby lots and set up an outdoor screen, which locals referred to as the "Airdome," where patrons could watch shows from benches or in parked cars. They later built the Broncho Theater at Main Street and Broadway (the Spearman Building) during the Depression for $200. In 1947, Edmond's first hospital was located on the second floor of the Broncho building. Spearman graduated from Central State Teachers College and was a school superintendent in the Big Four and Piedmont School Districts. He sang with the Edmond Quartet as a tenor and was active in many community organizations. The Edmond Chamber of Commerce named him an Outstanding Citizen in the 1990s. (Below, courtesy UCO Library, Archives/Special Collections; opposite, courtesy the *Oklahoman* archives.)

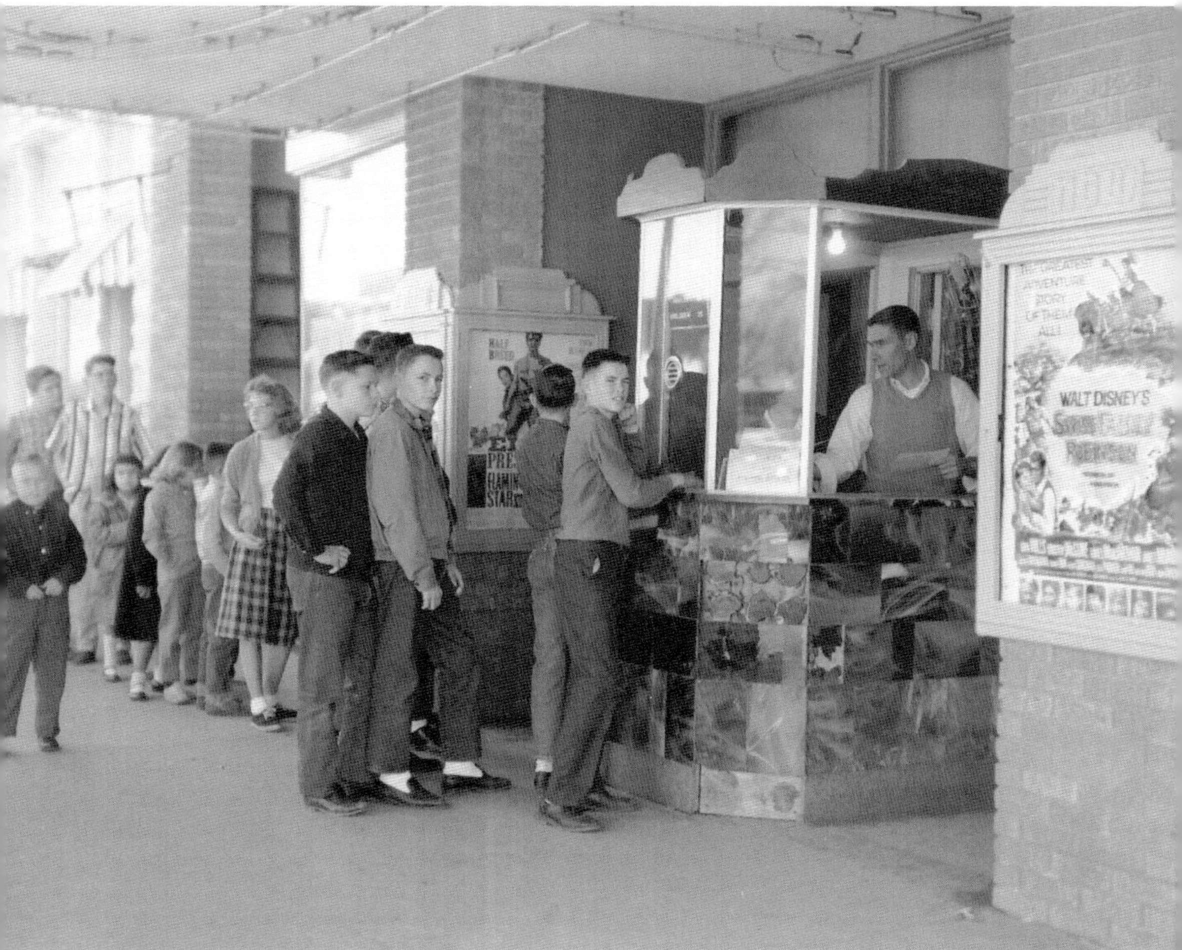

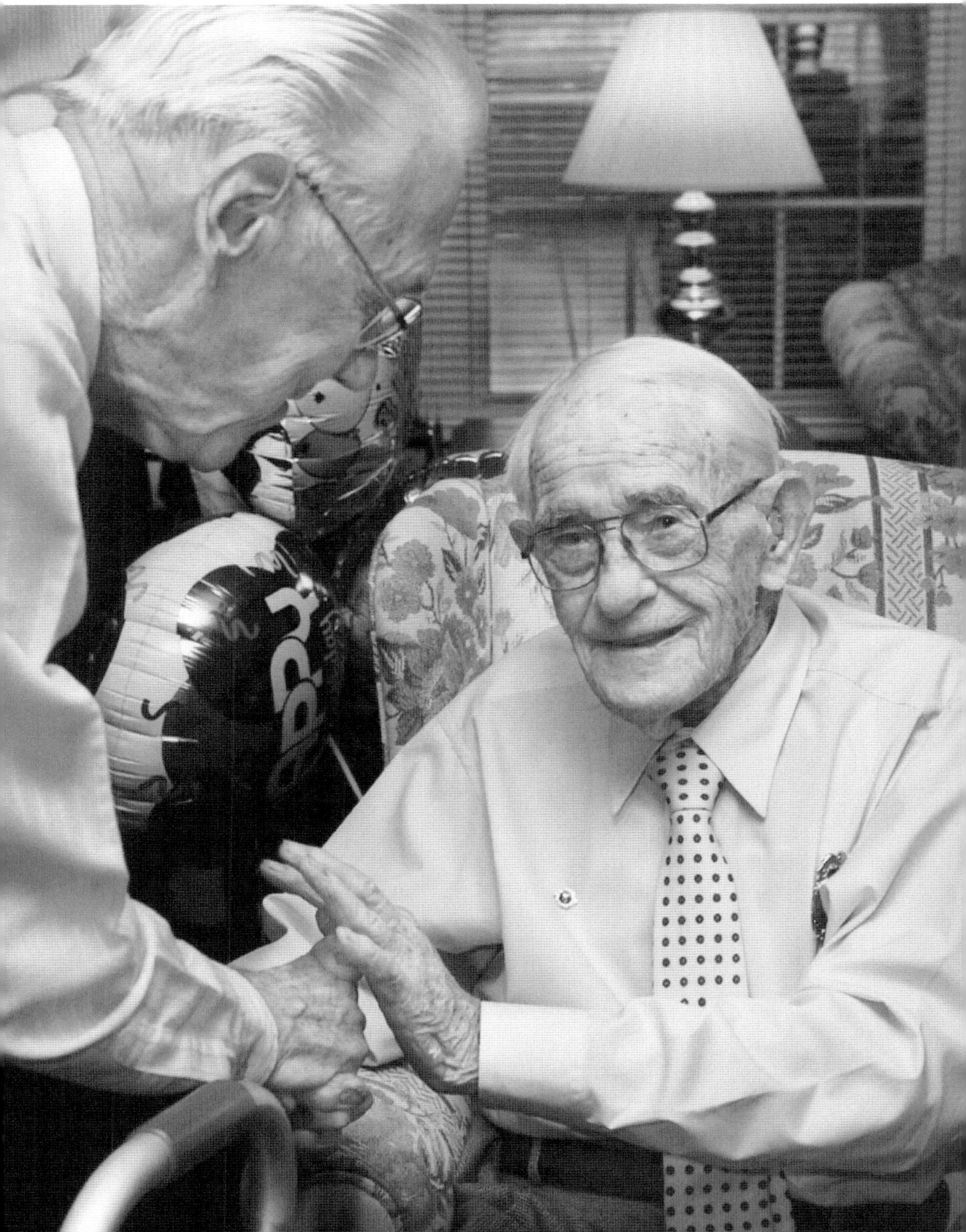

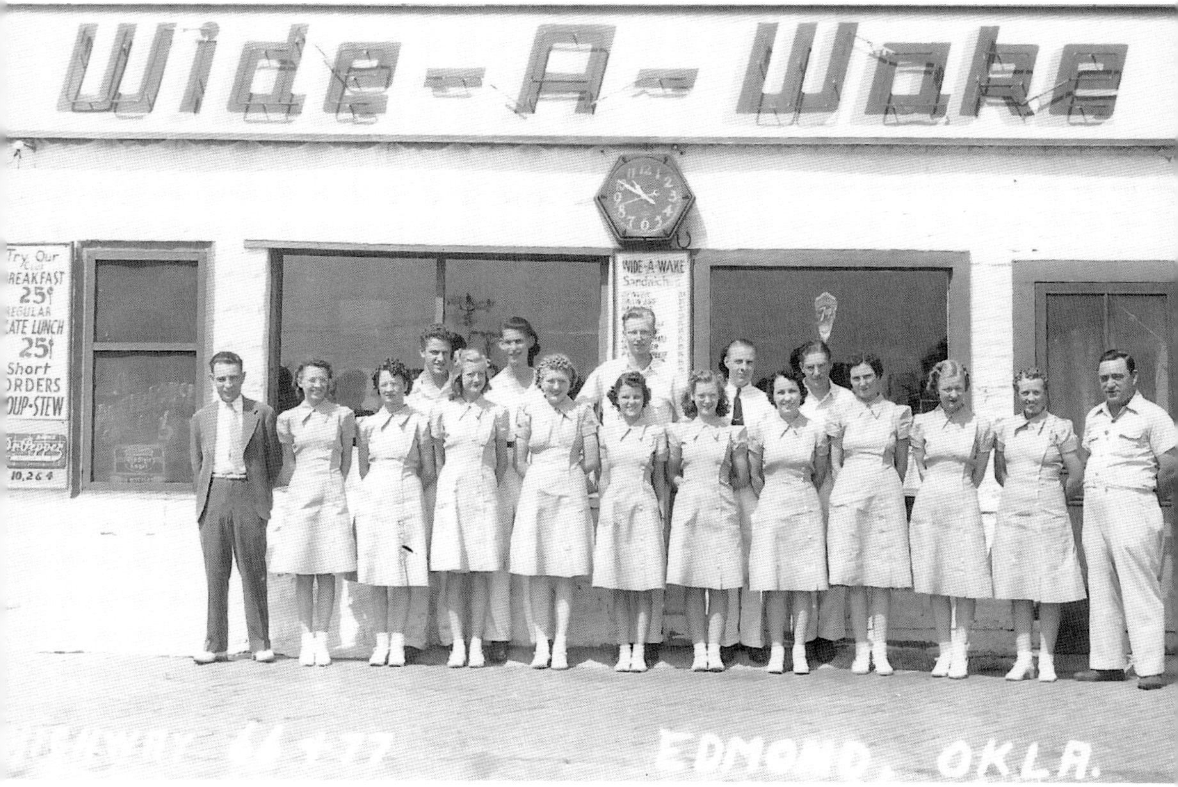

Cleo and Crawford Noe

"Good Food, Well Served" was the promise on the menu at the Wide-A-Wake Café, which began serving its famous chow in 1931. Located at 213 South Broadway near the intersection of Route 66 and Highway 77, Cleo Noe and husband, Crawford, along with other family members, opened the doors with $13 in leased space. The Wide-A-Wake became a tradition for more than 40 years. Historian Stan Hoig, in his book *Edmond: The First Century*, wrote, "Soon the café became a regular stopping place for many truckers who could leave pictures and notes on the cafe's bulletin board. . . . The Wide-A-Wake was never robbed, even during the trying days of the depression." Cleo, who died in 2010 at almost 103 years of age, recalled in an interview with the *Edmond Sun* that the café was open 24 hours a day, seven days and week, and was hard work. She told James Coburn of the *Edmond Sun*, "Everybody was so friendly that you just felt like part of the family." Crawford died in the 1950s, and Cleo operated the café until 1972. The building was demolished in 1982. (Courtesy Edmond Historical Society Photographic Collection.)

Royce and Neva Adamson

Royce Adamson, shown below standing far right, was in the newspaper business and was a great friend of Crawford Noe, owner of the Wide-A-Wake Café. Adamson heard how much fun Noe was having in the café business, so he sold his part of the *Edmond Booster and Enterprise* to partner Don Banzett and opened his own café at Fourth Street and Broadway in 1934. The two men remained good friends in spite of being competitors, according to Royce's daughter Louise Johnson. Adamson and his wife, Neva, "put their two teenage daughters to work and hired all the good-looking girls he could find as waitresses," Johnson wrote in a letter to author Marian Clark, who featured the restaurant in her Route 66 cookbook. The oil business was starting to flourish in the Edmond area, so the restaurant was soon enlarged. Open 24 hours a day, seven days a week, many local groups held meetings and ate at the café. One advertisement urged customers to "Win her heart the easy way. Dine in style at the Royce Café." Celebrities were known to stop in. One account recalls the night when gangster John Dillinger stopped by for coffee at the café, located at the Route 66 and Highway 77 crossroads. Adamson was warned not to alert authorities at risk of his life. As legend has it, he saw two guns pointed his way from a black car and was more than willing to comply. Adamson's son-in-law, Jimmy Tindall, managed the café and prided himself on being a superb cook. Writer Duncan Hines recommended the Royce Café in his book *Adventures in Good Cooking.* Jimmy's chili recipe and his trademark Royce Café salad dressing were featured in the book. Royce Adamson died in 1936, but Neva ran the restaurant until selling it in 1958. The building stands today but is unrecognizable from its days as the Royce Café. (Courtesy Edmond Historical Society Photographic Collection.)

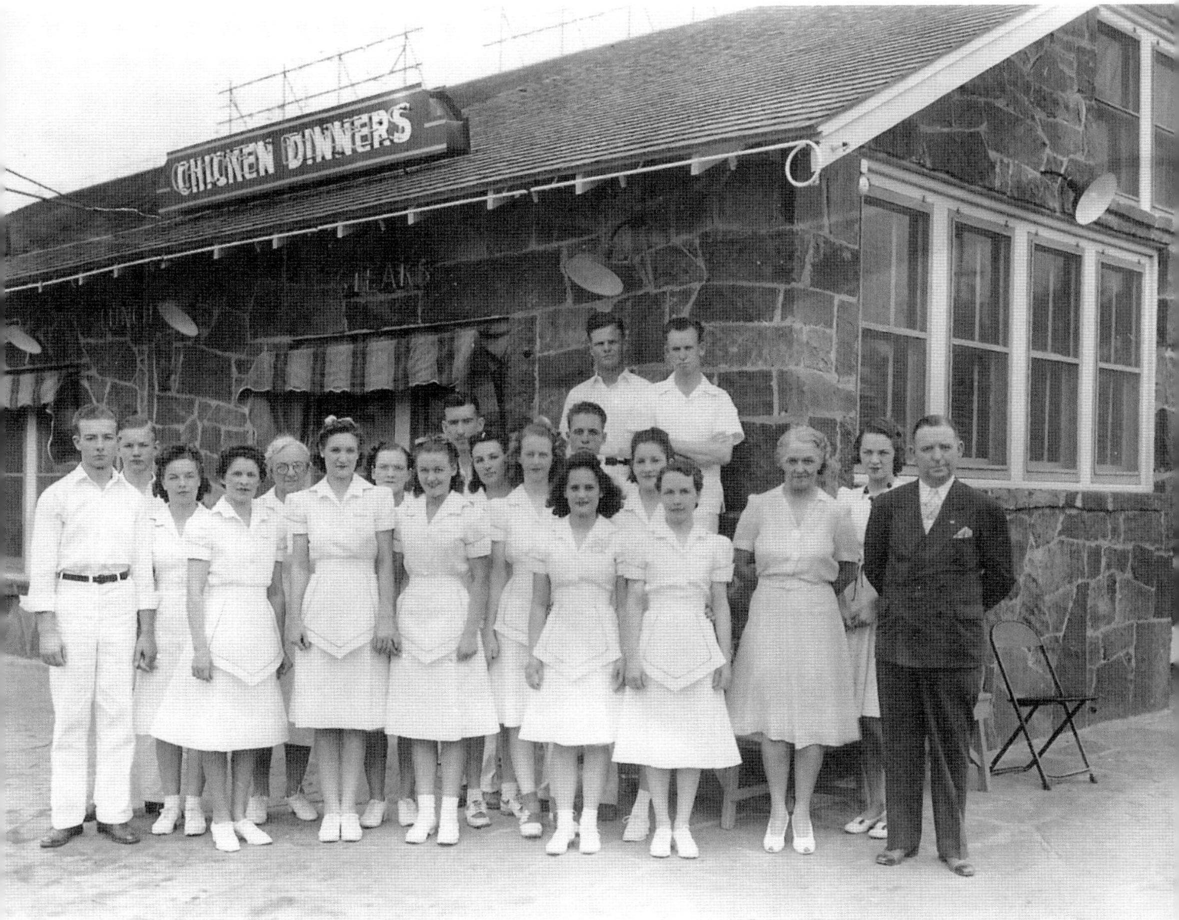

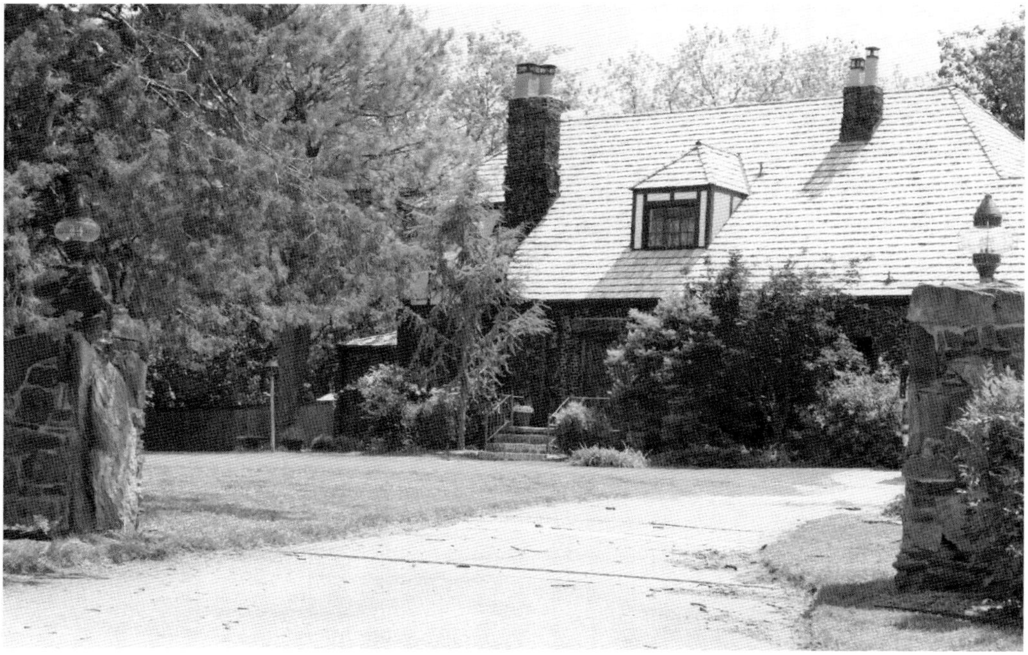

Harry W. Clegern

Real estate developer Clegern's mantra was, "Buy land near a growing city if you want to get ahead." He came to Edmond shortly after the land run and organized a land company. He was instrumental in the growth of several residential areas, including Capitol View, Normal Heights, and Highland Park. He built a stately home in 1929 that stands just as beautiful today on East Fifth Street. Clegern donated land in his Capitol View addition for an elementary school. (Both, courtesy David Fisk.)

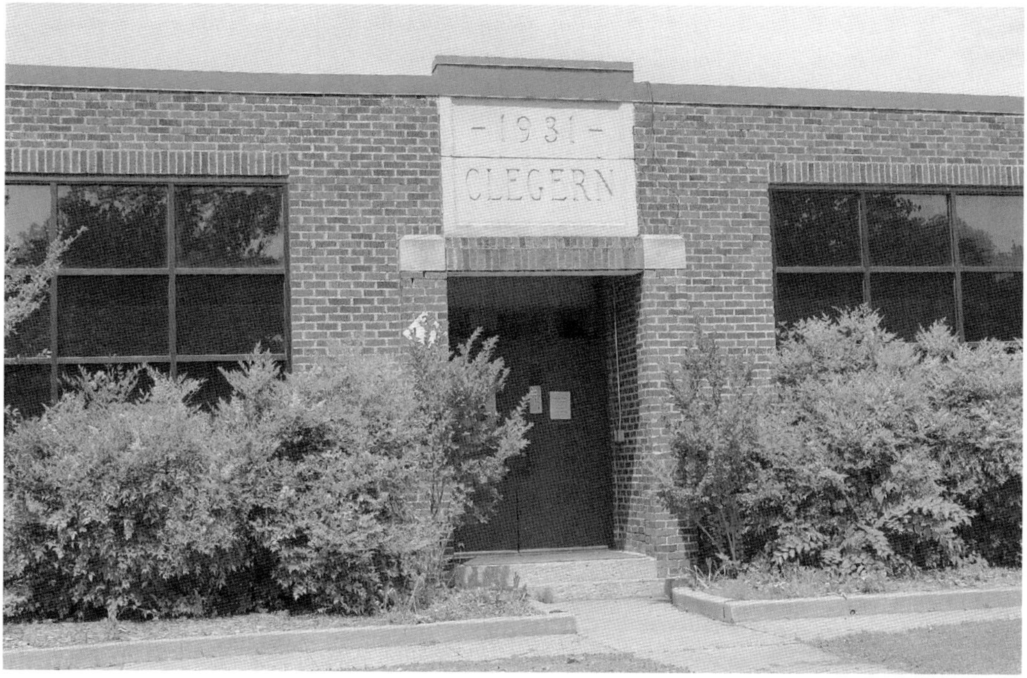

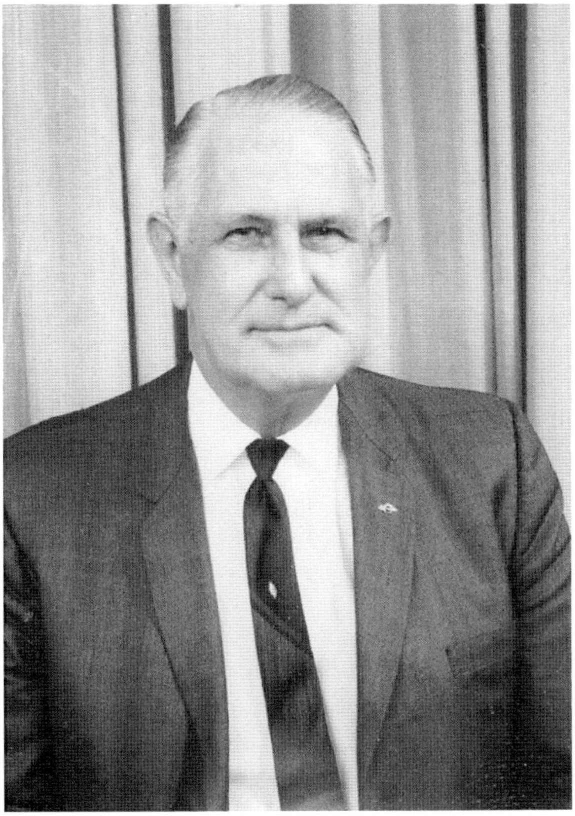

Everett Bryant

The acting postmaster in the 1930s, Bryant's push to upgrade the city's gravel roads and Bryant Avenue serves as a testament to his hard work. He played a major role in getting Broadway Extension built. Bryant Square bears the name of the charter Edmond Hall of Fame member, who was president of the Edmond Chamber of Commerce in 1952. Bryant owned and operated Central Cleaners and Laundry until his retirement in 1962. He was in the dry-cleaning business for 50 years and was chairman of the Oklahoma State Dry Cleaners, serving under five governors. (Both, courtesy Edmond Historical Society Photographic Collection.)

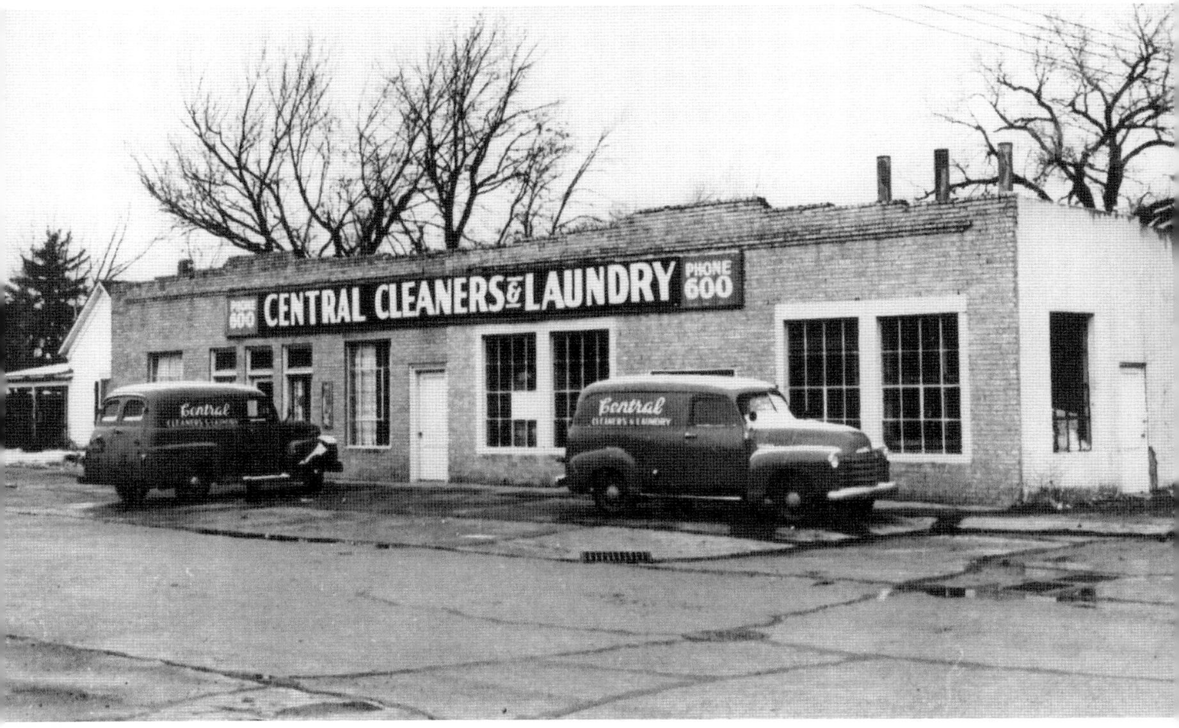

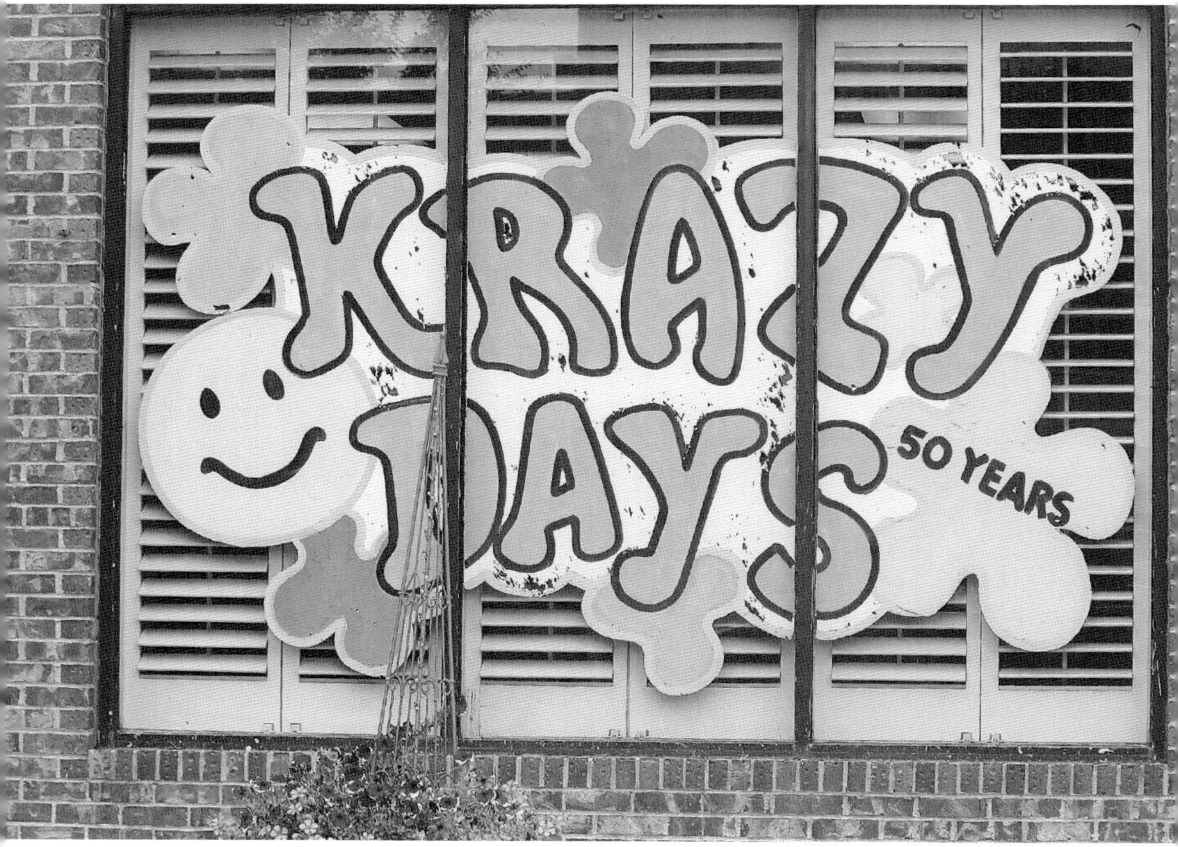

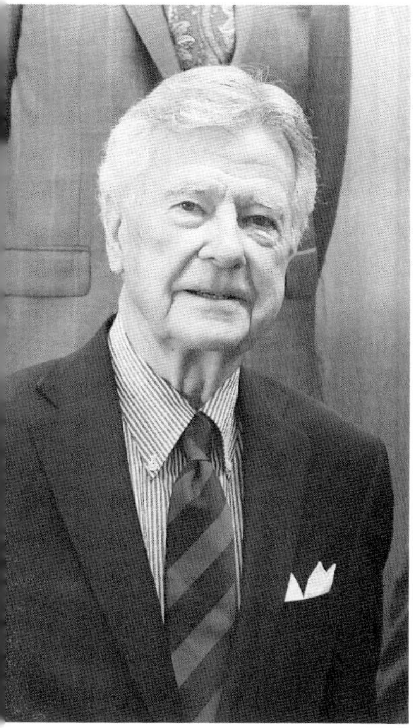

Morris "Hoot" Gibson

Edmond retailers go "Krazy" because of Gibson. The clothing store founder, whose son Steve now owns McCall's in downtown Edmond, started the first "Krazy Daze" promotion in the early 1960s. Gibson was a founder of the Downtown Edmond Business Association, which was formed to ensure the area prospered after the variety store TG&Y moved to the new Edmond Plaza Center in 1962. Gibson had worked at McCall's men's store in Norman when he decided to open his fine menswear store in Edmond with financial backing from Lewis McCall. Twenty years later, he became sole owner, selling to his son several years ago. In 1989, Gibson was inducted into the Edmond Hall of Fame. "Semi-retired" at 90, Gibson was still putting in time at the store in 2013. When he opened the store in the 1950s, a young man named James Bumgarner helped him renovate the store at 21 South Broadway, where it still operates. That man moved to Hollywood and became famous under the name James Garner. (Both, courtesy David Fisk.)

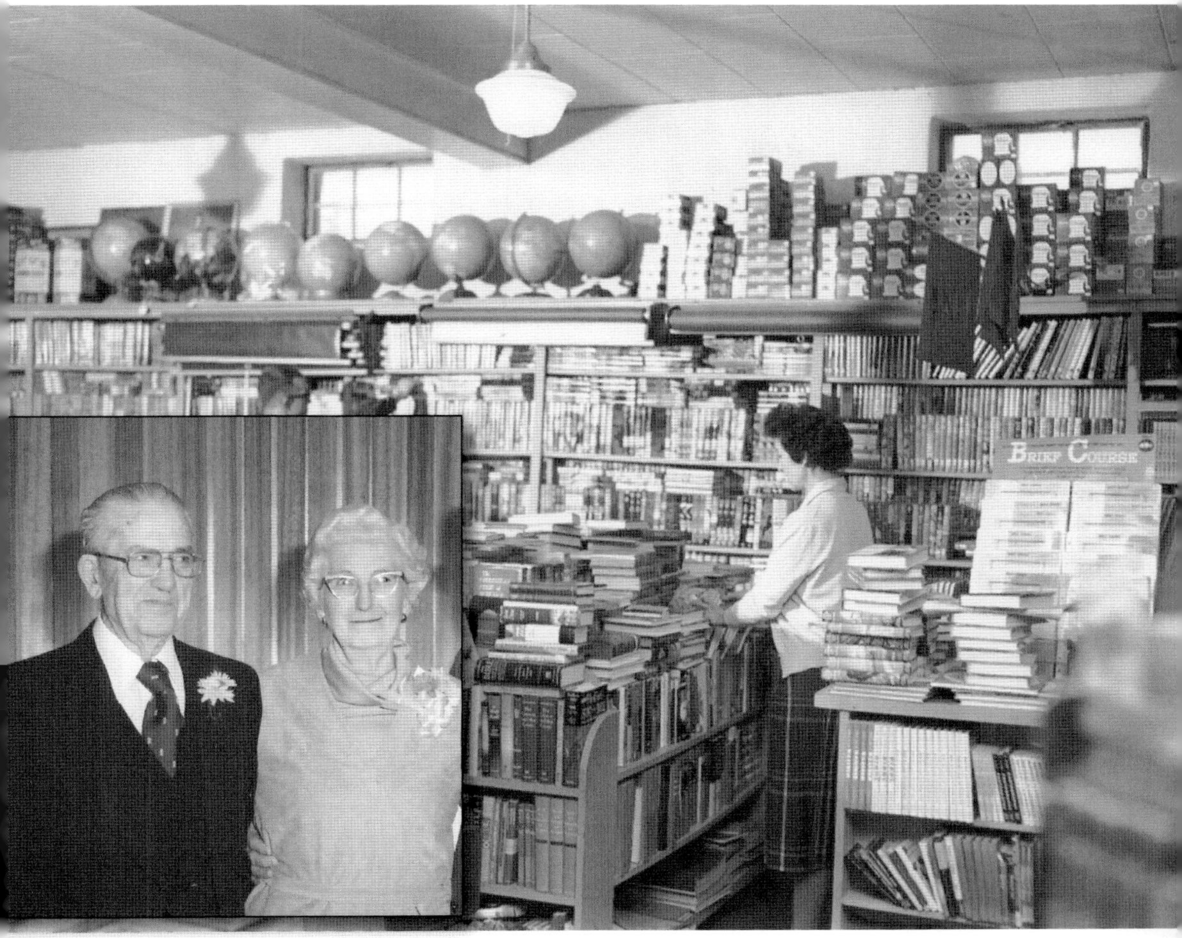

Bill and Alice Thompson

The Thompsons opened Thompson's Bookstore in Edmond in 1929 near Central State Teachers College. Several generations of Thompsons ran the store, which was a mainstay of the university community until closing its doors in 2013. Four generations of Thompsons attended UCO and in 2002 were named the "Family of the Year" at the university. Bill and Alice Thompson's first store was at 117 North College Street, and they lived across the street in a house called English Hall. The store seen in this photograph from the UCO Library Archives Special Collections was eventually located at 201 North University Drive, remaining there until its closing. Former employees said Alice "was the glue that kept the store together." She dedicated 55 years to the business before she died in 1997. A relative said she reviewed every textbook the store sold after hearing complaints about some questionable material in a book. Bill Thompson died in 1983. The campus faculty newsletter, the *Territory*, said Thompson was considered by many to be a UCO legend. The bookstore helped many college students pay their way through school. When they first opened the store, the Thompsons sold gum, aspirin, cigarettes, some school supplies, and books. Students could rent typewriters from the store for $2 for one weekend. The store was famous for kind words and small favors. When World War II and Korean War soldiers returned home, the Thompsons let them buy books on credit until their checks came in. Their son, Lowell, managed the store beginning in the 1960s. The original store was in Ada, with another in Durant. Their grandson, Mike Thompson, owns and operates Thompson Educational Furnishings, which is based in Edmond. He told of delivering books to customers from a basket on his bicycle when he was a youngster. (Courtesy UCO Library Archives/Special Collections; inset, courtesy Mike Thompson.)

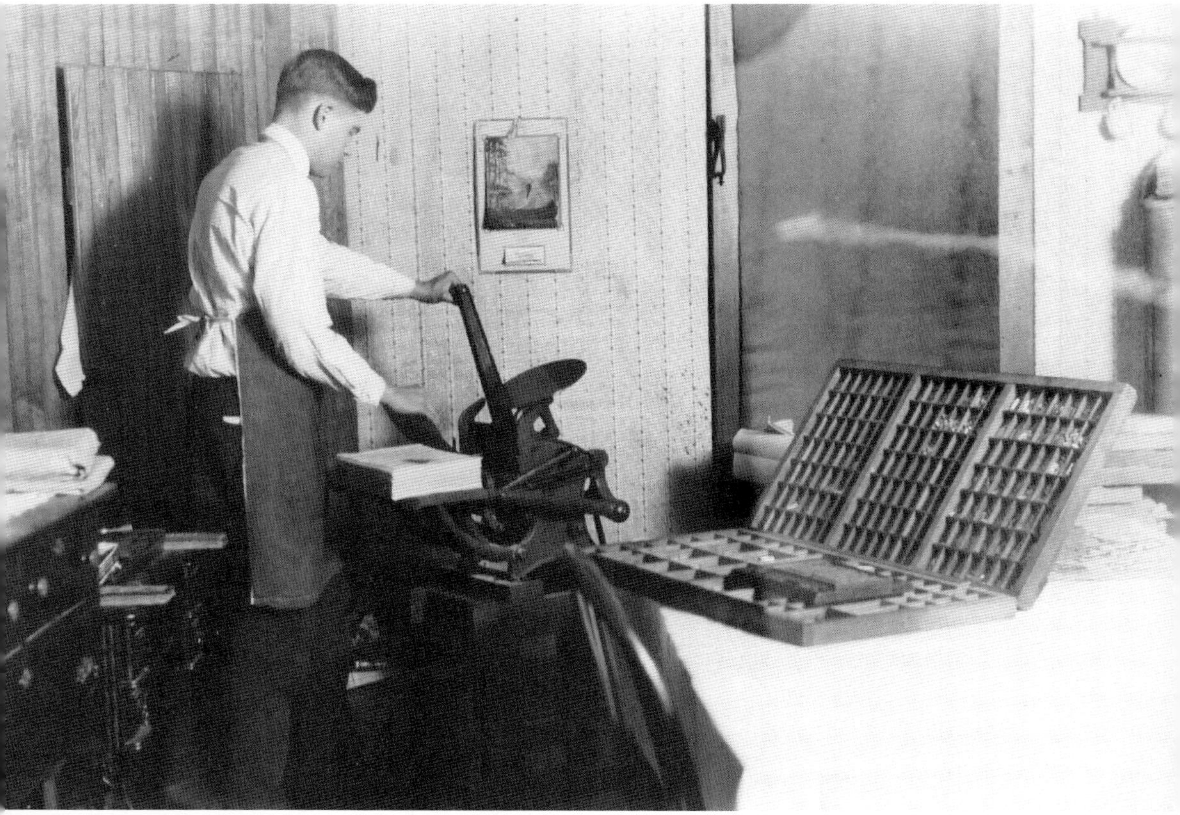

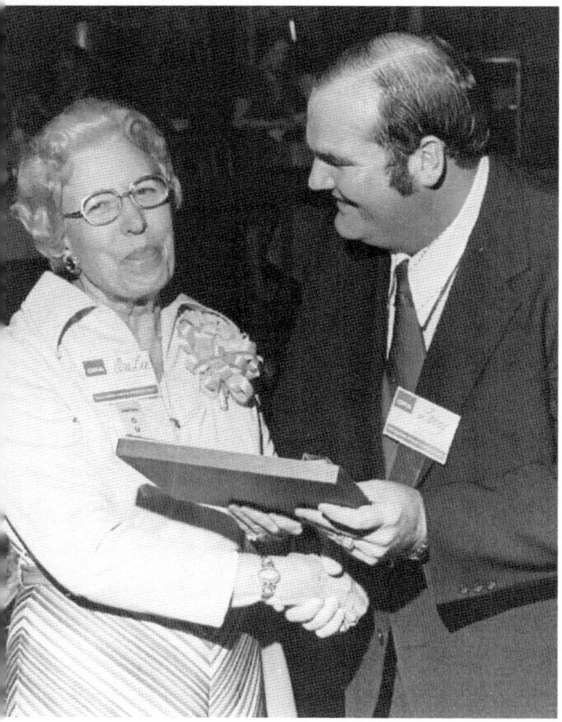

Osa Lee and Donovan Banzett

As a nine-year-old, Donovan "Don" Banzett made two-page tablet-page newspapers and sold to his neighbors for a nickel. When he grew up, he founded the *Edmond Booster* in 1925. A few years later, he married Osa Lee Pope, who became his copublisher and wife for the next 50-plus years. After the wedding, they used the $100 her father gave them to buy a linotype. They called it the *Booster* because they were always "boosting" Edmond every way they could. Both are members of various halls of fame, including the UCO Journalism Hall of Fame. Donovan served as president of the chamber of commerce and during World War II was chairman of the Oklahoma County Draft Board. He tried to buy the *Edmond Sun* but was thwarted. After 25 years, they sold the *Booster* and all their businesses, which included Central Office Supply. They travelled for two years and later owned several newspapers in Arkansas and Oklahoma. In 1983, they moved back to Edmond, where Donovan, who was in ill health, died seven weeks later. Osa Lee, shown at left receiving an award from the Oklahoma Press Association, lived until 1997. (Both, courtesy Edmond Historical Society Photographic Collection.)

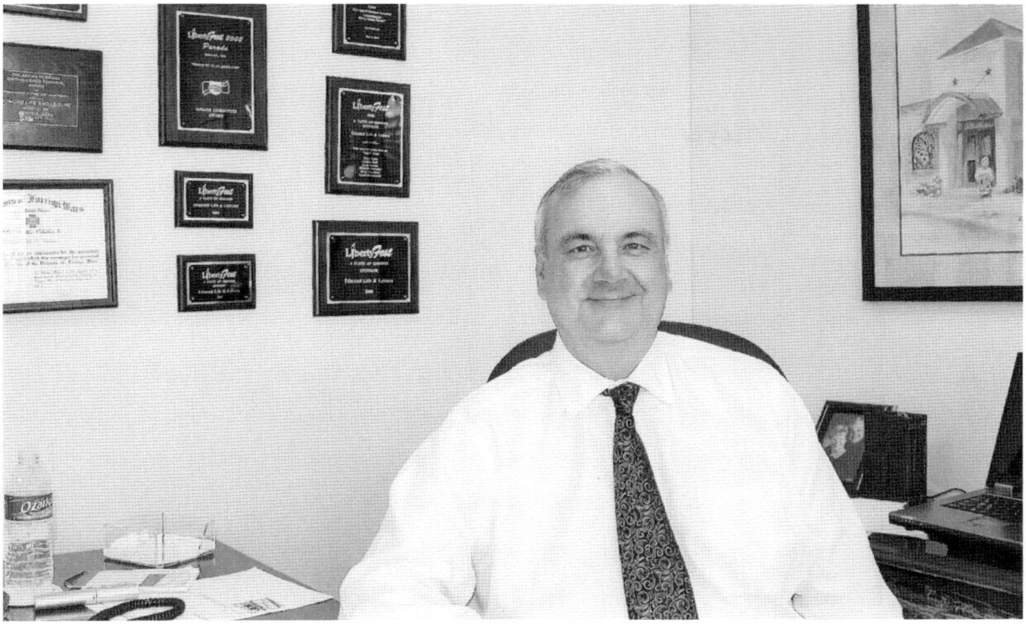

Ray Hibbard
Hibbard is one of those men that succeeds by defying conventional wisdom. In 2000, Hibbard and partner Chris Hoke decided to launch a new newspaper in Edmond during a time when traditional newspapers were suffering from declining circulation and advertising. *Edmond Life and Leisure* has done the opposite. Hibbard started the weekly paper after he left his post as publisher of the *Edmond Sun*. The only locally owned newspaper, Hibbard wrote in a column, *Life and Leisure* has a "local heart and conscience toward uplifting Edmond to the best of our ability." In 2005, Hibbard was awarded Citizen of the Year status from the Edmond Area Chamber of Commerce. He has been in charge of and involved in many organizations, including the chamber of commerce, Rotary, Edmond Arts and Humanities, and Edmond Historical Society. Community leaders are quick to point out that Hibbard is always there to help, noting that he always says "call me if you need help." (Courtesy David Fisk.)

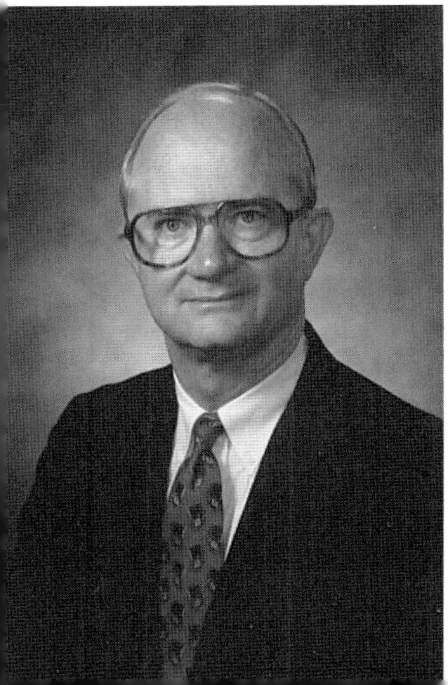

Ed Livermore Jr.
Livermore owned the *Edmond Sun* for almost 30 years. His father and a partner bought the newspaper when it was the *Sun and Booster* in 1965, and Livermore Jr. took over in 1970, when he was 26. *Booster* was dropped from the masthead in 1976, and the newspaper was renamed the *Edmond Evening Sun*, beginning a five-day-a-week publication. Active in the community, he was named Citizen of the Year in 1980. Livermore sold the paper in 1999 and retired to Texas. (Courtesy *Edmond Life and Leisure*.)

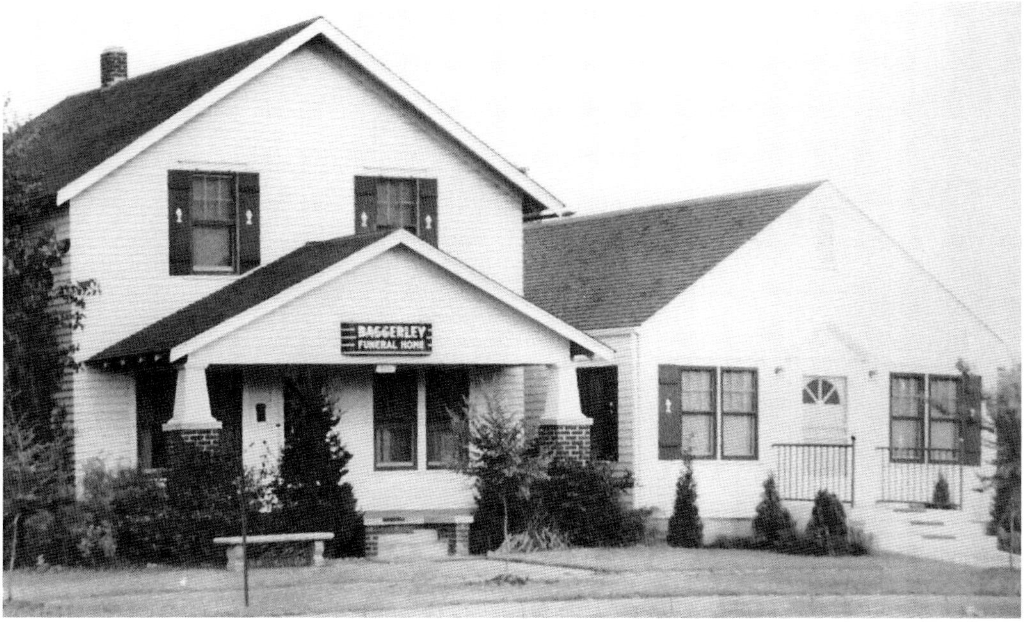

Morey Baggerley

Longtime funeral home operator Baggerley had a "reputation for square-dealing with his fellow man," the *Edmond Sun* reported in 1930. He came to Edmond in 1910 and operated a hardware store for many years and was a deputy sheriff. He opened Baggerley Funeral Home at Third Street and Broadway in 1929 and operated there until 1951, when he relocated to Boulevard Street. The home provided ambulance service for the city until 1967. At one time, ambulance drivers gathered at the business, and Baggerley was known to have fish fries for his drivers out back. Shown below is the funeral home in its present location on South Broadway, where it has been since the 1960s; the business is now owned by a national chain. Baggerley died in 1965, but the business still bears his name. (Above, courtesy Edmond Historical Society Photographic Collection; below, courtesy David Fisk.)

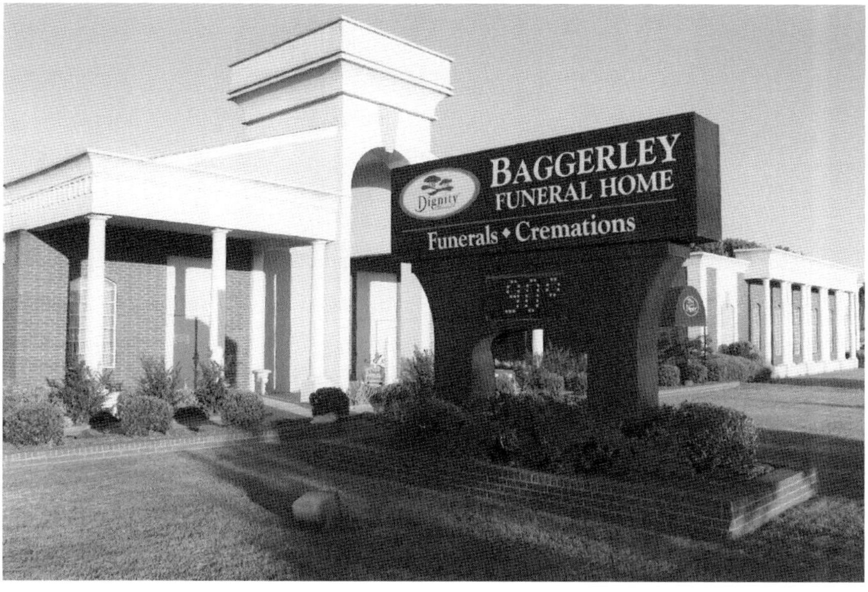

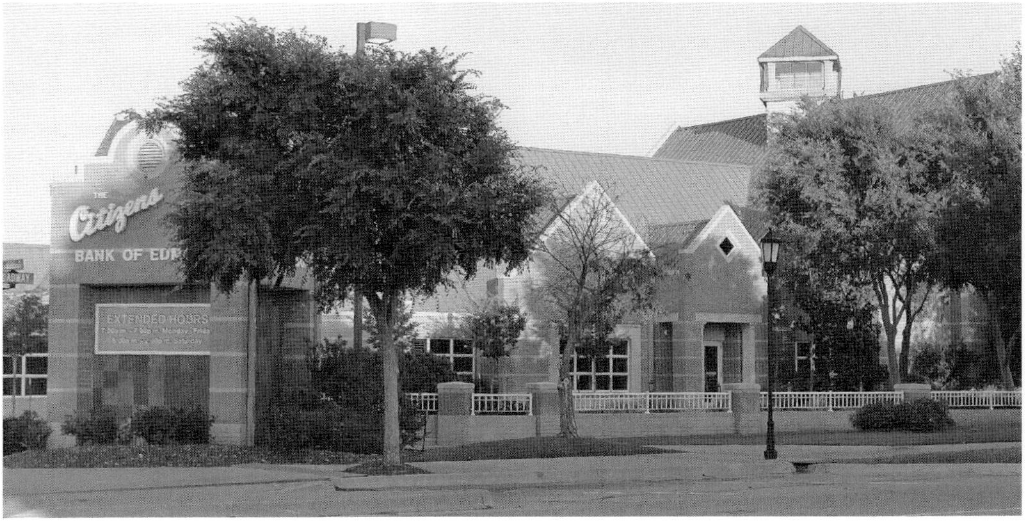

Granzow Family
Citizens Bank sits just a few blocks north of the original bank, which opened its doors at First Street and Broadway in 1901. A common thread in the bank's history since its early days has been the Granzow family, beginning with Henry Granzow in 1909, who was president of the bank. He was followed by his son, Gordon Granzow, who ran things as president and chairman of the board until he died in 1995. Gordon's son, Randy Granzow, was chairman of the board for many years until retiring. A fourth generation is represented by Jill Castilla, Randy's stepdaughter, who is a vice president and chief credit officer at the bank. The bank has been partly owned by the Granzow family for three generations. Mike Thompson is now chairman of the board at Citizens, which has historically been important in the economic growth of Edmond. (Courtesy David Fisk.)

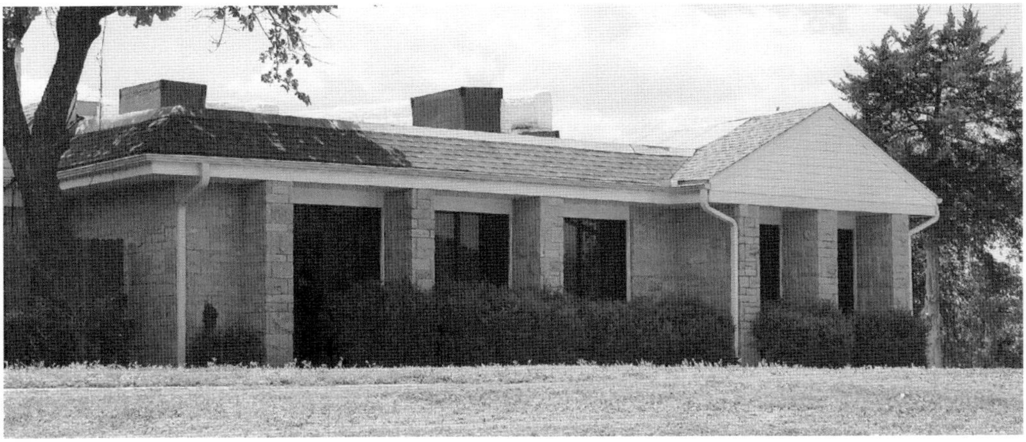

O.A. Cargill Sr.
Cargill, a longtime defense attorney who was also a mayor of Oklahoma City, liked his hobbies "wild." During the 1940s, he built a house using Arkansas greystone at Second Street and Sooner Road, east of town. Drivers on the highway regularly stopped to watch his herd of nine buffalo roam the property, known as the "Buffalo Ranch." Relatives said he got the first two from Pawnee Bill's herd. Years later, Virginia Lamb bought the house and converted it into the popular Greystone restaurant. In 2001, the Petroleum Club bought the property. Cargill was a big man at 6 foot, 6 inches, and was known to dominate the courtroom. Cargill died in 1967. His grandson was Henson Cargill, a country singer. (Courtesy David Fisk.)

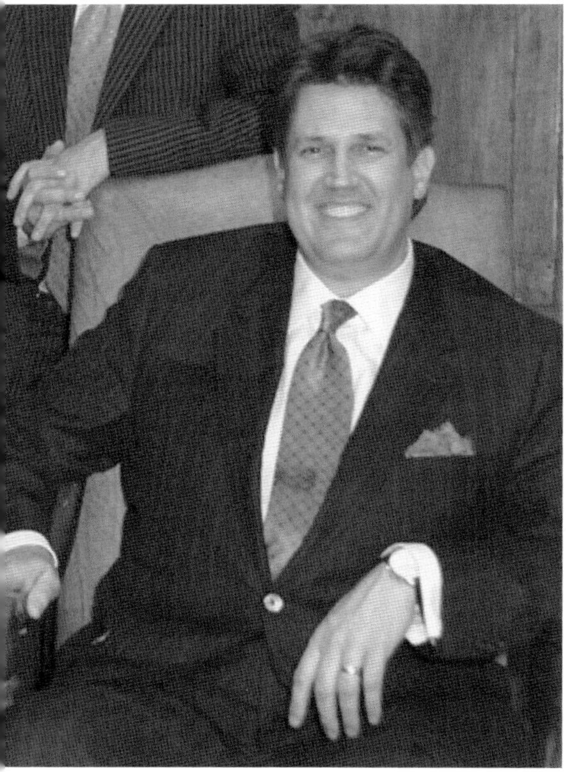

Mark Neighbors

In 1959, when he was a year old, Neighbors's father, Ed, and uncle Buck opened Parkway Cleaners. Mark Neighbors now owns Parkway with his brother, Brian. Neighbors has built the business from its original 1,100-square-foot building into three businesses and operates more than 35,000 square feet of retail space and leases out 100,000 square feet of space. Neighbors has developed the area at Fifth Street and Littler Avenue into what is called the Central Business District at the edge of downtown. *Edmond Life and Leisure* wrote, "In 2002, the Neighbors donated the land and about a third of the cost of the University of Central Oklahoma Jazz Lab. In 2000, Neighbors also took over the production of the Edmond Jazz and Blues festival and has built the event into a top event attracting 15,000 music fans on Memorial Day weekend." The *Edmond Sun* applauded Neighbors's work "to bring the exciting mix of retail, quality dining, and night life to this area." The Neighbors family has made things happen around Edmond for more than 50 years. *Edmond Life and Leisure* said, "They don't make a lot of noise about it. They just set about the business of getting the work done." (Left, courtesy Mark Neighbors; below, courtesy David Fisk.)

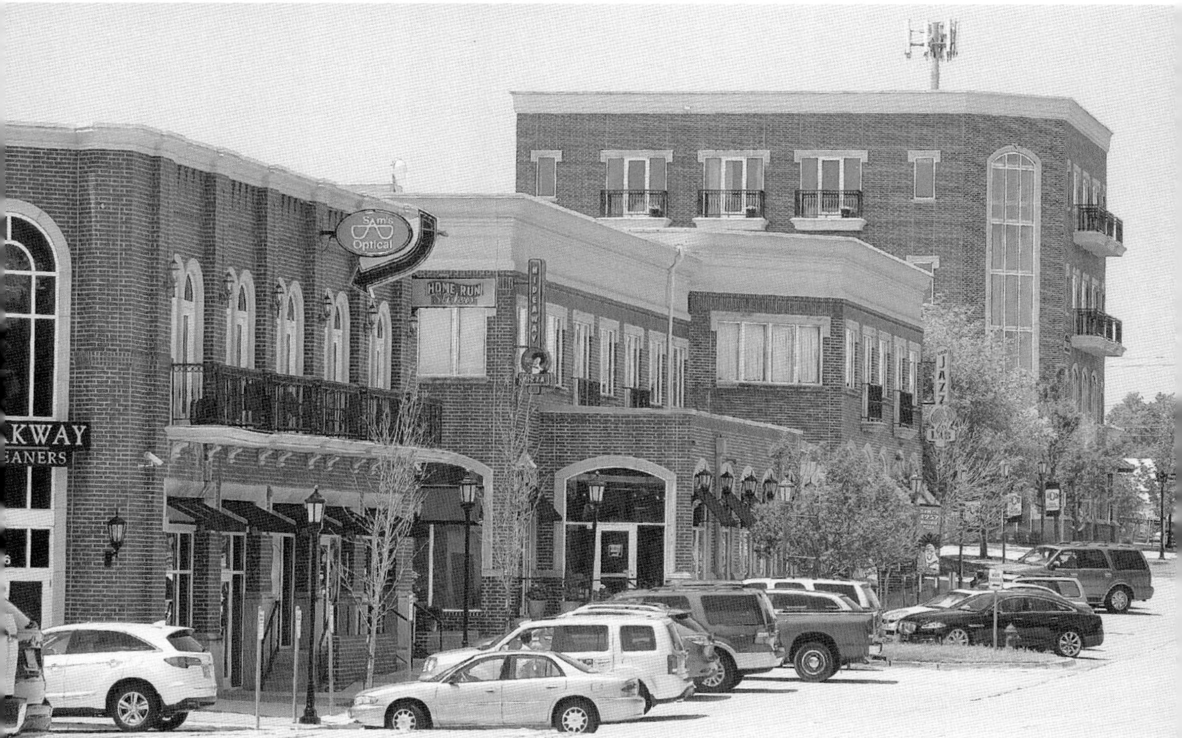

CHAPTER SIX

Modern Leaders

A leader is a person who influences a group of people towards a specific result. It is not dependent on title or formal authority. Ronald Reagan said, "The greatest leader is not necessarily the one who does the greatest things. He is the one that gets the people to do the greatest things." Leadership is organizing a group of people to achieve a common goal. The founders and early leaders of Edmond paved the way for modern-day mayors, politicians, and citizens who have shaped Edmond into the thriving and forward-thinking community it is today.

Mayors like Custer Service, Fred Snyder, Bob Rudkin, Carl Reherman, Randel Shadid, Saundra Naifeh, and Charles Lamb carried the torch for Edmond into the 21st century. Arcadia Lake, Edmond Memorial Hospital, Bryant Square, improved roads, public safety, and much more were made possible by the tireless efforts of many mayors and leaders.

Mayor Charles Lamb, for instance, helped bring the new safety center complex to existence. Crawford Spearman Jr. helped a college become a university. Mitzi Hancuff brought a greater awareness to the fine arts, as did Shadid, who is a chief reason Edmond has so much public art. Alvin Alcorn knew how to budget a dollar, and Sidney Bray helped direct war bond sales during World War II. E.C. Hafer helped shape the lives of many young athletes, while Guy Rankin was doing everything he could to make Edmond a "worthwhile place to live."

George Nigh led the University of Central Oklahoma to bigger things after serving as Oklahoma governor for a number of years. Businessman and politician Neal McCaleb has worn many hats, including his current role as a special ambassador for the Chickasaw Nation. Maj. Gen. Rita Aragon leads the state's office of military and veterans affairs. Judge Alan Synar created a juvenile court system in Edmond before his untimely death.

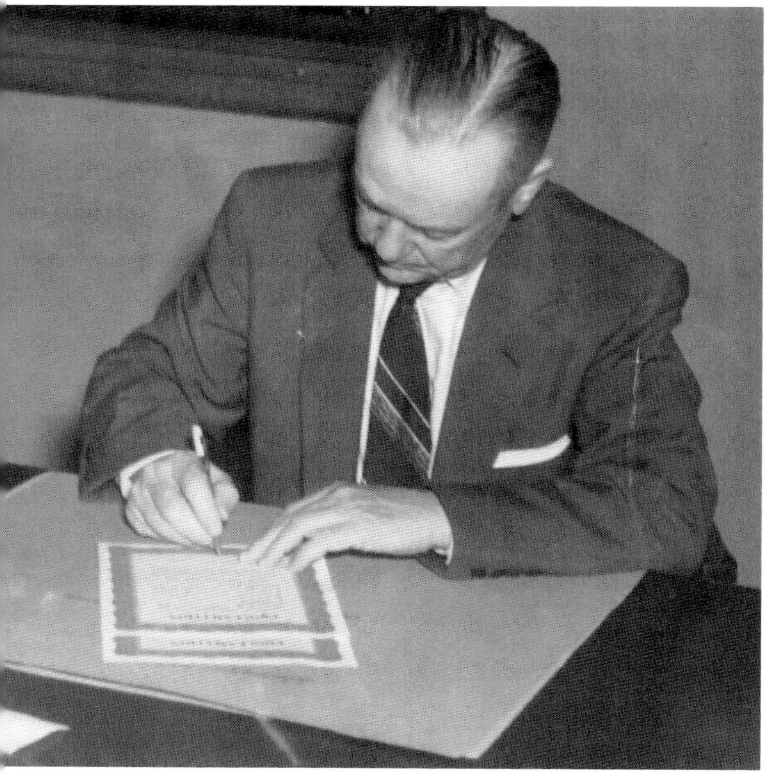

W. Custer Service

Service was mayor of Edmond from 1955 to 1965. The longtime lawyer and civic leader helped annex area for Arcadia Lake and get the Second Street underpass built. A new city hall was built during his tenure. The city council approved the site for Edmond Memorial Hospital at Second Street and Bryant Avenue, even though he favored a location across the street. His wife, Louise, said, "he took time to do the human thing." W. Custer Service Soccer Park bears his name. Inducted into the 1981 class of the Edmond Hall of Fame, Service "really made it possible for Edmond to be the size it is today," a friend said. (Left, courtesy Edmond Historical Society Photographic Collection; below, courtesy David Fisk.)

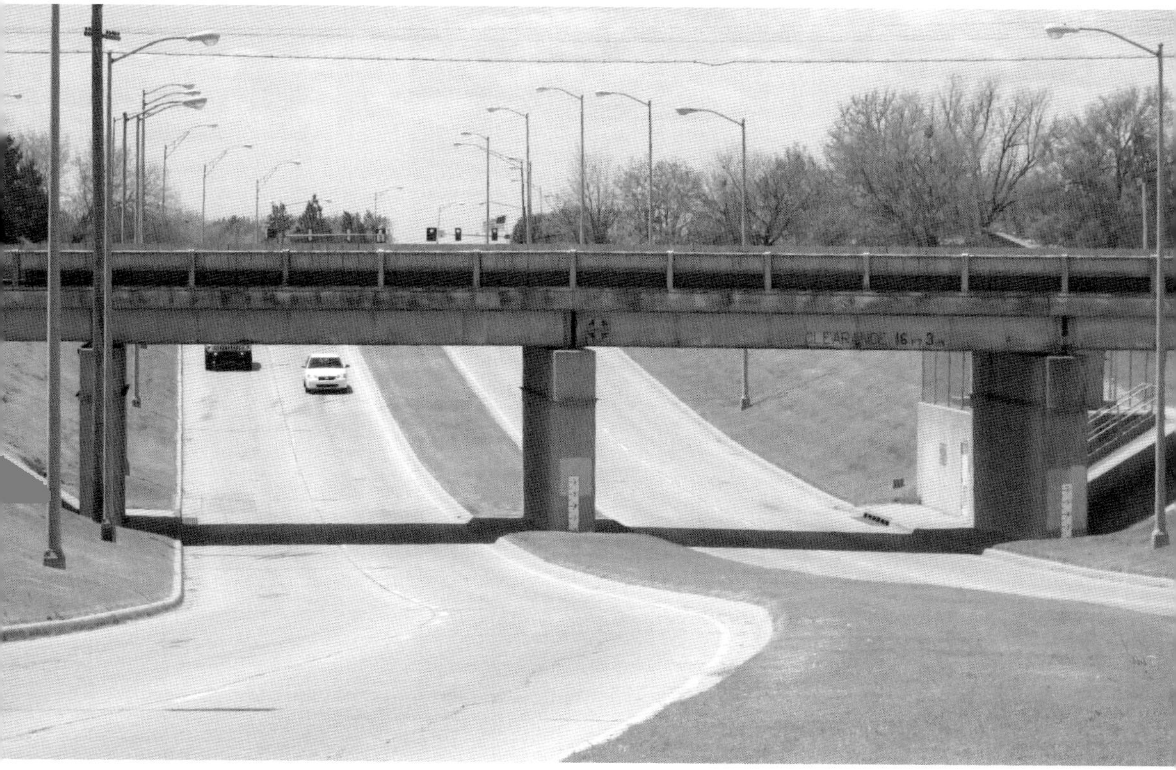

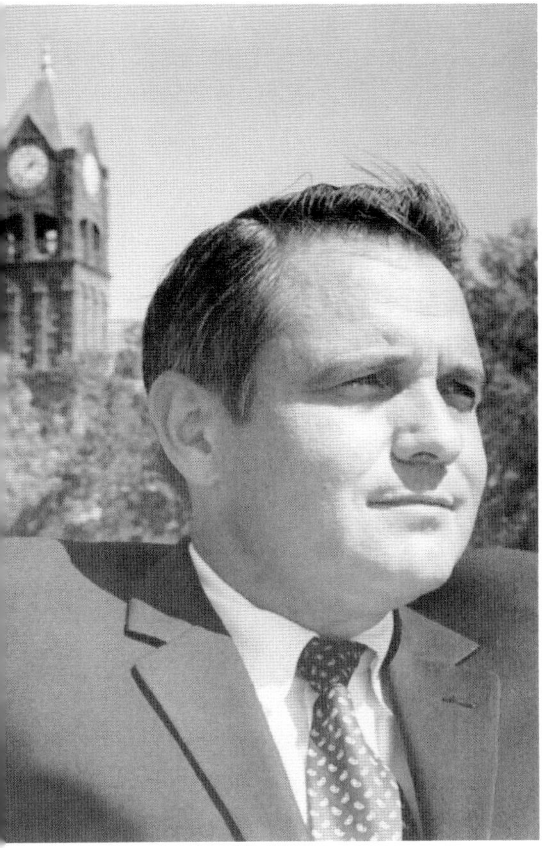

C.H. Spearman Jr.
Crippled by polio since childhood, Spearman carried on as the third generation of his family to leave their mark on Edmond. A graduate of Oklahoma University Law School, he practiced law before being elected in 1964 to the Oklahoma House of Representatives, where he served six years. He is best known for getting the bill through that changed his alma mater, Central State College, to a higher status as Central State University. It took three attempts, because Gov. Dewey Bartlett vetoed the measure twice. Finally, when David Hall became governor, it was approved. He penned an autobiography called *God Isn't Finished With Me*. He also helped get Broadway Extension turned into a four-lane highway instead of a two-lane road. (Courtesy UCO Library, Archives/Special Collections.)

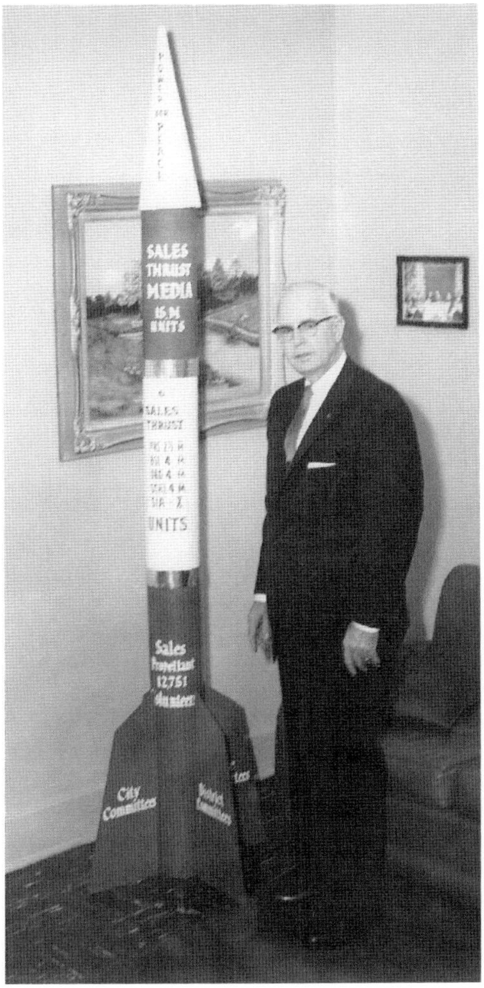

Sidney C. Bray
Bray was the man behind the idea of a veterans' memorial at Edmond's Gracelawn Cemetery. In fact, the antique bell sitting above the monument was donated by Bray. Bray was Oklahoma and regional director of the US War/Savings Bond Sales Program from 1942 until 1965. A World War I veteran, he was recruited to run the bond sales effort from General Motors, where he was sales manager. After his retirement, he was active in many Edmond organizations. He helped establish the Edmond Historical Trust and was named 1974's Outstanding Citizen by the City of Edmond. Considered an "idea man," he told the *Edmond Sun* his motto was, "Better to wear out than to rust out." (Courtesy UCO Library, Archives/Special Collections.)

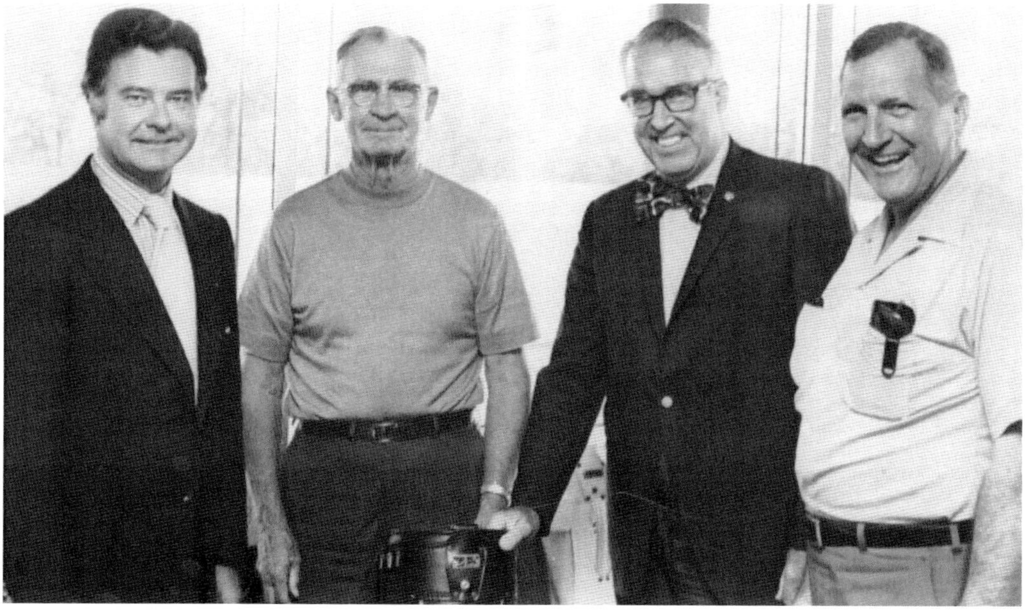

Everette Carl Hafer

E.C. Hafer Park is named for the longtime athletic director of Edmond Public Schools. "Hafe" had a love for young people that permeated his career as a coach and teacher. Hafer directed Edmond's summer recreational program and initiated the Kickingbird Golf Tournament. Pictured above at the opening of Kickingbird Golf Course are, from left to right, Hoot Gibson, Hafer, Oren Lee Peters, and Asbury Smith. Hafer started little league baseball in Edmond and was a mover behind the city's acquiring 120 acres for a park. Active in many civic clubs, he was also the first coach for future professional golfers Dave and Danny Edwards. (Courtesy Edmond Historical Society Photographic Collection.)

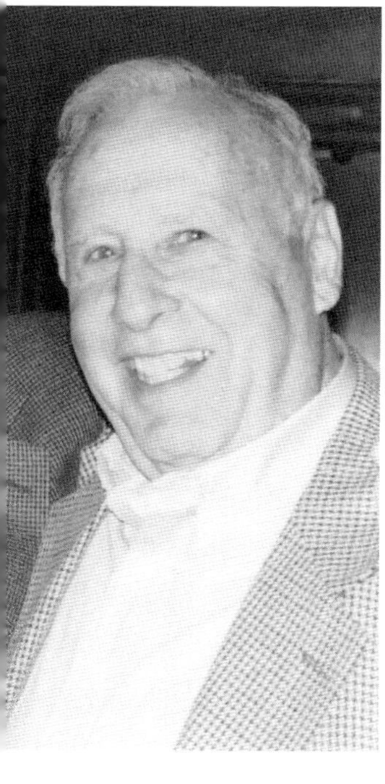

Fred Snyder

Snyder retired as an Oklahoma County commissioner in 1994. Before that, he wore many hats. He was a commander of the 179th Infantry Regiment in World War II as a lieutenant colonel and served again as a major with the 45th Infantry Division in Korea. In 1997, a bridge on Waterloo Road was named the 179th Infantry Regiment Memorial Overpass. Snyder had started the bridge project as a commissioner almost 10 years before. After he had returned from World War II to Edmond, he was an electrical contractor. After a dispute with the city, he ended up becoming city manager for several years. Years later, in 1967, he ran for mayor after the liberal mayor at the time "riled him" and was elected and served six years. In 1953, Snyder bought a hardware store at 104 South Broadway that was operated by his family for 37 years until it was closed in 1990. His son, Mark Snyder, said it was one of the few remaining family-owned hardware stores in the state. The *Daily Oklahoman* said, "Over the years, the business became known to many people in Edmond as the hardware store where they could find what they needed." (Courtesy Edmond Historical Society Photographic Collection.)

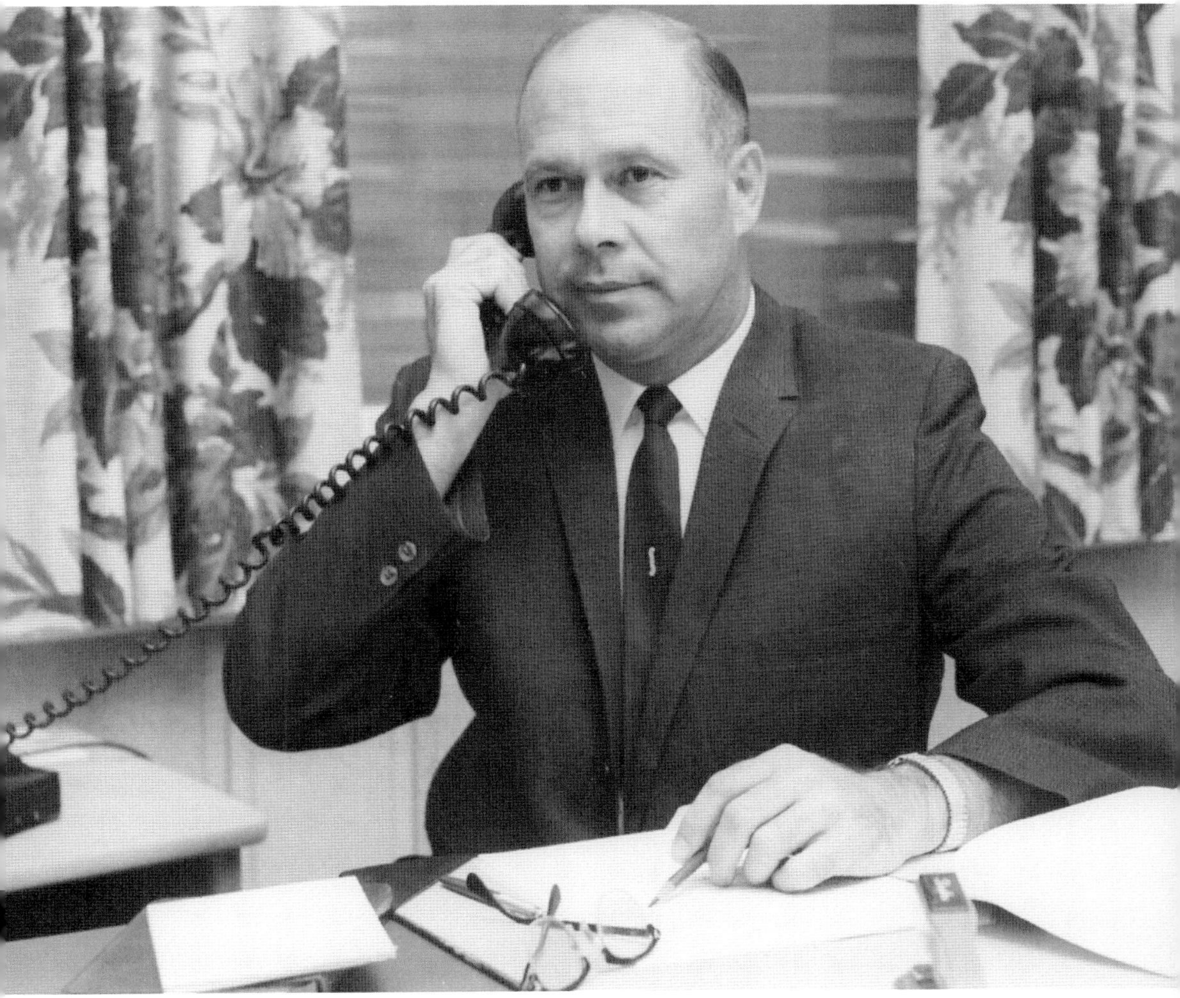

Alvin Alcorn

Alcorn was Central State University's "money man" for many years. He came to the university as comptroller in 1959 and was there almost 25 years, also serving as vice president of administration and executive vice president. "I'm tighter than hell—I have to be," he once told the *Tulsa World*. He helped buy land for the university, which grew from 40 acres to 200 acres under his guidance. He managed finances and oversaw the construction of more than 20 buildings on the campus, including the football stadium, field house, the Broncho Apartments, and many more. He was considered the "dean of business officers" in Oklahoma and was responsible for much of the university's growth. He also served on the Rose State College Board of Regents. The World War II veteran was a prime mover in establishing the Urban Renewal Authority in Edmond. A leader in Edmond for 40 years, he was president of the Edmond Chamber of Commerce in 1972 and on the chamber board for 15 years. Citizen of the Year in 1976, he went into the Edmond Hall of Fame in 1983. According to friends and family, he was tight-fisted and always looking for bargains. His pet peeve was lazy people. He told *Edmond Sun* writer James Coburn, "I hate lazy people more than anything else in the world." (Courtesy Edmond Historical Society Photographic Collection.)

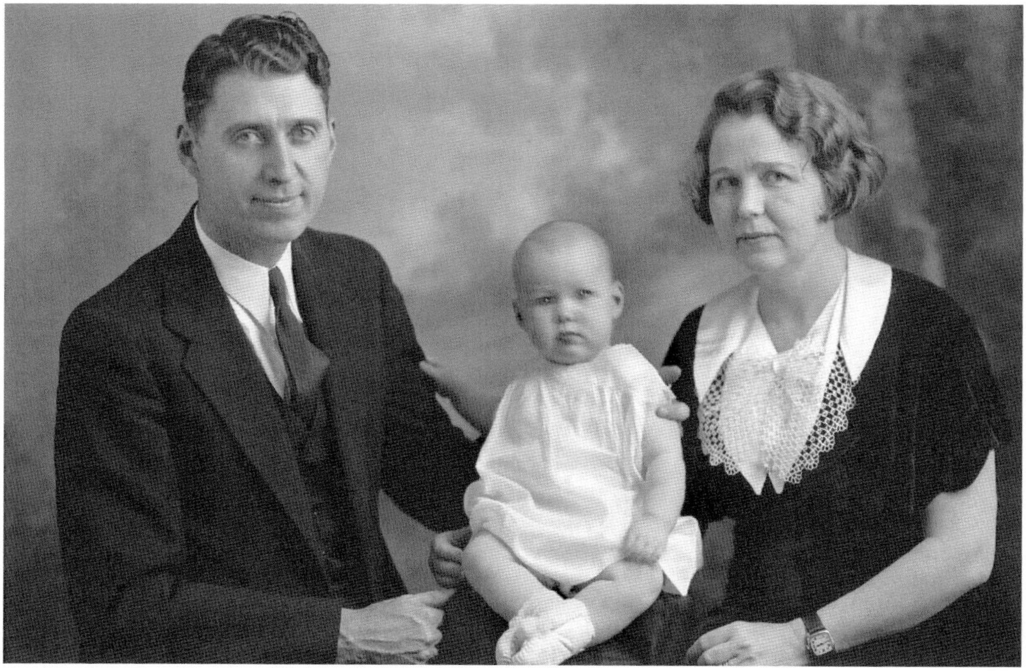

Guy M. Rankin

Rankin was too busy helping to make Edmond "a worthwhile place to live" to ever play golf. He moved here in 1924 with his wife, Maye, an Edmond girl, and taught economics at Central State College for 17 years. Pictured above with his family, he was a well-known civic leader. Rankin always had a great interest in the children of the community and was a founder of and fund-raiser for the Edmond YMCA. A longtime Democrat, he served on the city council and also was mayor pro tempore. He was a Rotarian since 1946 and served on the local library board. A staunch supporter of business, he believed "we've got to keep the trade in Edmond." He was inducted into the Edmond Hall of Fame in 1983. (Courtesy UCO Library, Archives/Special Collections.)

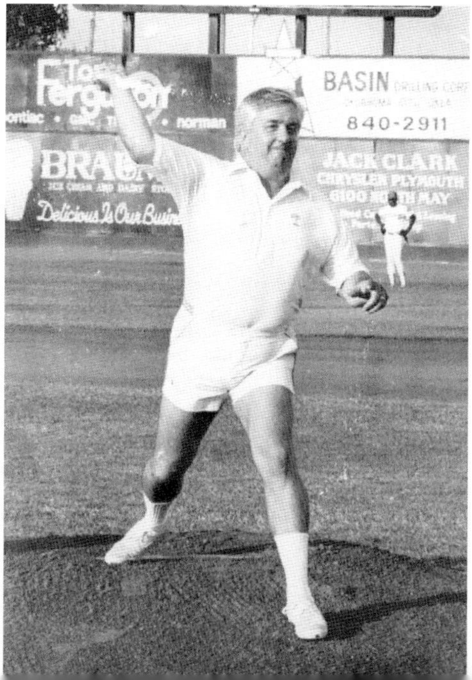

Carl Reherman

Reherman was mayor of Edmond from 1979 until 1989. One of the major accomplishments during his 10-year tenure was establishment of the Edmond Historic Trust in 1982. A longtime political science professor at the University of Central Oklahoma, he was a city councilman and member of the planning commission before becoming mayor. The 1981 Citizen of the Year, he helped secure funds for development of Arcadia Lake. Inducted into the Edmond Hall of Fame in 1984, he also helped raise funds for the post office memorial and chaired the committee to fund the Shannon Miller statue. The city got a new administration building, police station, and two new fire stations when he was mayor. (Courtesy Edmond Historical Society Photographic Collection.)

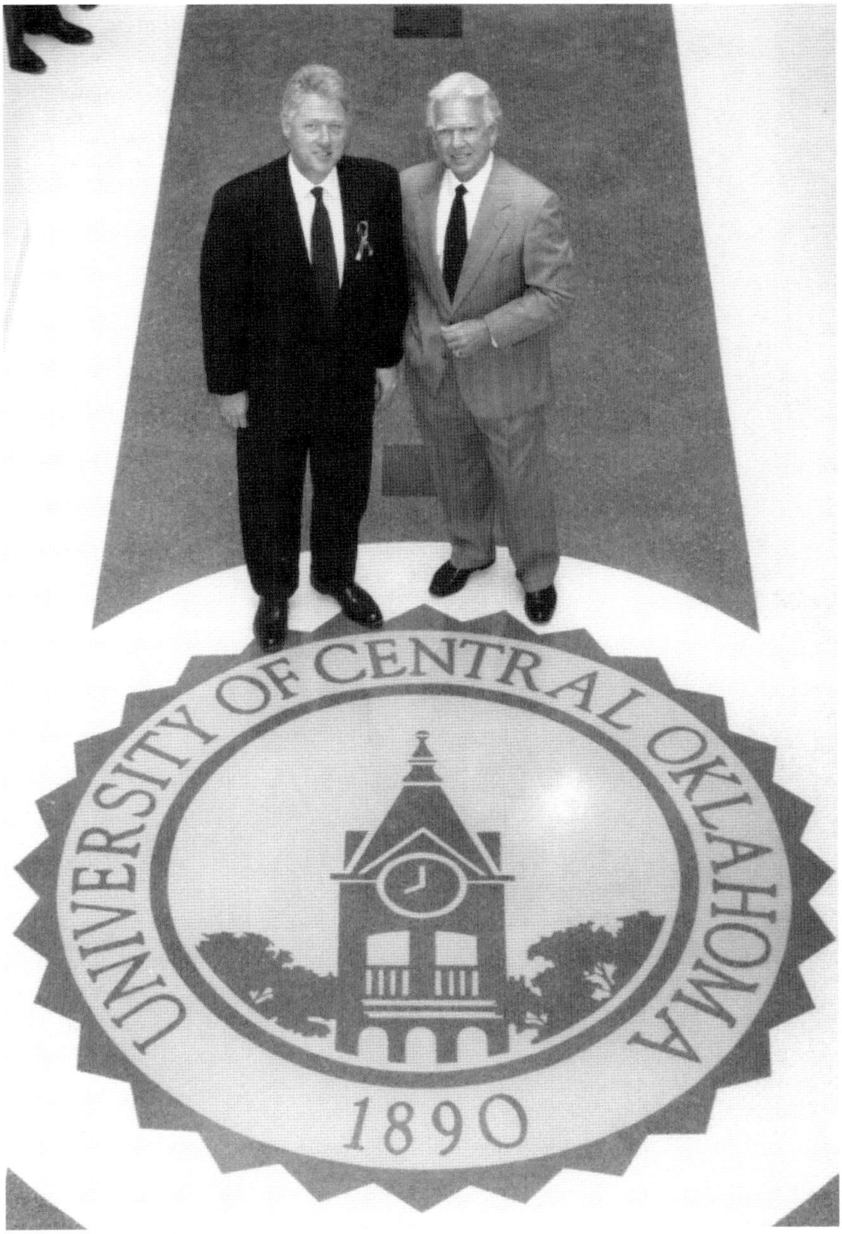

George Nigh

Before serving as president of the University of Central Oklahoma from 1992 to 1997, Nigh was governor of Oklahoma four terms. He was elected lieutenant governor in 1958, the youngest in the state's history at age 31. He worked to increase state tourism, and in 1963, he served an unexpired nine-day term as governor following the resignation of Gov. Howard Edmondson. He was later elected governor in 1978 and served until 1987 as the top official. He joined UCO's faculty in 1987 as distinguished statesman in residence. In 1992, he was named UCO's president. Pictured with Pres. Bill Clinton, he is credited with starting a building boom and bringing international attention to the university. His autobiography is called *Good Guys Wear White Hats: The Life of George Nigh.* He is in the Oklahoma Hall of Fame and won the Jim Thorpe Lifetime Achievement Award. (Courtesy Edmond Historical Society Photographic Collection.)

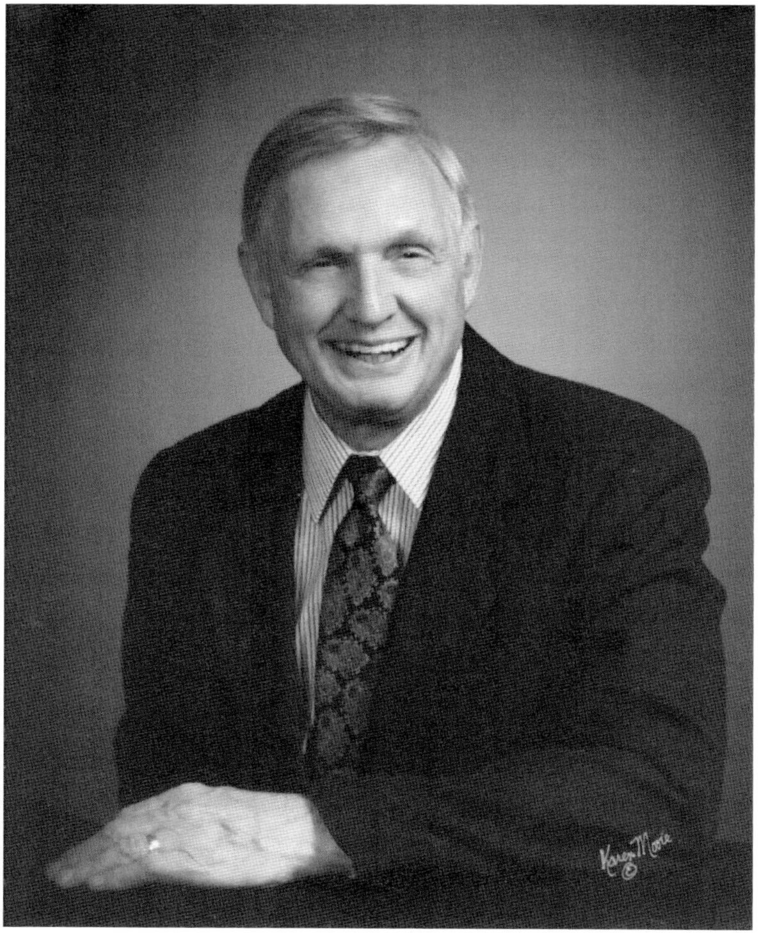

Bob Rudkin

Rudkin, a man who wore many hats in Edmond, including that as mayor, lived in Edmond for most of his 80 years. Rudkin played a major leadership role in Edmond's history and prosperity, as a story in the *Daily Oklahoman* acknowledged. An attorney by profession, he was a municipal judge, president of the school board, president of the Edmond Educational Endowment, a banker, president of Edmond Jaycees, president of the UCO Foundation, and mayor for six years. Former state secretary of transportation Neal McCaleb told the *Edmond Sun*, "every time there was a community project, Bob was there. And he was there because people sought his endorsement, because he was respected and trusted in the community." After serving 25 years on the school board, 10 as president, he became mayor in 1995 and served three terms. He told a reporter he was still involved in public service because "My wife says I need a hobby or I can't retire. Having grown up in Edmond, I've enjoyed public service here. We have a spirit of community." As mayor, he helped push for the 46-acre development on Second Street where the Lowes and Super Target store are located. He helped promote library expansion and helped forge an aggressive road-building program as the city grew to more than 70,000 residents by the time he left office in 2001. Rudkin's first law office was in a building shared by Neal McCaleb. As a teen, his first job was sacking groceries in a downtown Edmond market. He also worked at the historic Broncho Theater to help pay his way through college. Rudkin died in 2011, and a park bears his name in tribute to his years of service to Edmond. He once told the *Edmond Sun* that his philosophy was "leadership with integrity." One thing he did as mayor was reinstate the "Mayor's Prayer Breakfast." Former mayor Randel Shadid called Rudkin one of the "best public servants in Edmond's history." (Courtesy *Edmond Life and Leisure*.)

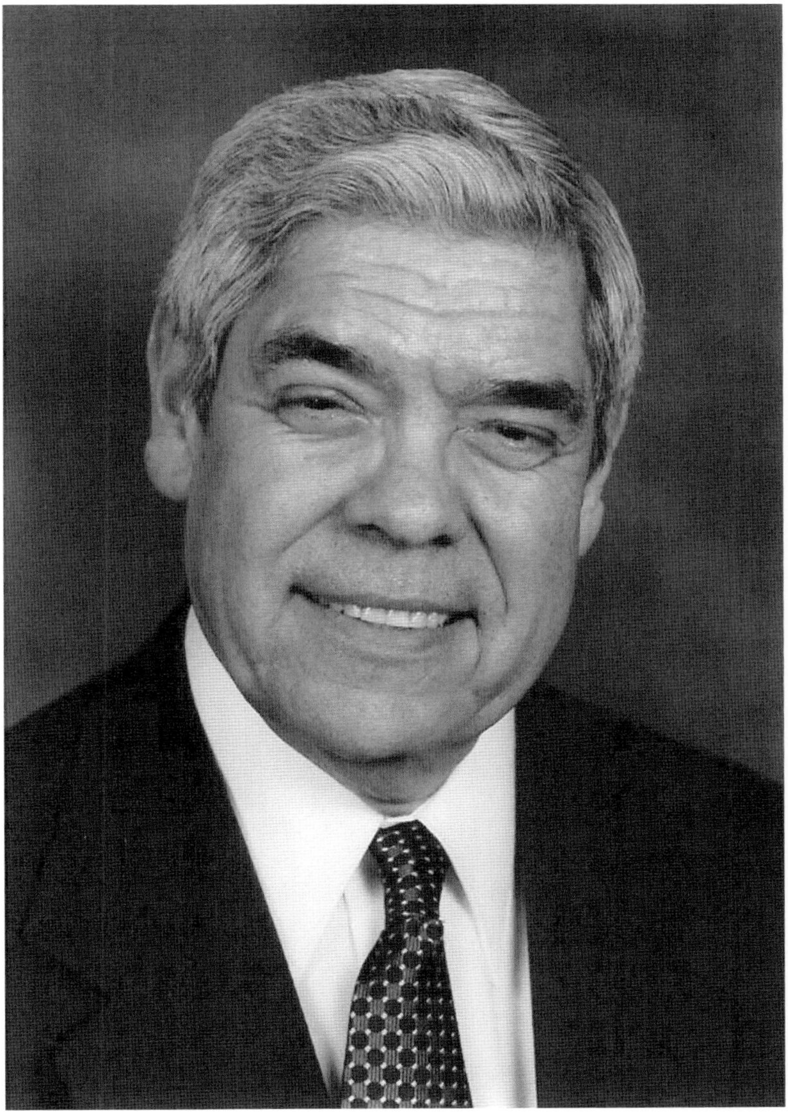

Neal McCaleb

Proud of his Chickasaw Indian heritage, McCaleb has been a leader in many areas. A civil engineer by profession, he was a real estate developer and engineer for many years in Edmond. McCaleb was president of the Edmond Chamber of Commerce before his election to the Oklahoma House of Representatives in 1974. He was the house minority leader as a Republican from 1978 until he retired from the legislature in 1983. He mounted a failed bid for governor in 1982 after leading a successful effort to eliminate the sales tax on prescription drugs in the legislature. He was Oklahoma's secretary for transportation under Gov. Henry Bellmon from 1987 to 1991 and again for Gov. Frank Keating from 1995 to 2001. He was also director of the Oklahoma Turnpike Authority before serving as Pres. George W. Bush's assistant secretary of the interior for Indian affairs. Never one to mince words, he once called Gov. George Nigh "Ole Marshmallow Nigh" and a monarch. McCaleb has served on the Chickasaw Nation Industries (CNI) board of directors since 2003 and as its chairman since 2007. CNI is a wholly owned sub entity of the Chickasaw Nation that promotes economic growth for the tribe. He was appointed ambassador-at-large for the tribe in 2013. (Courtesy Neal McCaleb.)

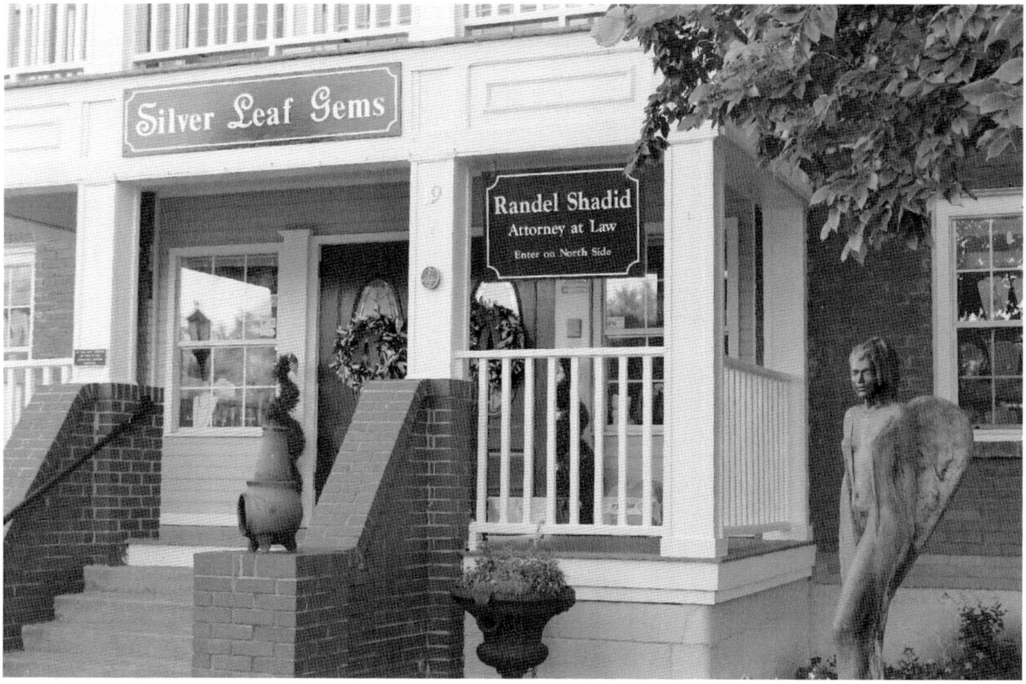

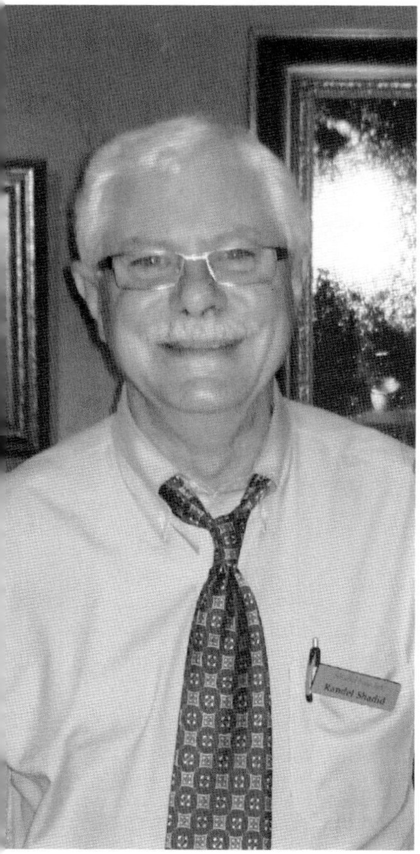

Randel Shadid

Always one to speak his mind, Shadid has been a familiar face around Edmond since 1973. The Altus native was a longtime city councilor and then mayor for four years before stepping down in 1995. A lawyer and art gallery owner, Shadid crusaded to make Edmond attractive and helped fortify "Green Edmond" polices in zoning. Maintaining a high profile after leaving public office, Shadid made it clear in an article in the *Edmond Sun* that "no one is going to forget Randel Shadid." As mayor, he refused to remove the cross from the city seal until a Supreme Court judge ordered it. He was behind the non-smoking ordinance and also a major force behind development of Mitch Park. Not one to shy from controversy, he was shadowed by police detectives, and that led to a scandal that brought about the ousting of police chief Bill Vetter. He told a reporter for the *Daily Oklahoman*, "I've never been afraid to tell people what I think on issues, and I've never been afraid to take controversial stands." He was inducted into the Edmond Hall of Fame in 1995 and once served as president of the Edmond Chamber of Commerce. The building that houses his art gallery was once the Caskey Apartments, the first multi-family apartment house in Edmond. The Methodist Episcopal Church once stood on the site and the first classes at the Territorial Normal School (now UCO) were held there. Shadid, an avid art collector, was a natural pick to head the first Visual Arts Commission. He was a huge proponent of the Art in Public Places program adopted by the city. There are more than 130 pieces of art scattered around Edmond because of the program, many in the downtown area. Edmond has made a name for itself with its collection of public art, much of it funded by private citizens and donors. (Above, courtesy David Fisk; left, courtesy *Edmond Life and Leisure*.)

Saundra Gragg Naifeh

Edmond's first female mayor, Naifeh was an organizer of the Edmond Women's Club in 1983 and founder of Keep Edmond Beautiful. Elected in 2001 to the city's top job, a post she held six years, Naifeh has long been active in the community. Edmond's Citizen of the Year in 1982, she was also a longtime executive director of the Oklahoma Association of Optometric Physicians. Naifeh championed membership of youth on city boards and commissions. She also worked for a youth council program which introduced young residents to the workings of city government. Naifeh led the way in getting a city ordinance passed that holds adults criminally responsible if they allow minors to drink alcohol at parties they host. Edmond became the first city in the state to have a "social host" ordinance. She was mayor during the controversy over the rezoning of 30 acres on Bryant Avenue south of Hafer Park for the proposed Bridges at Spring Creek development. Citizens petitioned for an election after the council voted 3-2 to rezone the property from single-family to commercial. She and husband Frank help raise funds for the Edmond Historical Society, serving as honorary chairs for Wine Through Time events. Her motto is "Embrace Life, encourage excellence, and inspire hope." (Courtesy City of Edmond.)

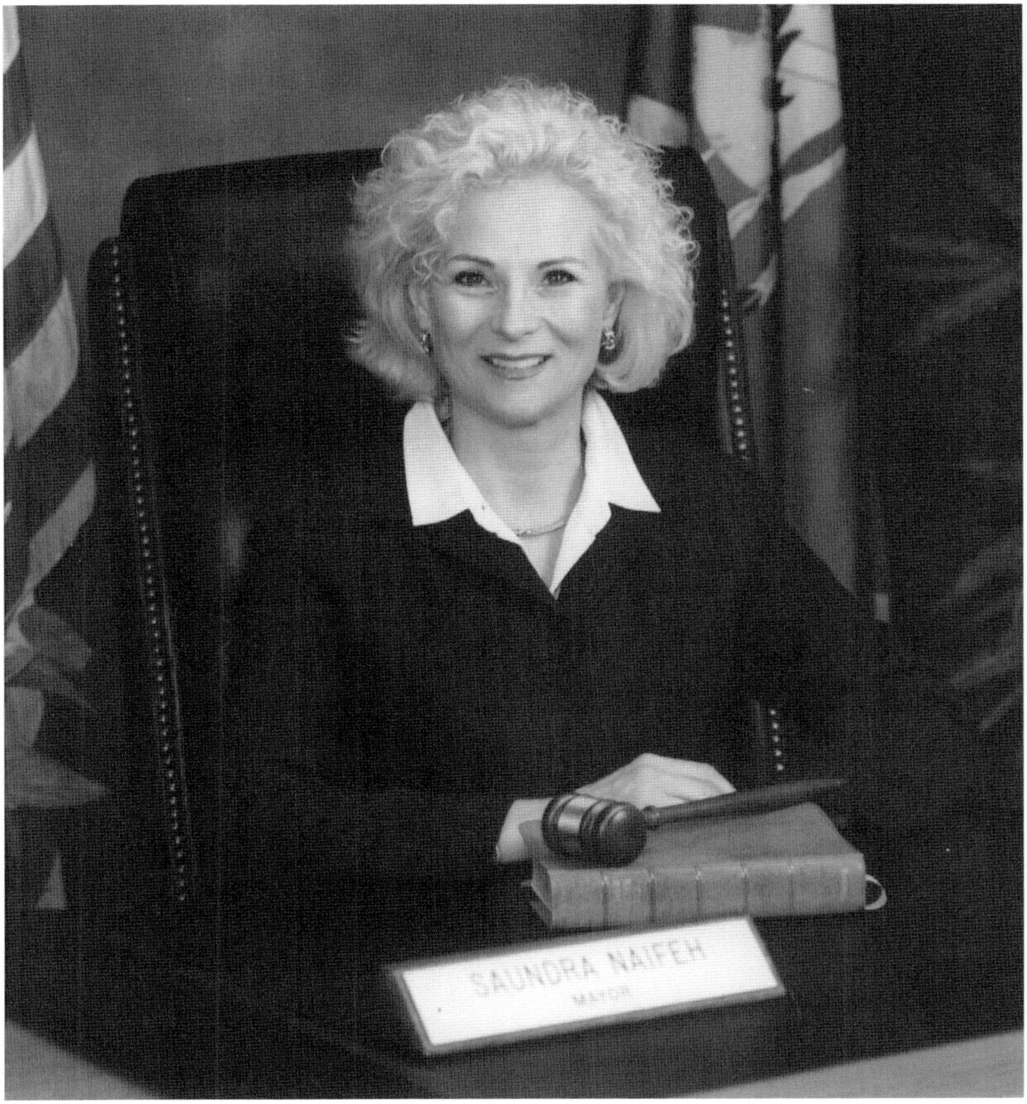

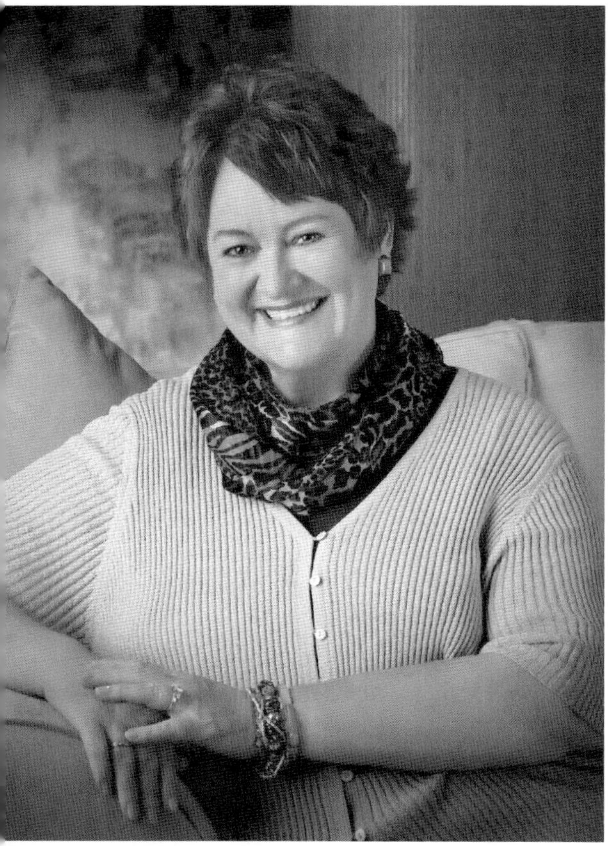

Mitzi Hancuff

Hancuff retired from the Fine Arts Institute of Edmond in 2013 after 25 years with the nonprofit arts organization. Under her leadership as executive director, the institute owns its own debt-free building and park. Enrollment has grown from 96 students in 1988 to almost 3,000 in those years. In 1988, the organization's budget was $18,000. Today, the budget is more than $500,000. *Edmond Life and Leisure* publisher Ray Hibbard wrote, "It is fair to say that nothing good happens in this town without the help of Mitzi Hancuff." The park at the arts institute is named Mitzi's Park in her honor. She was Edmond's Citizen of the Year in 2002 and was named the *Journal Record*'s Woman of the Year in 2012. In 2009, she received the Oklahoma Governor's Arts Award from the Oklahoma Arts Council. (Left, courtesy *Edmond Life and Leisure*; below, courtesy David Fisk)

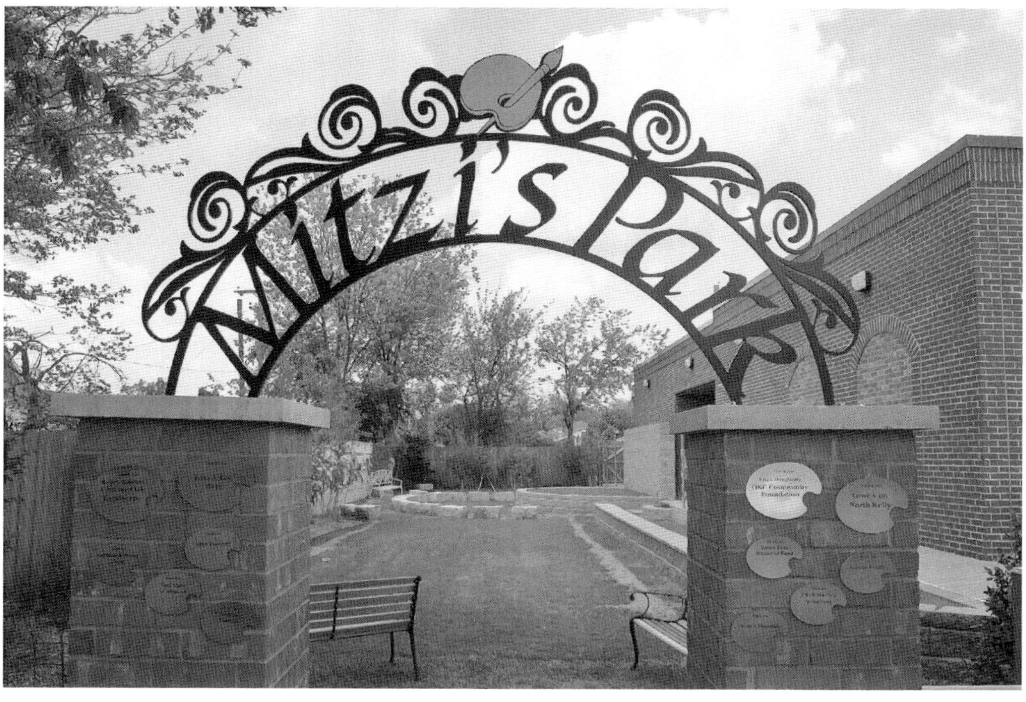

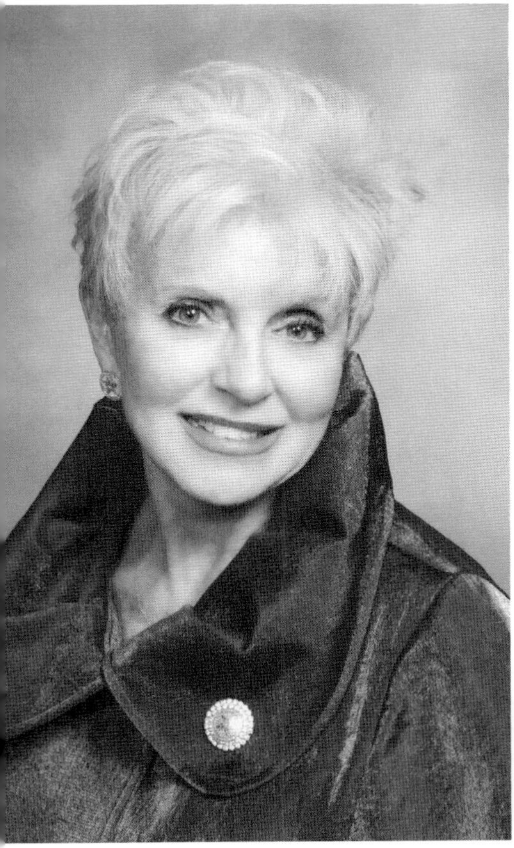

Rita Aragon
Major General Aragon was the first female secretary of military and veterans affairs for Oklahoma. Aragon was also the first female commander of the Oklahoma Air National Guard And the first Native American female to become a general officer. She is a member of the Edmond Hall of Fame and Oklahoma Women's Hall of Fame. The major general has won many awards and serves on many boards, including Integris Health Edmond, Pros for Vets, and Women's Foundation of Oklahoma. She is involved in many organizations, including Edmond Fine Arts and YWCA Purple Sash. (Courtesy Rita Aragon.)

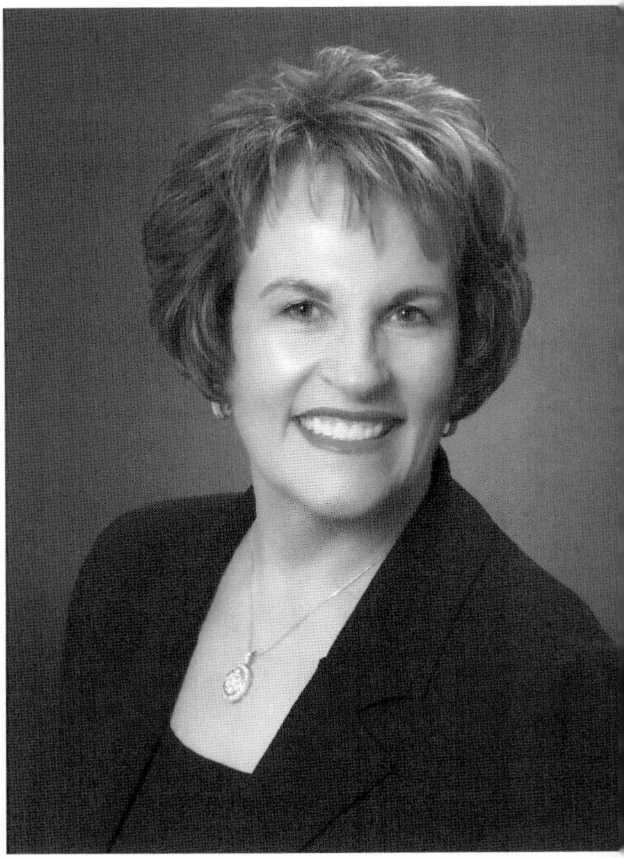

Mo Anderson
"Above all, keep Edmond Beautiful" was Anderson's philosophy as the first female president of the Edmond Chamber of Commerce in 1982. Once the president and CEO of Keller-Williams Realty, she is now a top executive with the firm. She was a music teacher 14 years before entering the real estate business. Her first office was a Century 21 franchise in Edmond in 1975. Her bio on the Keller-Williams Web site calls her the "Velvet Hammer" for her "uncompromising approach and leadership." She is in the Edmond Hall of Fame and was the 1983 Citizen of the Year. She serves on the boards of many local organizations, including the Daily Living Center and Francis Tuttle Vo-Tech Foundation. (Courtesy Keller-Williams.)

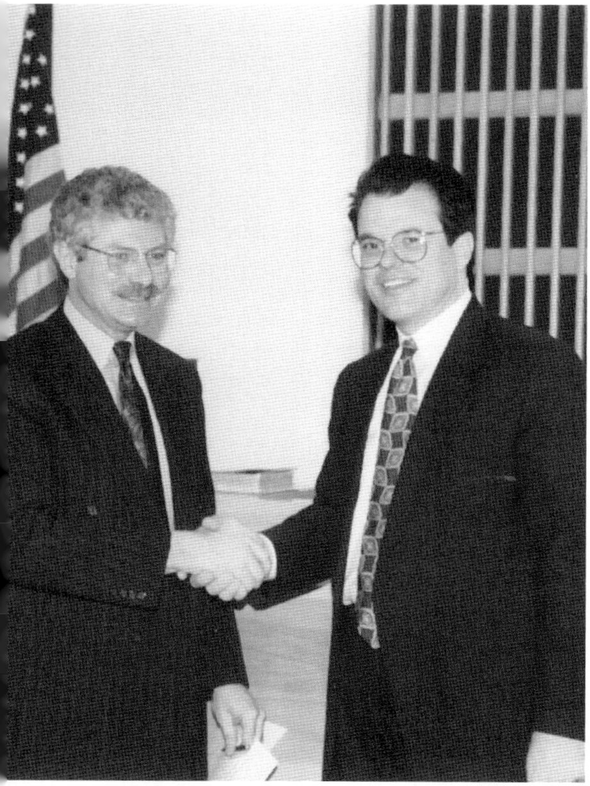

Alan E. Synar

Synar's most notable legacy is the creation of a juvenile court system in Edmond during the 1990s. Synar was the second municipal judge in Oklahoma to handle juvenile cases. Synar was named associate judge in 1988 by Mayor Carl Reherman, replacing Ray Vaughn, who retired to became a county commissioner. Several years later, Synar became presiding judge in Edmond. Synar, who died in 2011 at the age of 56, made many contributions to Edmond. Synar told reporter James Coburn of the *Edmond Sun*, "Teenagers biggest fear when coming to this court is the whole ordeal. And, really, it's all designed. I'm here to help you. I'm not such a mean person." Synar would assign juvenile offenders community service, requiring youths to take an art class at the Fine Arts Institute of Edmond. Offenders had to bring a piece of art to Synar when their probation was completed. Many of the pieces of artwork decorated the halls and judge's chambers at the court. City attorney Steve Murdock told the *Oklahoman*, "He cared about the young people." He loved to cook out on the grill, and his friends laughed about all the grills, cookers, and smokers he owned. Synar is pictured at left with Mayor Randel Shadid, left, and below at his desk. (Both, courtesy of Lisa Synar.)

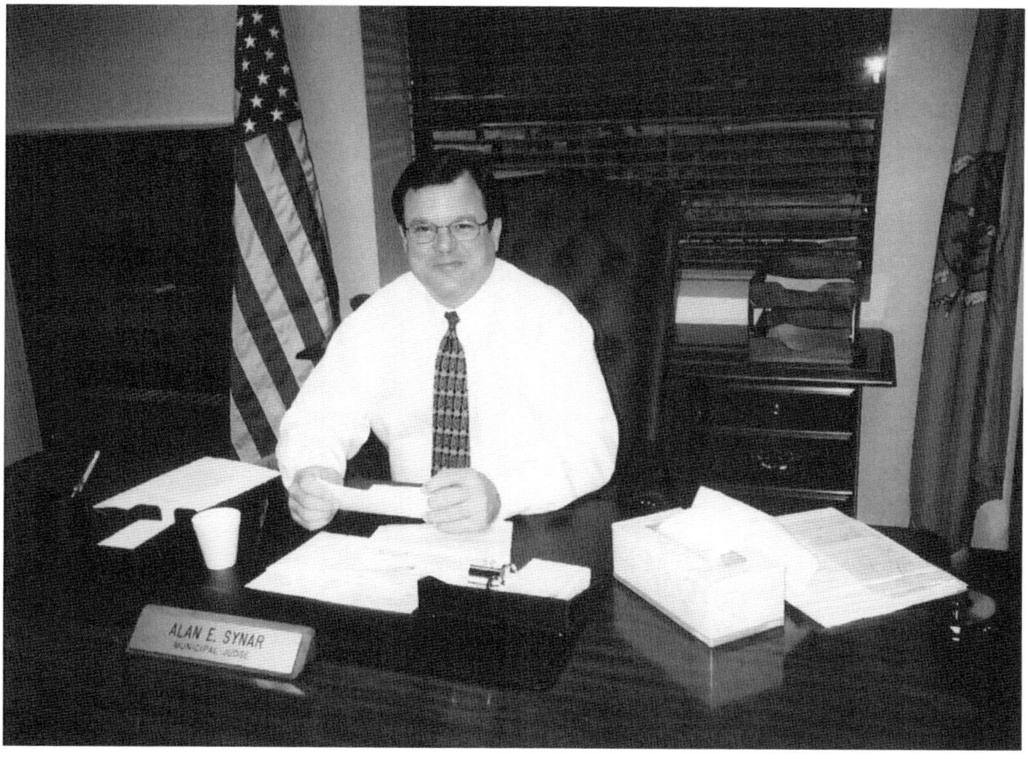

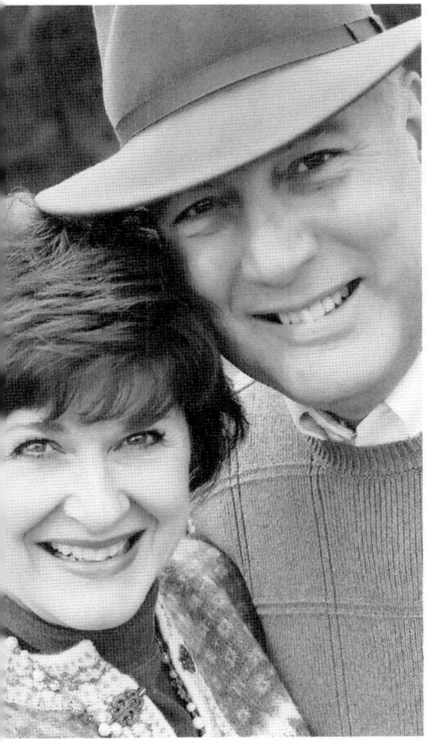

Ray Vaughn Jr.
A member of the Oklahoma House of Representatives from 1988 to 2004, Vaughn was inducted into the Edmond Hall of Fame in 2010. He told the *Edmond Sun* that his "inspiration for public service is to serve and not be served." A county commissioner for District 3 since 2006, Vaughn has been described by his family as a man of great character and integrity, someone who never uses foul language, and a dedicated family man. A founding member of the Edmond law firm Vaughn, Winton & Clark, he has been an Edmond Citizen of the Year and has many awards, including Legislator of the Year, the Oklahoma Bar Association's Liberty Bell award, and the UCO President's Medal of Honor. He is a trustee of the University of Central Oklahoma Foundation and Oklahoma Christian University. In 2013, he was chairman of the board for the Oklahoma County Commissioners. As commissioner, Vaughn helped lead the acquisition of the closed General Motors plant and the leasing of that facility to the Air Force, thus creating the Tinker Aerospace complex, which he said helped create more than 1,700 new jobs on the base. Vaughn says he owes his success to others, especially his father. (Courtesy Rick Buchanan.)

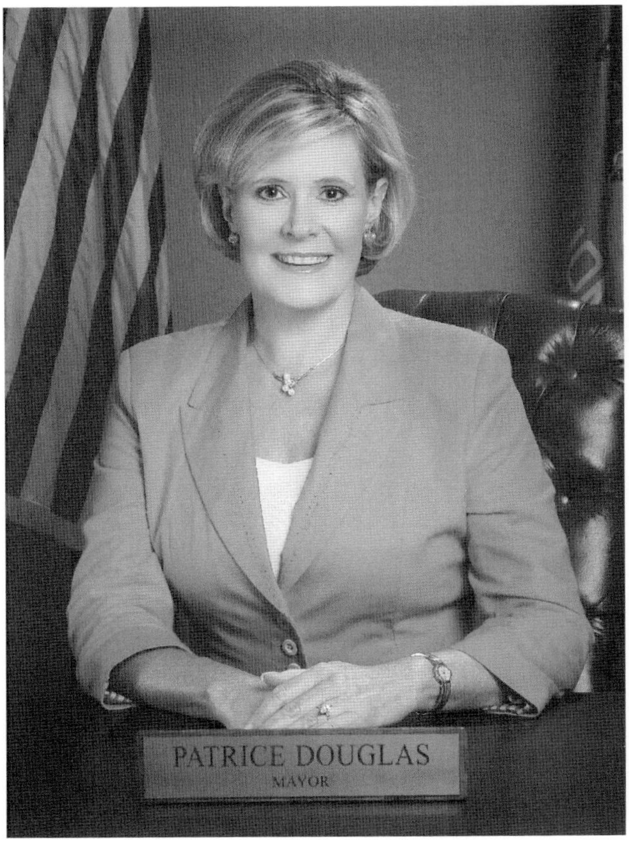

Patrice Douglas
Douglas was mayor of Edmond from 2009 to 2011. She only held one term as mayor because she resigned a short time into her second term to take a position on the Oklahoma Corporation Commission. Appointed by Gov. Mary Fallin, Douglas was named commission chairwoman in 2012. As mayor, Douglas defied a warning from a religious watchdog group and joined others to participate in a National Day of Prayer. (Courtesy City of Edmond.)

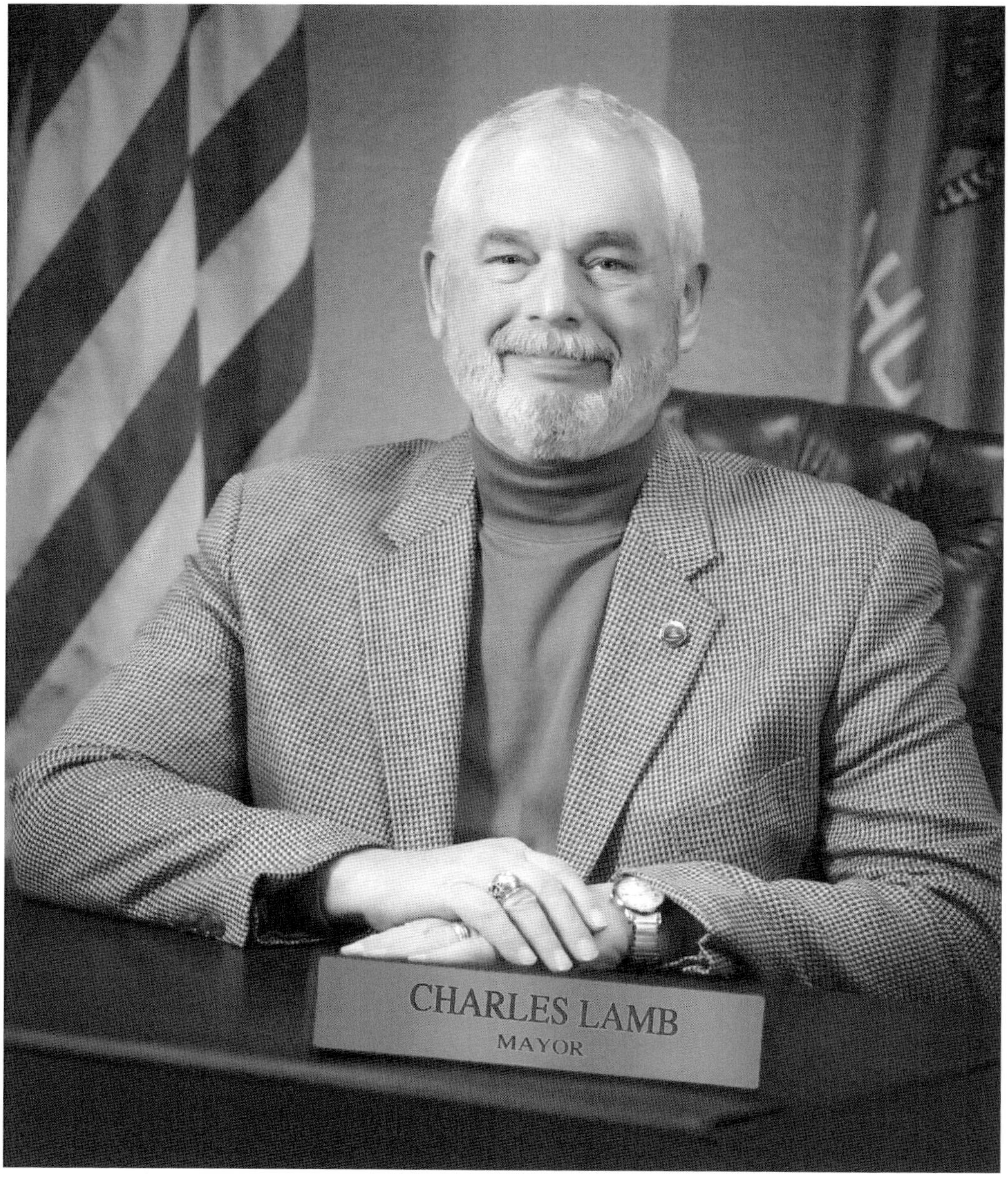

Charles Lamb
Lamb loves Edmond. Since 1959, he has lived in the same house, and he has been mayor of his beloved city since 2011. After serving out a term for Patrice Douglas, who resigned to be on the State Corporation Commission, Lamb won the post again with almost 82 percent of the vote in 2012. The 1999 Edmond Citizen of the Year has served on 24 Edmond boards, commissions, or committees. He was a councilman for 16 years before taking the mayor's job. In 2006, he was inducted into the Oklahoma Hall of Fame for City and Town Officials. Lamb has been a longtime supporter of the redevelopment of downtown Edmond. Former mayor Saundra Naifeh called Lamb "an open-minded yet resolute leader and someone who doesn't like to be the center of attention." A new city service center is being built, and a $24-million swimming pool and recreation center—a partnership of the city, YMCA, and Edmond public schools—was finished in 2014. (Courtesy City of Edmond.)

CHAPTER SEVEN

Neighbors

In 125 years, Edmond has grown from its original town site to a city of varied neighborhoods. In those neighborhoods live many varied characters, each of whom has a unique story. Here are a few of those "folks next door."

Charles Boldin was a role model to young men for many years and became the ultimate model when he posed for Edmond sculptor Mary Lou Gresham's statue *The Reader*, which is seen by thousands of people every week at the Edmond Library. Quimby Enterline's 50 years service to the Boy Scouts of America is legendary.

Lucille Warrick led the drive to restore the public schoolhouse on Second Street to its original form after the building's many years as a camera shop. Ted Anderson wore many hats in Edmond, helped organize the YMCA, and was once called "Mr. Edmond." Restaurant owner Charlotte Worsham once chained herself to trees in downtown Edmond to try and save them.

And then there is young Ella Turner, an elementary student with a heart of gold that raised money by jumping rope in memory of her little sister who died of a rare heart disease. Lucille Fancey and Joy Milligan's therapeutic horse riding center has enabled many youngsters to enjoy horses while learning to ride. Musician and teacher Lee Rucker mentored young musicians for more than 30 years at UCO while entertaining many more with his trumpet playing.

Naturalist Bob Jenni shared his knowledge and love of animals with students across Oklahoma for many years. Martha and Gary Hall host many a guest at their restored Arcadian Inn Bed and Breakfast. Patsy Sandefur pinch-hit for city officials on many occasions while working as a loyal Edmond city employee. Hall "Dr. D." Duncan has touched many curious minds with his children's and humor books; by the way, he was also a World War II hero. Katrina Shaklee brought the Endeavor Games and Olympic training to UCO. Edmond's homeless man, Dwite Morgan, known as "Bicycle Bob," was a friend to many around Edmond until he was brutally murdered in 2009.

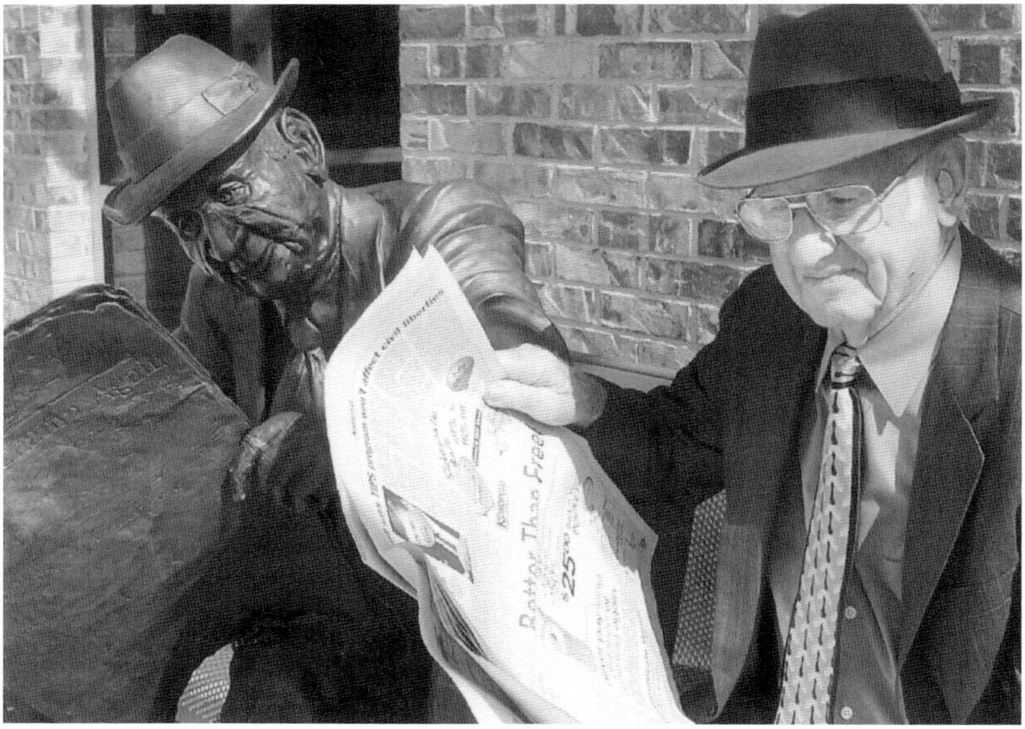

Charles Boldin

"Changing lives one boy at a time" was Boldin's way of life. Superintendent of the Boys Town Ranch in Edmond from 1956 until 1982, Boldin and his wife, Ellen, served as teachers and role models for more than 900 boys during their 26 years overseeing the home. He worked there more than 40 years and in 1996 was inducted into the Edmond Hall of Fame. At his funeral service in 2003, a friend said, "he has been a father figure, mentor and best friend to more young boys than any man in Edmond history." Edmond sculptor Mary Lou Gresham added to the legend by using Boldin as the model for *The Reader* statue, which sits on a bench at the entrance to the Edmond Library. She knew Boldin from First Baptist Church and said "I used a contemporary gentleman extraordinaire as my model, Charles Boldin. He was director of Boys Ranch Town and there are no finer men to remember in bronze." Her grandfather Maxwell Olsen served as her first inspiration for the statue, Boldin did the modeling and provided the hat, and the *Edmond Sun* provided the newspaper to be bronzed. (Above, courtesy Ellen Boldin; right, courtesy David Fisk.)

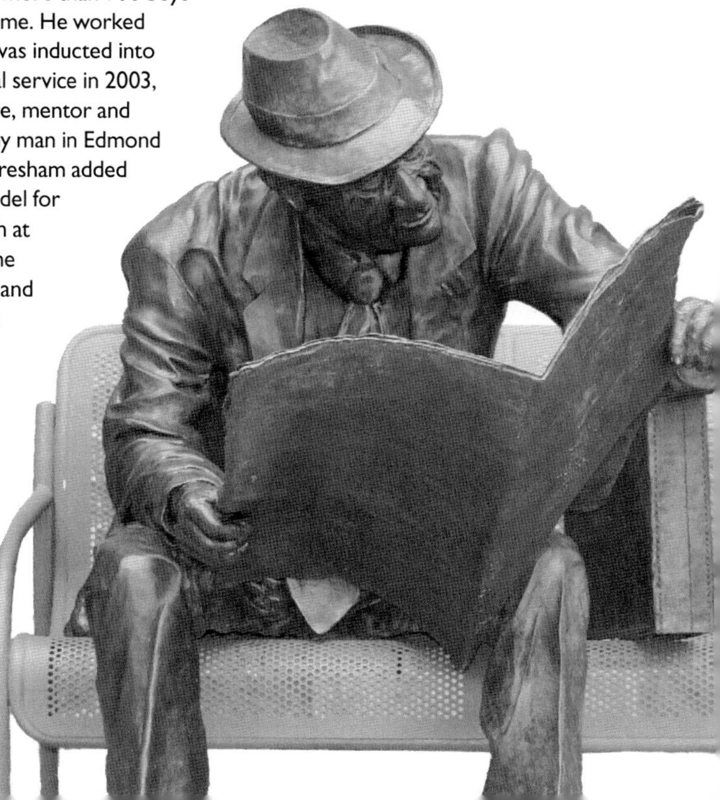

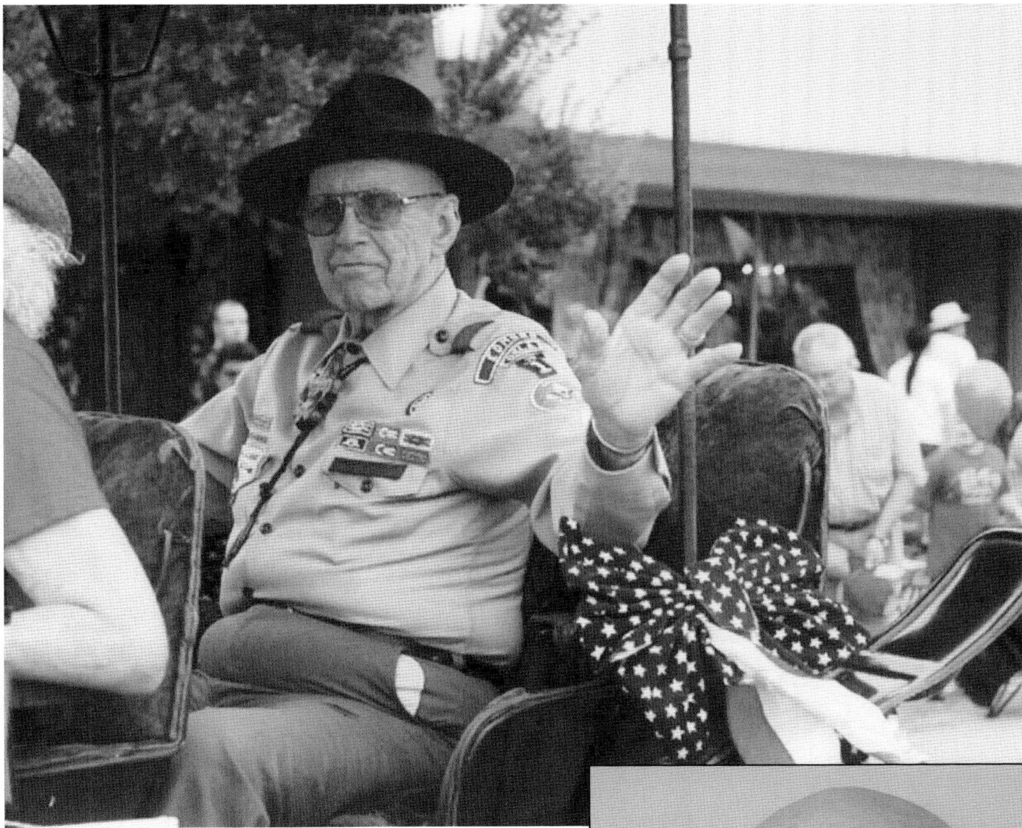

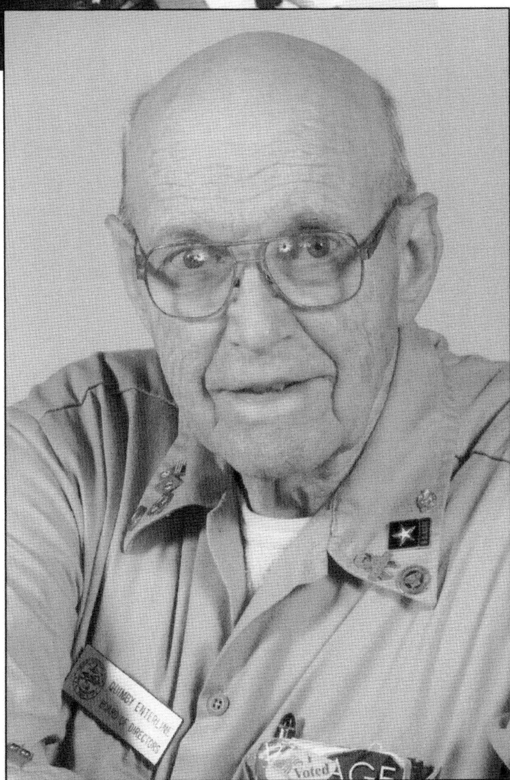

Quimby Enterline

Enterline, who retired from Tinker Air Force Base in 1980, has volunteered with the Edmond Historical Society Museum since 1984. His activities with Scouting are legendary. In 2010, he was honored for 50 years of service to the Boy Scouts of America. The Daughters of the American Revolution bestowed the Community Service Award on him in 2006. Active with Edmond's famed LibertyFest Parade since 1972, Enterline was parade marshal in 2010. His great-grandfather built what is considered the first two-story home in Edmond in 1902. He was in the 179th Infantry during World War II, fighting in Italy and France. He told a reporter, "I saw some of *Saving Private Ryan*, and it was a lot like that." In 2013, he was still helping out at the history museum. (Both, courtesy Edmond Historical Society Photographic Collection.)

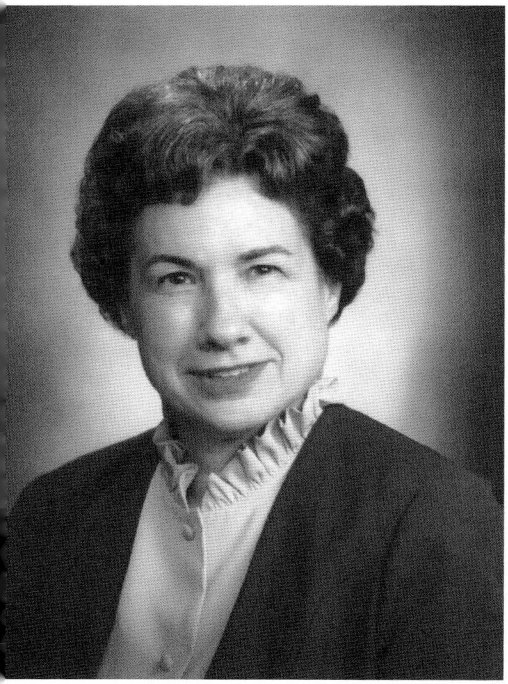

Lucille Warrick

A lifelong passion for history was Warrick's driving force behind her long and successful quest to save and renovate the first public schoolhouse in Oklahoma Territory. As a member of the Edmond Historical Trust, Warrick once said restoring the building was the first priority for the group, which was created in 1982. From 1950 until 1975, the building was Sanders Camera Store. The trust bought the building for $100,000 from the Sanders family in 2001 and raised $400,000 to restore the building to its original state. In 2007, it was dedicated as an official Oklahoma Centennial Project. Without a schoolhouse, Edmond might not have become a town, and without Warrick, the school might not have been saved. In 2010, the trust honored Warrick, who died in 2009, by dedicating the school's bell and bell tower in her name. This event happened appropriately on April 22, the anniversary of Oklahoma's land run. (Left, courtesy Taylor Made Photography; below, courtesy David Fisk.)

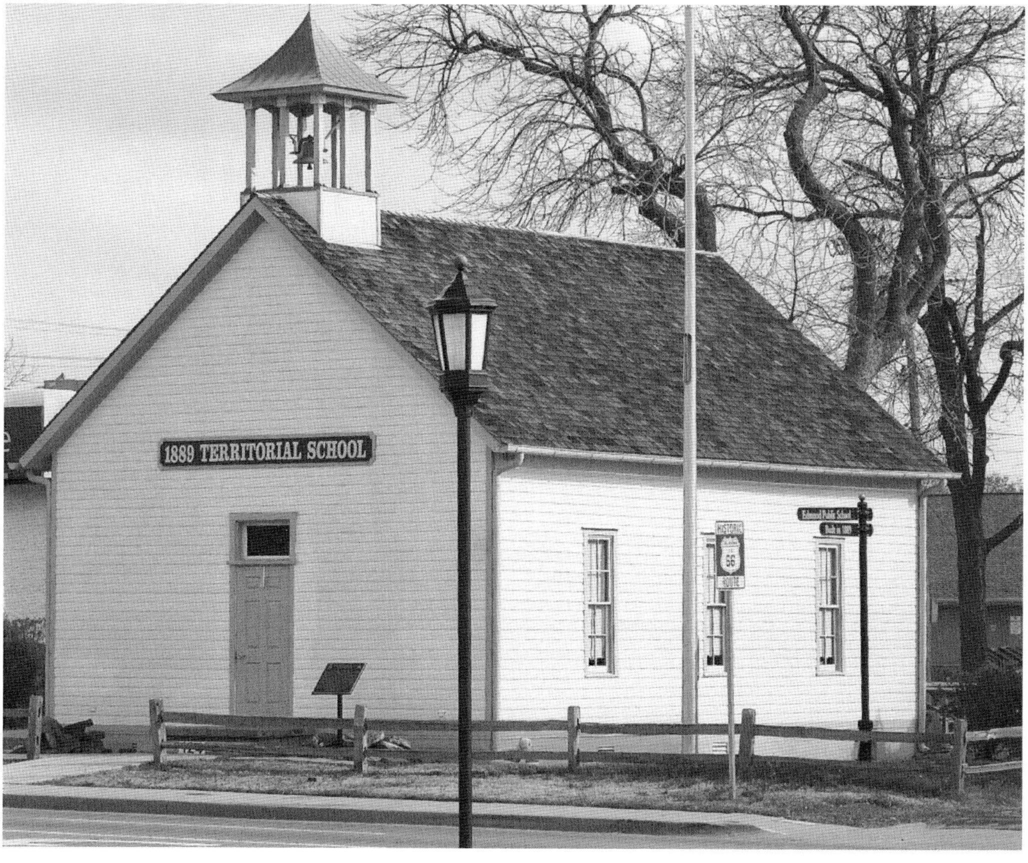

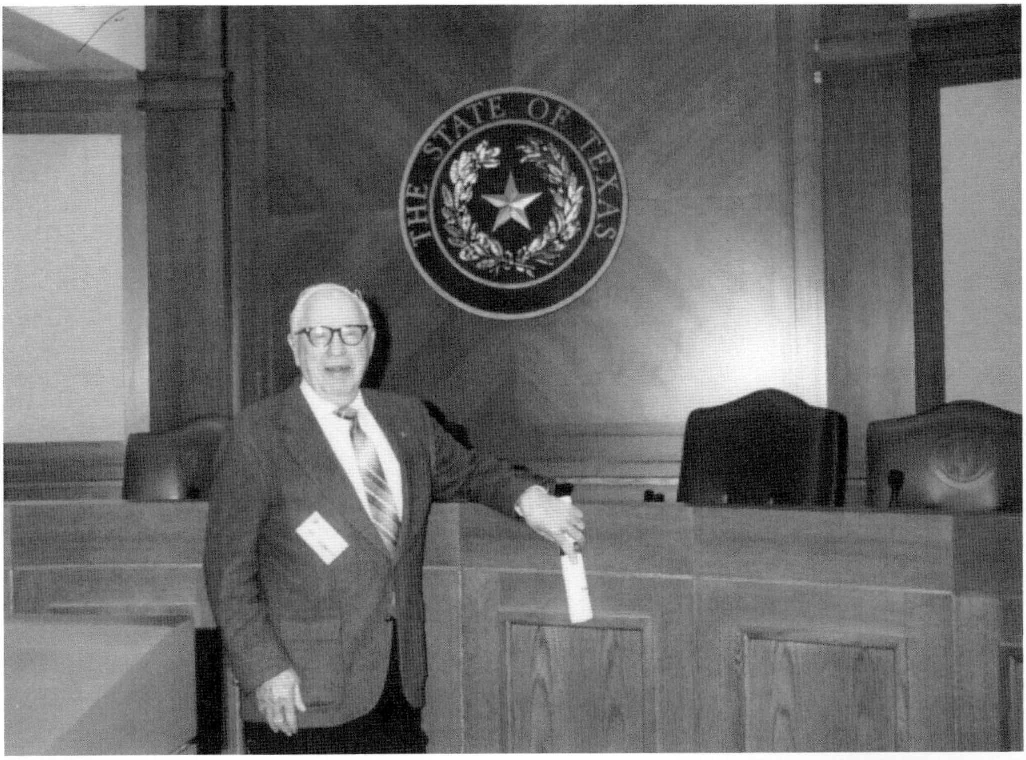

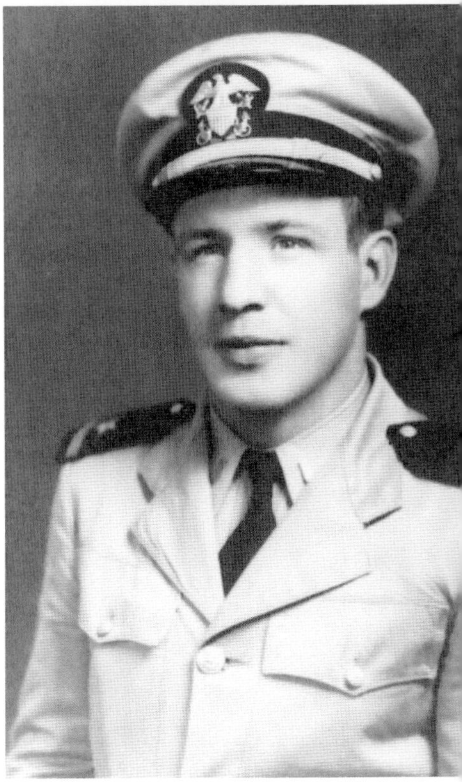

Ted Anderson

Wrestling was a major part of Anderson's life, but not everything. The 1936 NCAA wrestling champion graduated from Central State Teachers College in 1939. After volunteering for the Navy in 1942, the ensign was assigned as an athletic officer, charged with getting future pilots in fighting physical shape. He also taught them hand-to-hand combat. Anderson, who is in the UCO Athletic Hall of Fame, spent 35 years coaching and teaching math and retired as a principal. The park next to Orvis Risner School is named after him. While a wrestling coach at Edmond High School, he led the team to eight top-10 finishes at the state tournament. After retiring as a coach and educator in 1976, he stayed busy, serving from 1977 to 1985 on the city council. He was on the organizing board for the YMCA, a member of the Edmond Historical Trust, and active in many civic organizations, including Kiwanis and the Masonic lodge. He was Kiwanian of the Year six times and served as president of the Oklahoma County Teachers and the Oklahoma Wrestling Coaches Association. A headline on an article in the *Daily Oklahoman* called him "Mr. Edmond." He was 77 at the time. (Both, courtesy the Edmond Historical Society Photographic Collection.)

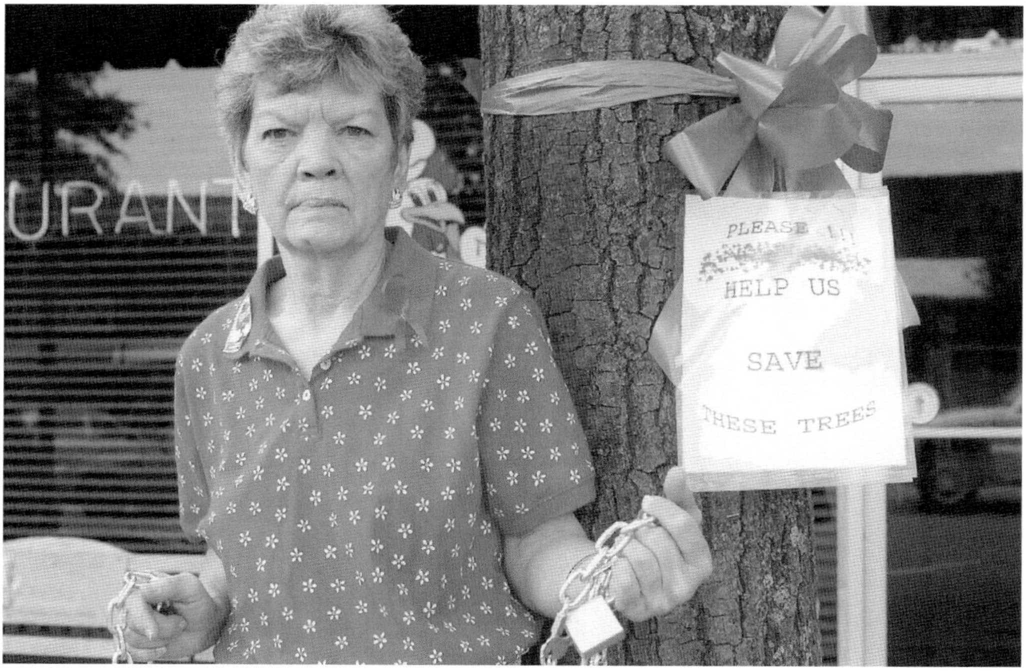

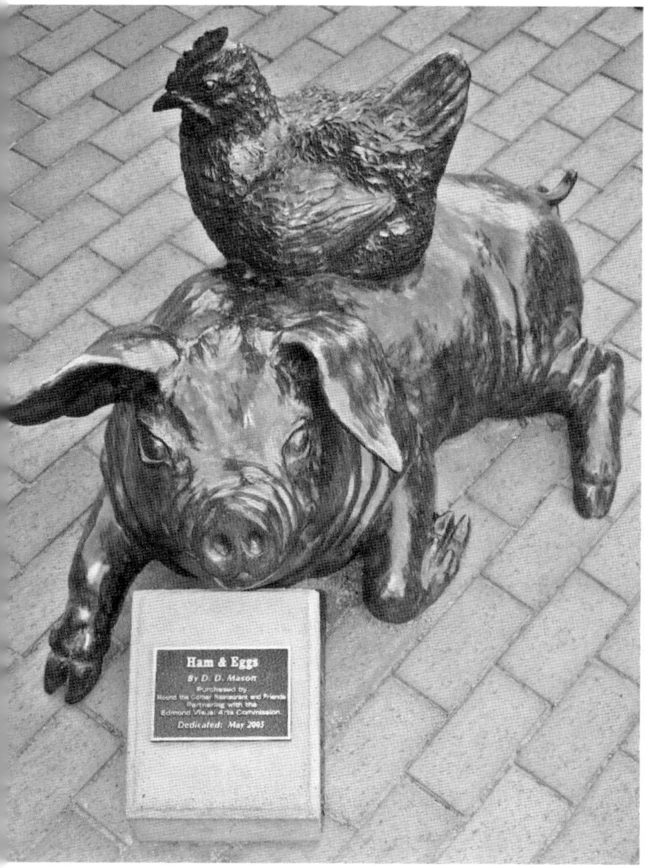

Charlotte Worsham

This popular restaurant owner once threatened to chain herself to a pole in protest of a city streetscape remodeling project. She also climbed into some trees (above) to try and save the trees from being cut down. Her Around the Corner restaurant was known to many as "the heart of Edmond" for 50-plus years. Worsham owned and operated the eatery for 24 years until her retirement in 2012. The family restaurant was the gathering place for business owners, politicians, retirees, and many more. Her customers pitched in and bought two statues to go in front. One is a bronze statue of a pig with a hen sitting on its back called *Ham and Eggs*; the other is *Girl Feeding Chickens*. In a newspaper story after her death in 2013, a friend said Worsham "didn't care about anyone knowing the good she did. She would just show up and do something for someone." (Above, courtesy the *Oklahoman* archives; left, courtesy David Fisk.)

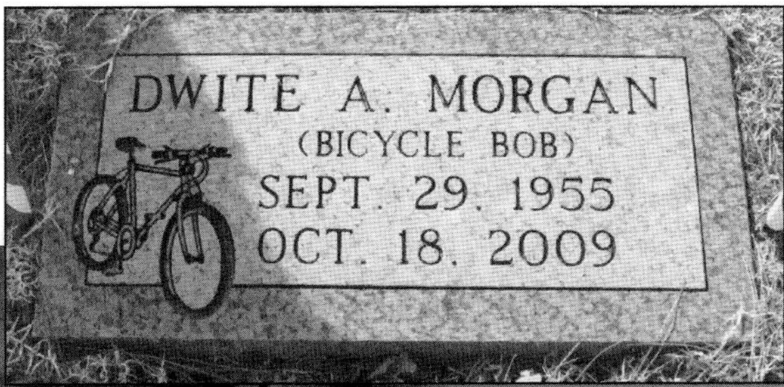

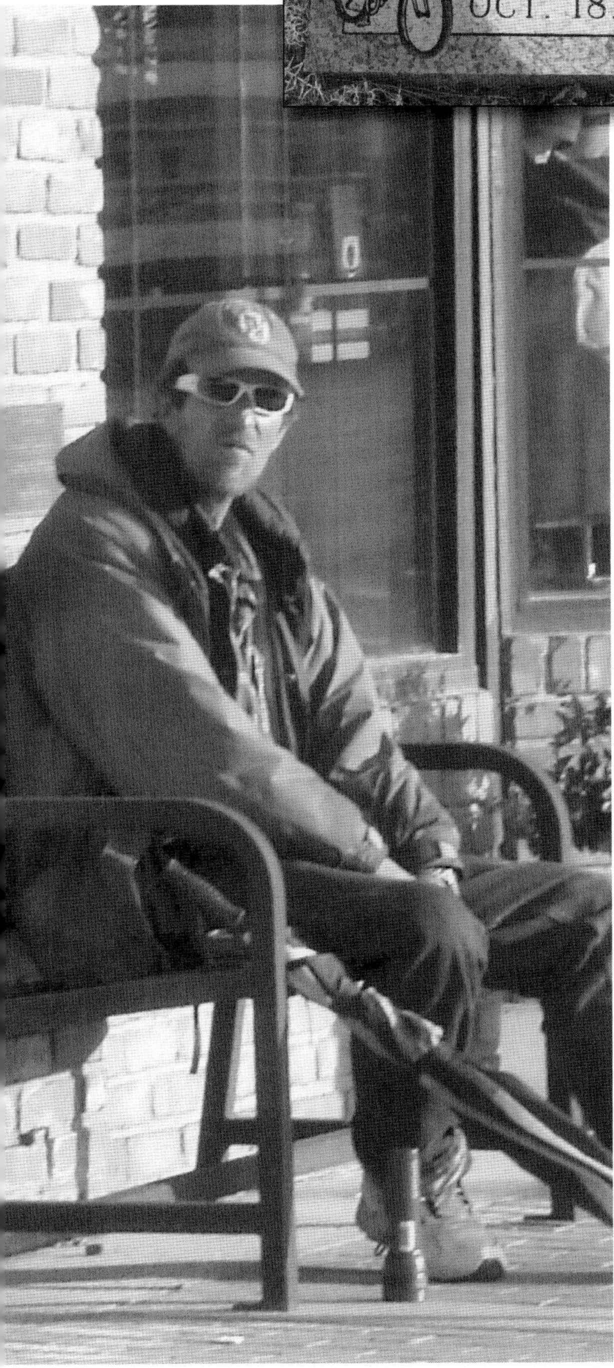

Dwite Morgan
Edmond's first homeless man was senselessly murdered in 2009. Morgan, known to many in Edmond as "Bicycle Bob," spent his days riding his bicycle around town for 25 years. Community members pooled money to pay for a funeral for Morgan. Nobody turned their backs on him. This photograph was taken on July 4 at First Street and Broadway at the LibertyFest Parade the summer before "Bob" was murdered. Citizens and Edmond police officers had helped Morgan, who was 54, for many years. Sgt. Scott Fees told reporters that officers checked on Morgan, who was mentally delayed, year-round to make sure he was ok. "Everyone has a Dwite story," Fees said. "He never bothered anyone. He was a good guy." Charlotte Worsham, who once owned the Around the Corner restaurant, said she fed Morgan biscuits and gravy and coffee every day for two years. She told the *Edmond Sun*, "I didn't charge him. That could be me someday." Morgan often visited Al's Bicycles, where customers had bought him bicycles, store manager Craig Cossey said, but he mostly was there to talk and visit. A bicycle is engraved on his marker at Gracelawn Cemetery. Nearly 350 people were at his funeral service at First Christian Church. Edmond police served as pallbearers. Senior Minister Chris Shorow, who helped officiate the service, wrote in an article in the *Edmond Sun* that Morgan "touched a nerve in this town like few before him." The Reverend Jerry Black said, "He inspired a sense of compassion and concern. He gave us reason to reach out beyond ourselves and be community. And, for that alone, I think we are forever in his debt." His killer was sentenced in 2013 to life with the possibility of parole by Oklahoma County district judge Jerry Bass. (Left, courtesy Scott Fees; above, courtesy David Fisk.)

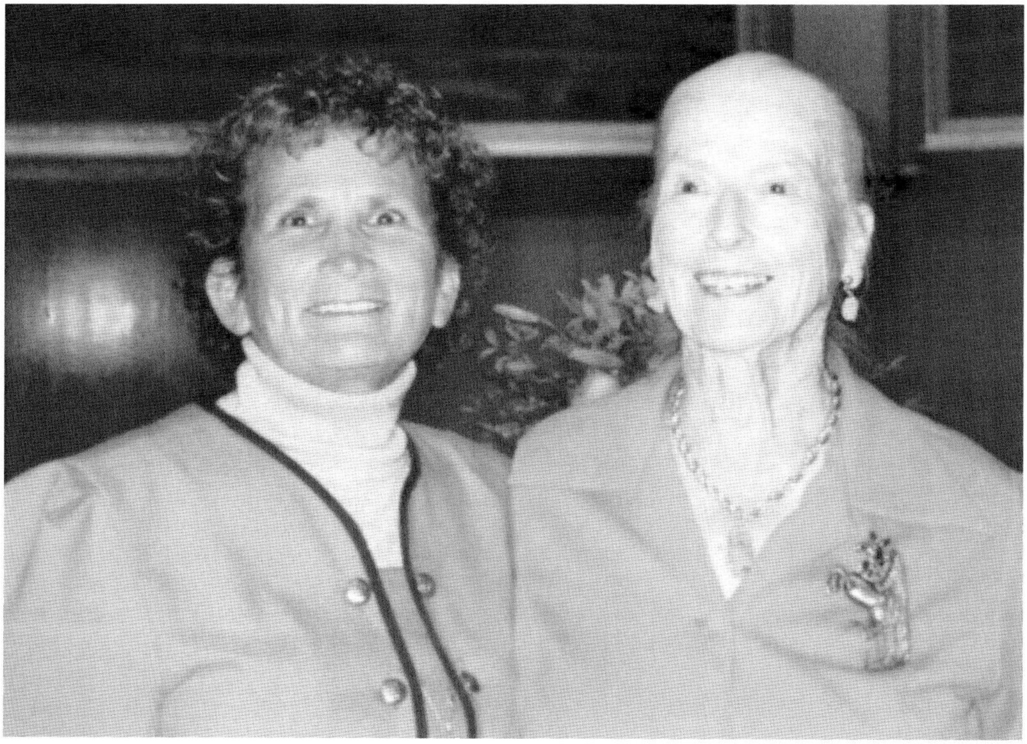

Lucille Fancey and Joy Milligan

This mother-and-daughter team has run the Coffee Creek Riding Center for the Handicapped since 1977. Fancey and daughter Joy Milligan have 15 horses that are in use at the therapeutic riding center for the disabled at no charge. In her 90s, Fancey still helps with the center, which receives some funding from the United Way. Fancey was the "Master of the Lost Hound Fox Hunt" for 35 years in Oklahoma, daughter Joy said. Milligan says her work "is a calling." She used to teach at Rose State College but says she "can't say no to God," so she instead teaches therapeutic horsemanship. A horsewoman since her younger days, Fancey's dream began to take shape when one of her riding students was paralyzed in an automobile accident in the early 1970s. A newspaper article explored the possibility of a riding center for the disabled and brought 10 students and a bunch of volunteers. Within six months, the center was operating full time with 50 students. An article in the *Edmond Sun* described their philosophy as "life is best lived by giving yourself to others." They have lived on meager means to ensure that others may enjoy and benefit from the Coffee Creek Riding Center. (Both, courtesy Joy Milligan.)

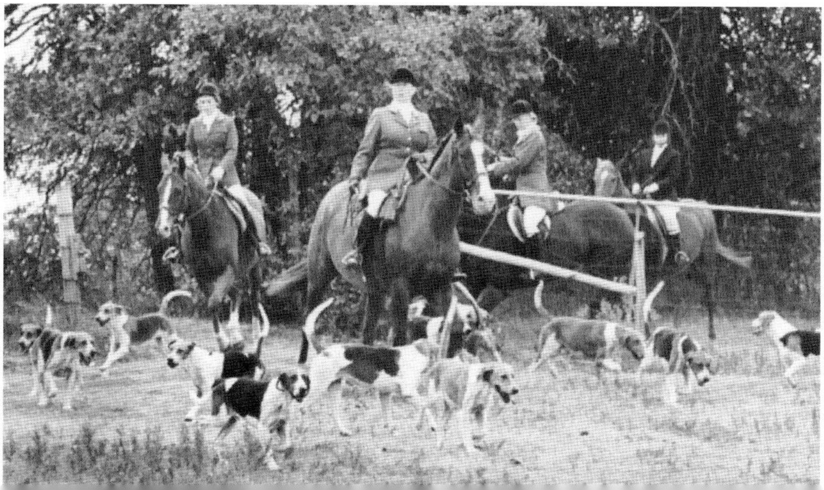

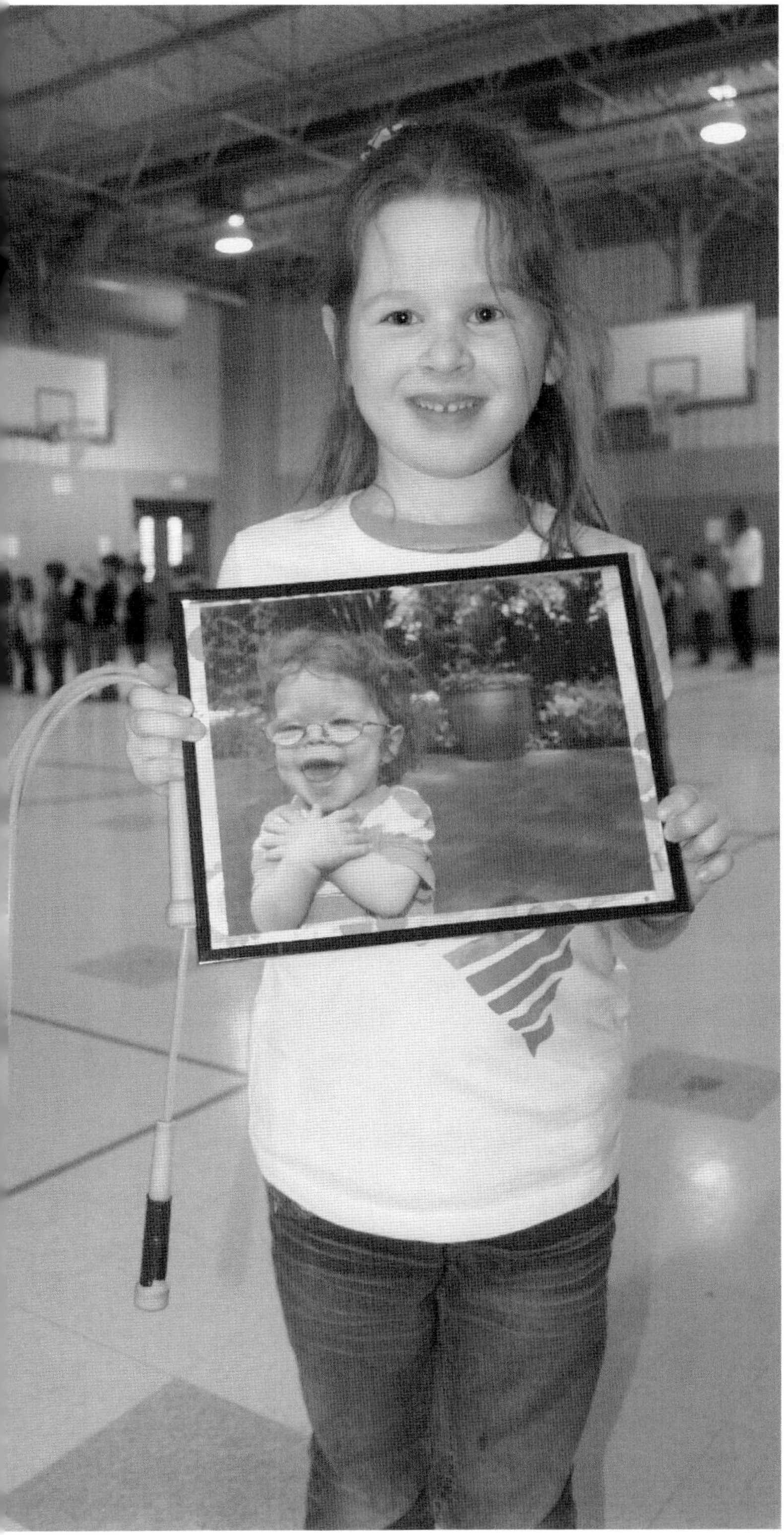

Ella Turner
This nine-year-old girl with a heart of gold raised more than $25,000 in three years for the American Heart Association. Ella's sister, two-year-old Colby, died of a rare heart disease in 2010 while the family was living in Texas. Ella learned about a program called Jump Rope for Heart in her physical education class there. She told *Oklahoman* newspaper reporter Diana Baldwin, "I came running out of school, I was so excited. I told my dad [Neil Turner] I wanted to raise $1,000." He told her she did not understand how much money $1,000 was. In a letter, her dad recalled how a determined Ella told him "No, you don't understand. They help kids with bad hearts. They help kids like Colby." When her family moved to Edmond at the end of 2012 and Ella started the spring semester at Centennial Elementary School, she continued her efforts as an ambassador for the AHA. Her goal was to find 1,000 donors for the 2013 Jump Rope for Heart program. Neil Turner said she raised another $10,500 by June 2013. With a big smile, the little red-haired girl told Baldwin, "My heart feels good when I do it because I feel like I'm doing something for other people." (Courtesy the Turner family.)

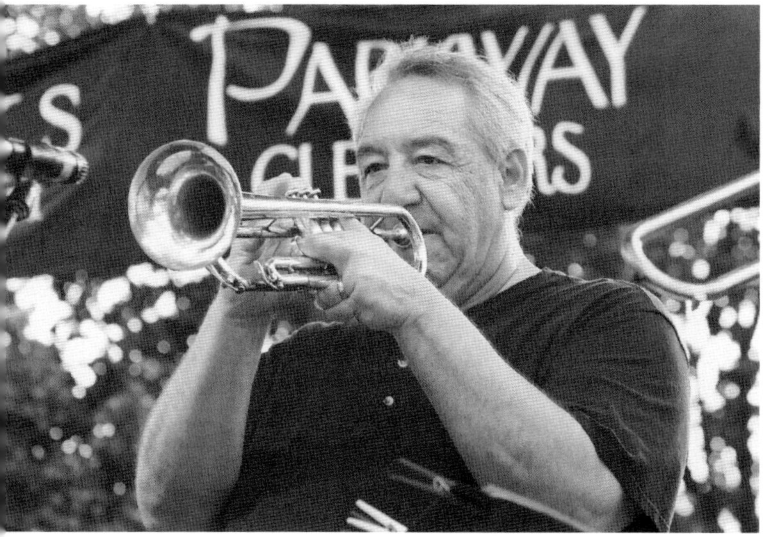

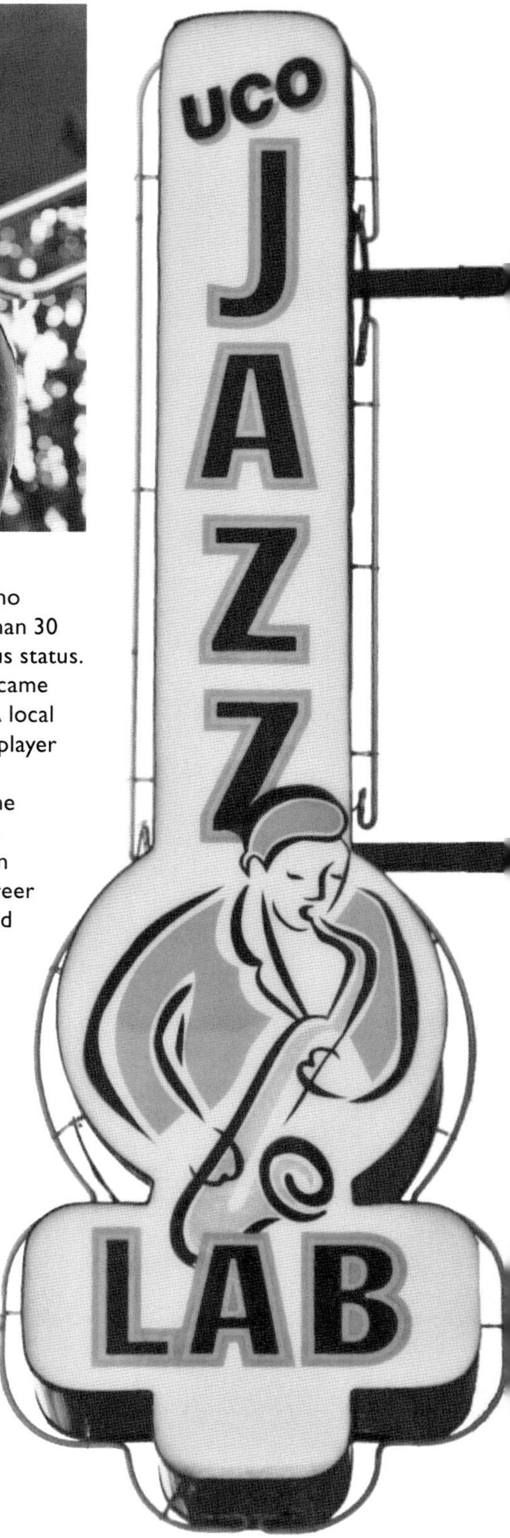

Lee Rucker

Music students have learned many a note from Rucker, who taught at the University of Central Oklahoma for more than 30 years. Rucker retired in 2012 and holds professor emeritus status. When the UCO Jazz Lab was created in 2002, Rucker became the director at the request of his mentor, Kent Kidwell. A local newspaper interviewed the nationally acclaimed trumpet player and he said, "this place is rich with goodness."

Besides operating the UCO Jazz Lab, Rucker has had the opportunity to make music with the Temptations, Aretha Franklin, the Four Tops, the Spinners, the Woody Herman Orchestra, and more. Rucker recalled highlights of his career that included traveling in the 1970s as a trumpet player and conductor with the Ice Follies, followed by the heartfelt responsibility of influencing more than 1,000 students as a UCO instructor, director of bands, and private teacher. "I sit here and look around and think—I can't believe how fortunate I've been," Rucker told the newspaper reporter. (Both, courtesy David Fisk)

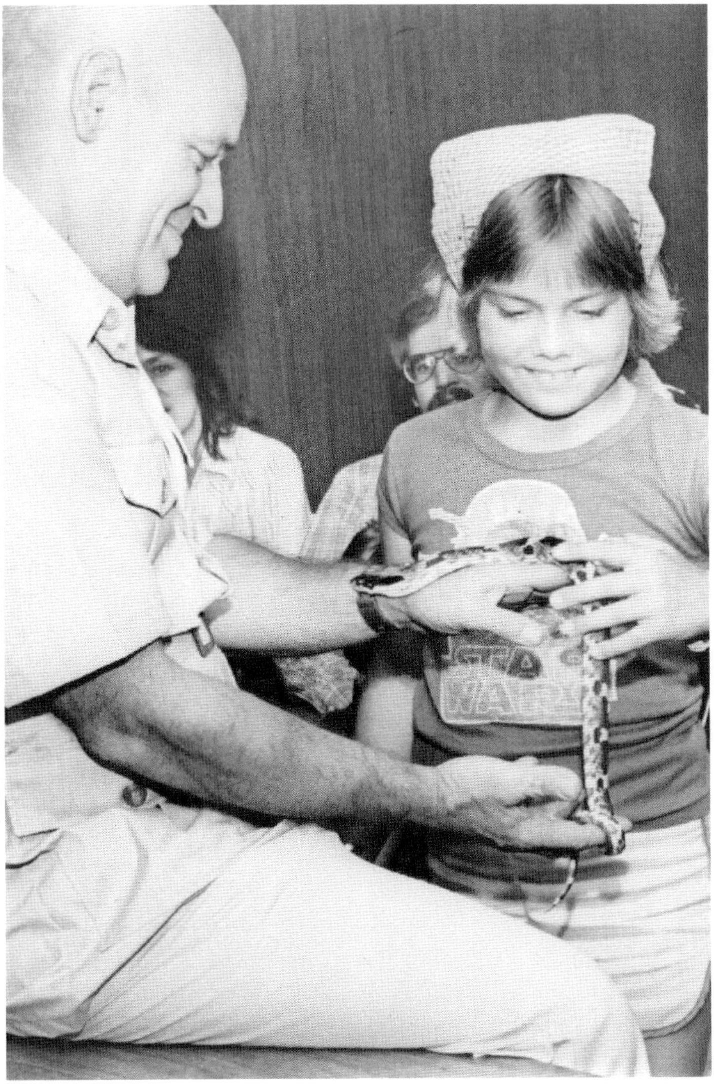

James Robert Jenni

James Robert "Bob" Jenni never met an animal he didn't like. Jenni was a nationally known naturalist and animal expert. In the early 1990s, he opened Bob Jenni's Nature Center east of Edmond on State Highway 66, and he operated it until his death in 2005. Many local youngsters grew up learning about animals from Jenni, who travelled across the state as a wildlife educator. He always had animals with him, and the sight of a snake curling around his arm was not uncommon. He worked for the Oklahoma City Zoo and state wildlife conservation department and began his career as a teenager at Tulsa's Mohawk Zoo Park. He established the first reptile exhibit with the Lincoln Park (now Oklahoma City) Zoo and had an aquatic show at Springlake Amusement Park, where youngsters learned to swim with the dolphins. He was often called to rescue animals, and his nature center had many occupants, including Sue the alligator, Apache the bobcat, Josie the black bear, and lots of snakes, raccoons, llamas, skunks, turtles, and other wildlife. Jenni and his wife, Natalie, took numerous photographic safaris to Africa and displayed photographs of animals in the wild at the nature center. He often appeared on local television stations with wildlife and nature features. He appeared on the *Ho Ho Show*, *Forman Scotty Show*, and many others. (Courtesy Edmond Historical Society Photographic Collection.)

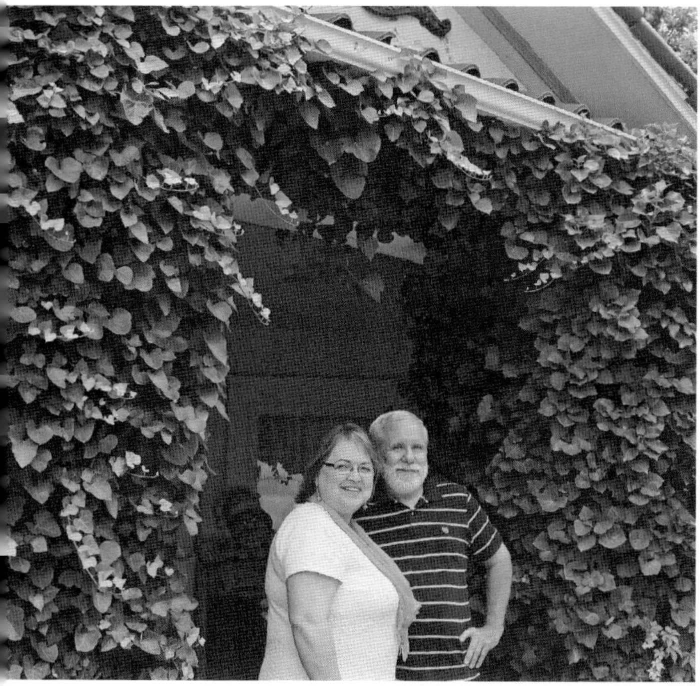

Martha and Gary Hall

The Halls are living their dream at their Arcadian Inn Bed and Breakfast. In 1990, the Halls (left) opened the boutique inn in the historic home of turn-of-the-century Edmond doctor A.M. Ruhl at 328 East First Street and University Drive. They raised and homeschooled their two sons at the inn. Gary is a contractor who does work on other bed-and-breakfasts. Martha has served on various industry-related boards and has been active in Edmond organizations and enjoys her role as a "glorified mother." Martha said, "Arcadian Inn has really set the standard for bed and breakfasts in Oklahoma." In the photograph below, Dr. Ruhl and his wife, Edith, sit in their Buick in front of the Ruhl home that is now the Arcadian Inn. (Left, courtesy David Fisk; below, courtesy Edmond Historical Society Photographic Collection.)

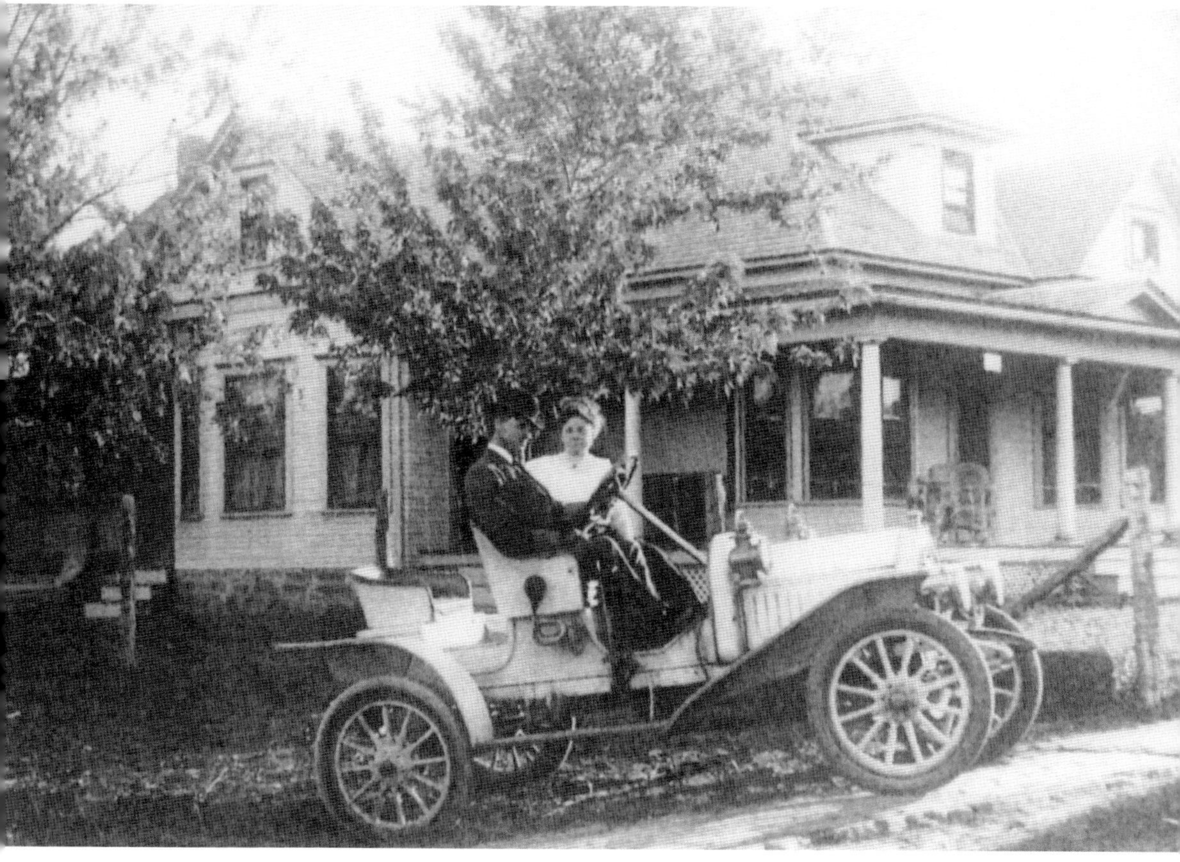

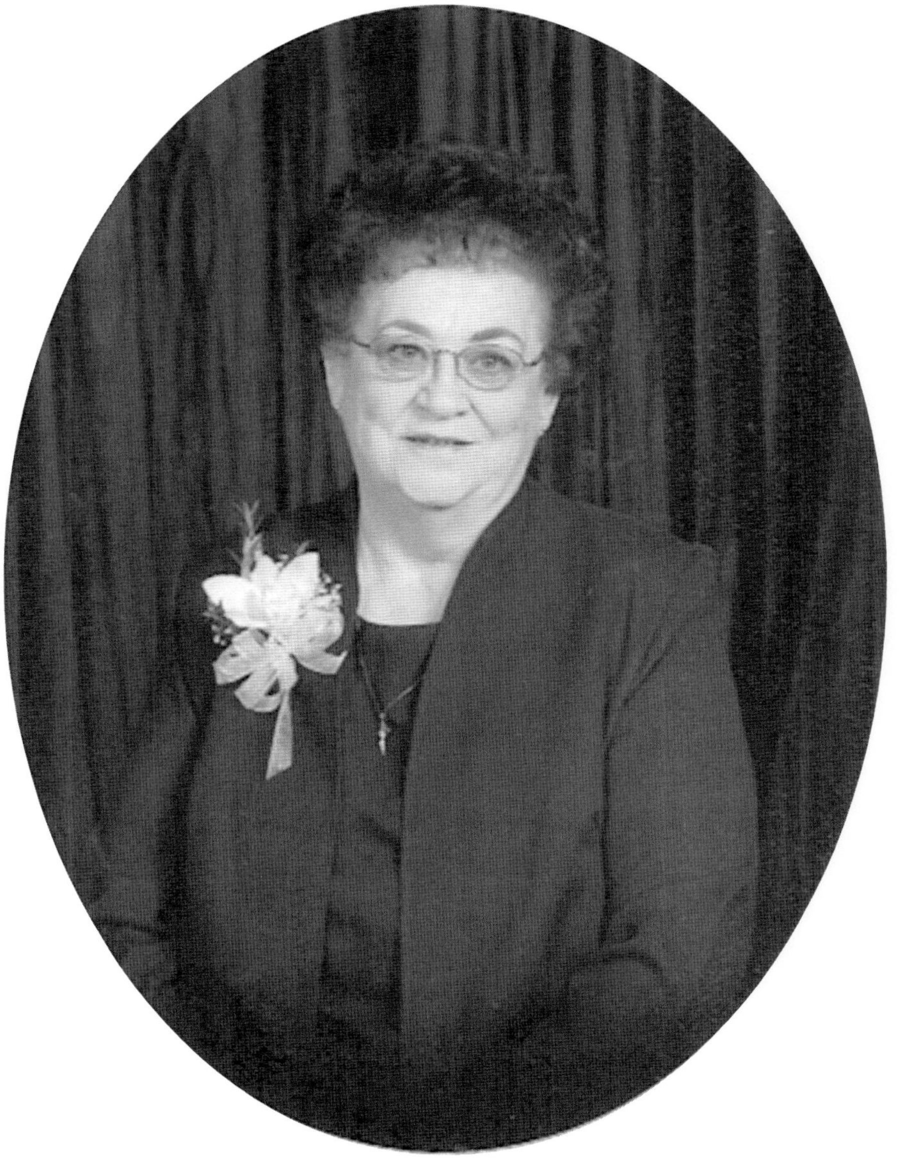

Patricia L. Sandefur

"Patsy" Sandefur cared a lot about Edmond. The longtime city employee died in 2006, but she left a long list of accomplishments during her career, which began in 1967 as secretary to the city manager. She became assistant city manager and city clerk in 1979 and held both jobs until retiring in 1989. She pinch-hit for Edmond as acting city manager twice while a permanent one was sought. Mayor Carl Reherman tried to get her hired for the job but was opposed by the city council. She served as city manager of Guthrie for several years after that. Former Edmond councilman Tom Kennedy said, "She had the interest of the city at heart. She was not just doing a job; she was very dedicated in her work." Sandefur was involved in many community activities, served on several city boards and committees, and was interested in city business even after she retired. She was a secretary for Edmond's first School House Trust and the Edmond Historical Society. She was a president of the Edmond Alumni Association and the St. Patrick's Cemetery Association. She grew up in Lockridge and was a third-generation descendant of the original land run settlers to the Lockridge area, just west of Edmond. (Courtesy Pam Timmons.)

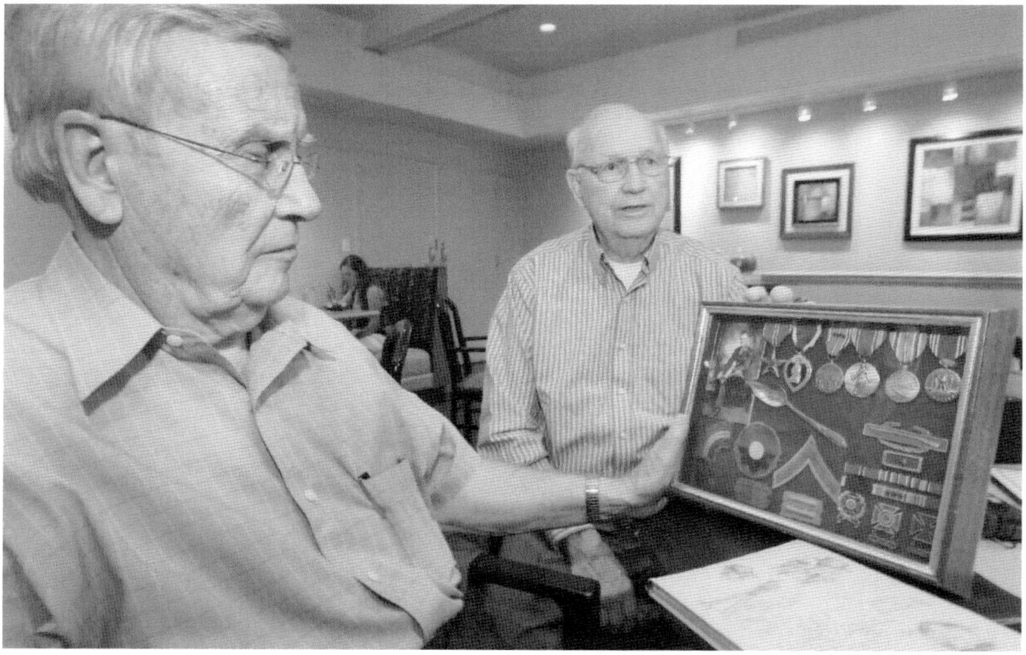

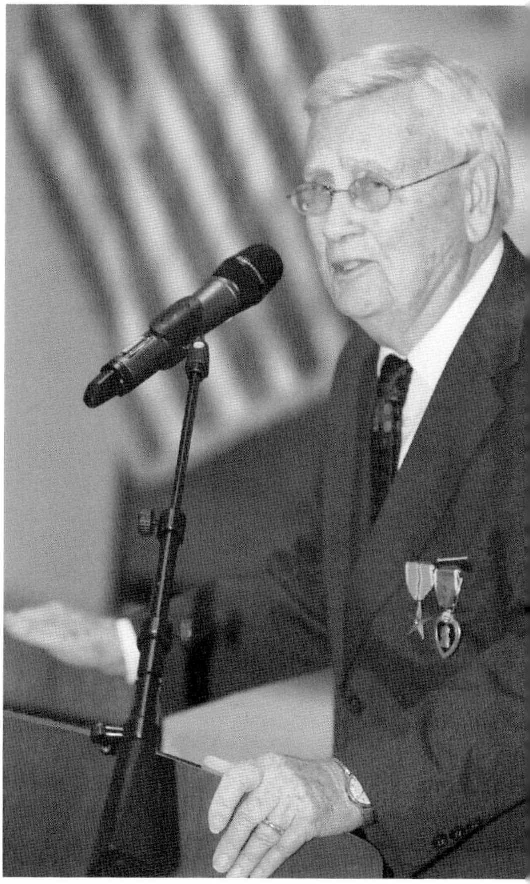

Hall F. Duncan
Duncan began his second career after retiring as an advertising design and cartooning instructor at the University of Central Oklahoma. He started a company called Humor and Communication Publishing, based out of his Edmond home. Since 1986, Dr. D., as he is known, writes and illustrates children's books and humor books. Duncan was a hero in World War II, receiving numerous medals, including the Bronze Star and the Purple Heart. However, it was not until 67 years after the war that he was given the medals. US Rep. James Lankford helped Duncan get his military records and presented the medals to him after Duncan inquired about the records so he could prove his qualifications for the French Legion of Honor. In 2013, Duncan was awarded the Chevalier of the French Legion of Honor. According to his Web site, Duncan's books are "filled with action-packed characters, delightful pictures and significant lessons." They try to bring to life the imagination and joy of childhood. Before teaching at UCO, Duncan was an advertising agency art director, teacher, and illustrator for the United Methodist Board of Global Missions. (Both, courtesy the *Oklahoman* archives.)

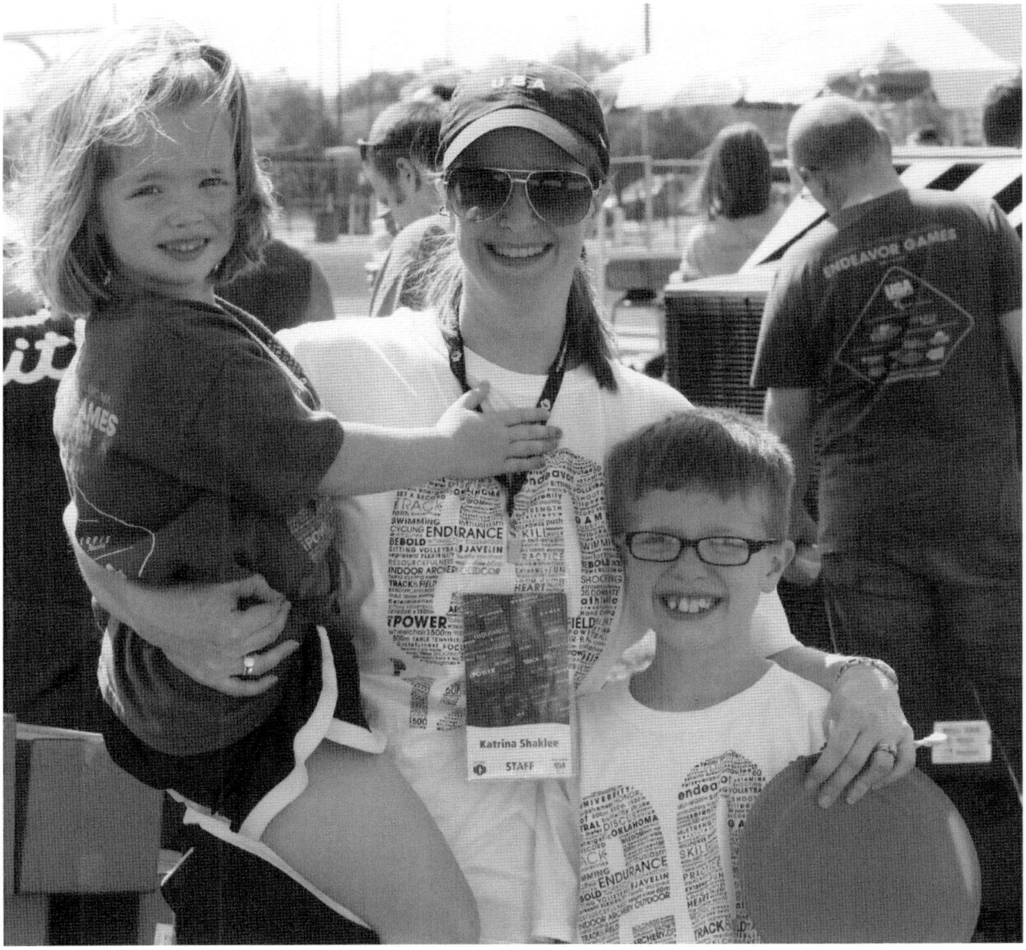

Katrina Shaklee

Shaklee works for the University of Central Oklahoma as director of the Wellness Center. When Shaklee learned she had multiple sclerosis in the late 1990s, she began to dream of an event in Oklahoma for athletes with physical disabilities. She began her career in 1994 as public relations coordinator for the Sooner State Games. She went back to school at the University of Northern Colorado to earn her master's degree in sports administration. She returned to Oklahoma in 1998 as assistant director of the Sooner State Games. She resigned from that post in 1999 and formed a nonprofit called Sports Group, Inc., which in 2000 hosted its first event in Edmond, the Endeavour Games for Athletes with Physical Disabilities. In 2004, the group was absorbed into UCO, and Shaklee joined the Wellness Center. The Endeavor Games has grown to include more than 550 participants from across the nation. She was a catalyst in UCO's involvement with the US Paralympics, which uses the university as an official training site. UCO is now an official Olympic training site as well. Shaklee has many awards and honors to her credit, including the Oklahoma Hospitality Club's Women in the News in 2011. She is on the board of Disabled Sports, USA, and was a torchbearer for the Salt Lake City Games in 2002. In 2000, she received the National Sportscasters and Sportswriters Heroes Award for Oklahoma. Shaklee is pictured above with her children, Katharine, 6, and Callahan, 10, at the Endeavor Games. (Courtesy Tom Means.)

INDEX

INDEX

LEGENDARY LOCALS

AN IMPRINT OF ARCADIA PUBLISHING

Find more books like this at
www.legendarylocals.com

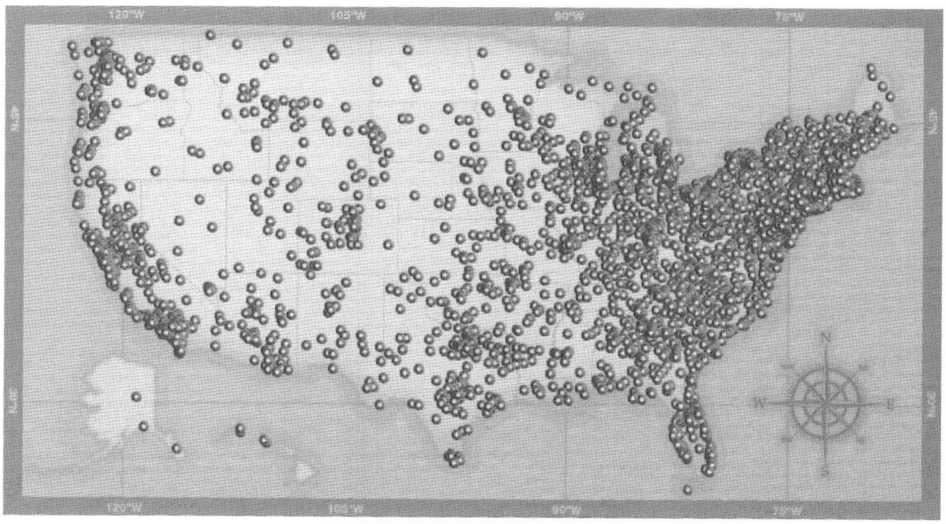

Discover more local and regional history books at
www.arcadiapublishing.com

Consistent with our mission to preserve history on a local level, this book was printed in South Carolina on American-made paper and manufactured entirely in the United States. Products carrying the accredited Forest Stewardship Council (FSC) label are printed on 100 percent FSC-certified paper.

MADE IN THE USA